Other Books by Joseph C. Goulden

THE CURTIS CAPER

MONOPOLY

TRUTH IS THE FIRST CASUALTY

THE MONEY GIVERS

THE
MONEY GIVERS

by Joseph C. Goulden

Random House   New York

For Lecta Mahon Everitt Goulden,
a nonfoundation philanthropist

CONTENTS

THE MONEY GIVERS

CHAPTER **1**

Introduction

EARLY ONE SWELTERING MORNING in the summer of 1969, a tottering old fellow in a Rutgers State University sweatshirt and mismatched tennis shoes stepped into an alcove on Tenth Avenue on New York's West Side and took the last gurgle, head thrown back, from a pint bottle of wine. He sat the bottle on the pavement, wiped his mouth with his sleeve, and walked, with cautious dignity, around the corner into the Lowenstein Memorial Cafeteria, 535 West 48th Street, past the inconspicuous sign by the doorway: "If you are hungry and without means come in and have a meal as my guest. If you can pay for your food please stay out and give others a chance." The breakfast the dere-

3

lict carried to his table was plain but substantial: scrambled eggs, hash-browned potatoes, toast smeared with margarine, and a heavy white mug of coffee. The same meal, if eaten in one of the dank hole-in-the-wall cafés in the neighborhood, would have cost him forty cents.

Later the same morning, at the opposite side of Manhattan, a former secretary of defense, the heads of U.S. corporations with assets totaling more than $8,000,000,000, the presidents of two leading educational institutions, and a U.S. district judge took their seats, in $500 swivel chairs, around the Honduran mahogany table that dominates the board room of the Ford Foundation. There was banter about the heavy agenda awaiting their action ("I hate these two-briefcase meetings," one of them said), and about the New York heat, which is kept off the Ford premises by a magnificent glass enclosure that soars eleven stories above a perpetually green garden across the rear of the building. Ford employees are perhaps the only people in Manhattan who work with their windows open in winter.

Soon they got down to business. The major item was approval, by voice vote and without expressed dissent, of a grant of $2,225,000 to the National Urban Coalition. This organization was formed by industrialists and black nationalists after the 1967 big-city riots to provide jobs, education, and housing for the urban poor. The trustees spent the rest of the meeting reviewing a 1970 budget of slightly more than $200,000,000 for grants and administrative and operating expenses.

In rural North Carolina, meanwhile, a retired Methodist preacher walked down his lane and found the postman had left his $47 monthly pension check from the Duke Endowment, in Charlotte.

In Chicago (or Houston or Pittsburgh or Oakland or Tampa) the owner of a small manufacturing company signed papers drafted by his lawyer transferring five percent of the stock of his firm to the "charitable foundation" bearing his name. The stock had paid no dividends since 1947, and it was not traded publicly. The executive's salary ($73,490 that year) varied annually so as to absorb the company's earnings. Nonetheless, after the transfer the lawyer did quick computations on a note pad and said: "This should knock about $14,700 off the tax bill, give or take a hundred."

In a federal court in Louisiana, an attorney employed by the NAACP's Legal Defense Fund, which is financed by a coalition of more than a dozen foundations, sighed wearily as he listened to an assistant state attorney general argue for further delays in school integration in northern parishes.

In Reno, Nevada, an officer of the Max C. Fleischmann Foundation signed a diverse stack of checks: $5,000 to a volunteer fire department in Genoa, Nevada, toward construction of a new firehouse; $9,000 for support of the Midnight Sun Council of the Boy Scouts of America in Fairbanks, Alaska; $100 for the National Braille Press in Boston; $100 for the American Merchant Marine Library Association in New York; $75,000 for the California Institute of Technology, for construction; $25,000 for the World Wildlife Fund, Washington, for land acquisition.

In New Haven the "secretary" of another foundation—who also happened to be office manager for the benefactor's business—read a report from the bank that the foundation's stock investments had returned dividend income of $371.95, and he promptly wrote a check for that amount payable to the local United Fund, thereby completing the year's philanthropic activity.

        As these paragraphs suggest, foundations are so diverse—in size, in *modus operandi,* in motivation, in fields of interest, in visibility, in the amount of serious attention (and money) they devote to philanthropy—that any categorical statement one chooses to make about them can be proved—or refuted.

> Foundations are altruistic institutions, the modern form of the Judeo-Christian tradition of helping one's neighbor and of using wealth for the common good.
>
> Foundations are tax dodges, created by the greedy rich to cheat the Internal Revenue Service.
>
> Foundations created the modern American university, hospital, and research institute.
>
> Foundations waste their time and money on impractical, inapplicable research of interest only to a handful of obscure academicians, and they are afraid to come down into the street to wrestle with the meaningful issues of society.
>
> Foundations are manned by unfettered social activists bent upon revamping America through support of radicals and their schemes; they ruthlessly unseat Congressmen and other elective officials, using tax-exempt funds in the process.
>
> Foundations are so big that they unsettle the normal balance of the marketplace, and their business and investment holdings are swelling so fast that a dangerous portion of the American economy is being placed beyond the tax collector's reach.
>
> Foundations play such a small role in the scheme of things in America that they could vanish overnight and not be missed by anyone other than the professional "philanthropoids" who operate them and the few persons dependent upon their support.
>
> Foundations are run by superior beings who know what's good for the country, and should be left alone while they do it for us.

Foundations are the playthings of social cranks and proven failures who should not be set at large with multi-digit bank accounts. (After all, the lay citizen asks, didn't the Vietnam war result from faulty advice of McGeorge Bundy, the White House national security adviser under Presidents Kennedy and Johnson, and now president of the Ford Foundation? Is control of a $3,028,644,744 foundation* Bundy's reward for his contribution to the ghastly Vietnam venture?)

Foundations are the only institution in America with the freedom of action essential to problem-solving. Bundy, recognizing the abysmal state of New York public schools, could spend Ford money as he wished to improve them, free of any fetters of responsibility to public agencies or the teacher-administrator bureaucracy or the public at large.

Actually, foundations are all these things—and more. Yet, despite their controversiality in Congress and elsewhere, no legal definition exists that tells us exactly what a foundation is.** For purposes of taxation, foundations are lumped with assorted other organizations granted exemption under Section 501 (c) (3) of the Internal Revenue Code of 1954:

Corporations, and any community chest, fund or foundation, organized and operated exclusively for religious, charitable, scientific, testing for public safety, literary, or educational purposes, or for the prevention of cruelty to children or animals, no part of the net earnings of which inures to the benefit of any private shareholder or individual, no substantial part

* The figure is as of September 30, 1969.
** Among the twenty-five largest foundations, which are listed in the appendix, we find an extraordinary variety of generic names: Ford *Foundation*, Duke *Endowment*, Pew *Memorial Trust*, Bernice P. Bishop *Estate*, Rockefeller Brothers *Fund*, Carnegie *Corporation* of New York, and Carnegie *Institution* of Washington. There are also the American Missionary *Association*, the A. W. Mellon *Educational and Charitable Trust*, the Carnegie Hero Fund *Commission*, the White Cross *Society*, and the University of Iowa *Facilities Corporation*.

of the activities of which is carrying on propaganda, or otherwise attempting, to influence legislation, and which does not participate in, or intervene in (including the publishing or distributing of statements), any political campaign on behalf of any candidate for public office.

F. Emerson Andrews, an elder statesman of the professionals who operate the nation's larger foundations, and retired director of the Foundation Center, their trade association, defines a foundation as "a nongovernmental, nonprofit organization having a principal fund of its own, managed by its own trustees or directors, and established to maintain or aid social, educational, charitable, religious or other activities serving the common welfare." [1]

A less somber man, who is a staff member at the Ford Foundation, defines the place where he works as "a large body of money surrounded by outstretched hands." Another says: "A foundation is a pile of money totally beyond the reach of the tax collector—and of anyone else we don't like." Still another says: "A foundation is proof that even if you can't take it with you, you can keep it away from the federal government."

The Ford Foundation is a "foundation." So is the Wilhelm Lowenstein Memorial Fund, established by a rich, unmarried New York fur dealer, which furnished the breakfast for the derelict we met in the opening paragraph of this chapter. The W. K. Kellogg Foundation, which occupies a low-slung modernistic building in Battle Creek, Michigan, is a foundation. So are the tax-avoidance family foundations whose headquarters consists of the upper left-hand drawer of a desk in an attorney's office.

GIVEN THE LOOSENESS OF DEFINITION, it is not surprising that foundation statistics suffer from a certain vagueness. Until Representative Wright Patman prodded it into compiling a list of private foundations in 1968, not even the Internal Revenue Service was certain how many there were. (The IRS list, when completed, contained 30,262 names.[2]) The Foundation Center, however, disputes this figure. It would exclude from the IRS list organizations "which make a general appeal to the public for funds; which act as trade associations for industrial or other special groups; which are restricted by charter solely to aiding one or several named institutions; or which function as endowments set up for special purposes within colleges, churches, or other organizations and are governed by the trustees of the parent institution." The Center estimates that there were 24,000 foundations in the United States at the end of 1969, compared with 22,000 at the end of 1968. It estimated their total wealth at $18,000,000,000 and annual grants at $1,600,000,000, compared with $20,500,000,000 and $1,500,000,000, respectively, at the end of 1968. The stock-market slump accounted for the decline in assets. The Center counted twenty-seven foundations with assets of $100,000,000 or more, and it estimated that more than ninety percent of all assets are held by less than seven percent of them. Finally, it figures that approximately two-thirds of the foundations have assets of less than $200,000.

Congressman Patman, in his continuing study of foundations, has used an accountant's nightmare of figures. His first report, issued December 31, 1962, said that "according to figures compiled for us by the Internal Revenue Service there were 45,124 tax-exempt foundations at the close of 1960 . . ."[3] Four years later Patman wasn't sure he should rely upon IRS' count: "It is very possible . . . that there are today hundreds of thousands of tax-exempt foundations operating in the country, some of them officially operating by exemptions and others enjoying a bootleg status [sic] with the same results." [4]

Whatever the definition and census, the number of foundations is steadily swelling. *The Foundation Directory*, the hefty biennial publication of the Foundation Center, lists only those foundations with assets of at least $200,000 or annual distributions of $10,000 or more. Between 1964 and 1967 the number of foundations large enough to be listed in the directory rose from 5,331 to 6,803, an increase of abou five hundred per year. Manning M. Pattillo, Jr., Foundation Center president, estimates that about two thousand new foundations "of all sizes" are being established each year, yet Attorney General Louis Lefkowitz of New York says new registrations of "foundations, trusts and other charities" totaled 2,563 in New York alone during 1968.[5] Pattillo admits that the figure on growth, standing alone, could lead one "to jump to the conclusion that the foundation field is growing by leaps and bounds and will soon gobble up the whole economy."

But Pattillo insists this is not so: according to Foundation Center figures, foundation assets were only about eight-tenths of one percent of net debt instruments and corporate stocks in the American economy. They were about seven-tenths of one percent of the value of all tangible U. S. wealth. They were less than the market value of at least two of the largest American corporations (AT&T and General Motors) and were less than ten percent of the aggregate assets held by domestic insurance companies. Furthermore, foundation grants are less than two-tenths of one percent of the Gross National Product and only nine percent of total charitable giving in the United States. Foundation grants amount to one-quarter of what Americans spend on toiletries and cosmetics, one-sixth of what they spend on tobacco,

one-tenth of what they spend on alcoholic beverages.[6] And
John Simon of the Yale law school faculty, an active philanthropoid, notes that the trust department of one New
York bank controls more money than all the foundations
combined.

Pattillo is indeed correct when he says foundation
wealth is a "small fraction" of the American economy. But
foundation assets can be an "action fraction," capable of
great leverage on American society. Paul Ylvisaker, formerly director of the national affairs division of the Ford
Foundation, has spoken of foundation spending (in this instance, to support community-action programs) as representing the "social application of the art of jujitsu: of exert-
ing smaller forces at points of maximum leverage to capture
larger forces otherwise working against us." [7] Dean Rusk,
president of the Rockefeller Foundation for almost a decade
before serving as secretary of state in the Kennedy-Johnson
administrations, has correctly quipped: "If all foundations
in this country were to commit all of their funds to what
may be called 'experimentalism' we could easily drive the
nation into a case of jitters." [8]

Dr. James A. Perkins, former vice president of the Carnegie Corporation of New York, and later president of Cornell University, avows that although foundations "represent
only a fraction of the total philanthropic dollars operative"
in any given field, "it is a fact that . . . [they] exercise an
enormous amount of leadership and influence on both the
persons and the institutions and the ideas in the areas in
which they work." [9] Perkins listed several reasons. Foundations, if they are wise, don't commit their money for years in
advance. Except for small administrative staffs, foundations
are not responsible (as is a university) for persons "who
must be paid for years to come." Foundations can begin

each year with a *"tabula rasa,* a fresh sheet, a new score to be made. It is one of the great ways whereby a small amount of money can have a great influence." Perkins compares the relative positions of Harvard, with $500,000,000 of endowment, and the Carnegie Corporation, with $250,000,000: "The fact of the matter is . . . that Carnegie has an enormous advantage, in that it has all assets and no liabilities, which is not the case with Harvard."

Furthermore, the money can be spent in almost any way that strikes the fancy of foundation trustees, and that does not violate the rather loose strictures of the Internal Revenue Code. President Alan Pifer of the Carnegie Corporation wrote in his 1968 annual report that a foundation, "unlike a business enterprise . . . is not subject to the discipline of the market-place nor, like public agencies, of the ballot box. In short, it [the foundation] enjoys less constraints by the usual forms of accountability to society than does perhaps any other type of institution."

McGeorge Bundy sent a shudder through the House Ways and Means Committee during its 1969 tax reform hearings with this off-hand remark: "The board of trustees of the Ford Foundation could give $3 billion tomorrow to any one of thousands of institutions in the country." [10]

TO WHAT USE DO FOUNDATIONS PUT THEIR WEALTH? As seed money for innovation. To support and accelerate the search for new knowledge which may expose the root causes of human suffering and want. To protect the weak and defenseless against ruthless exploitation. In an attack on basic human problems through a carefully focused program characterized by continuity of effort, flexibility, and readiness to innovate, and emphasis on quality in leadership and performance.

Each of these purposes was taken, in direct quotation or paraphrase, from a foundation annual report.

As is generally true with self-appraisal, stated intention often falls short of proven accomplishment. The vast majority of American foundations, despite the potentiality given them by unrestricted wealth, are nothing more than incorporated checkbooks, doling out a thousand (or a hundred thousand) dollars here and another thousand there. These grants can be a shotgun dispensation to all institutions in a given field, regardless of quality or need; continuing alms to a pet charity of the controlling party; or a random gift with no more forethought and definite scheme than a stray dog gives to his breakfast menu.

Because they have money, and because they do spend it, foundations *have* made contributions to science, to medicine, to education. Rare is the American campus unadorned by a research laboratory or by a professor financed in part or in whole by a foundation; even rarer is the American community whose hospital or United Fund or boys' club is not supported by one or more locally-oriented foundations. On a broader scale are such frequently-cited achievements as the reformation of American medical education (as a result of a study by Abraham Flexner for the Carnegie Foundation for the Advancement of Teaching); the so-called "green revolution" of improved farm production in poor nations (financed chiefly by the Rockefeller Foundation, joined later by Ford); the pioneering research in rocketry by Dr. Charles Goddard, financed by the Research Corporation and the Guggenheim Foundation, among others, when few persons accepted the totally daft theory that man could travel in space; the National Gallery of Art in Washington, constructed and stocked by the A. W. Mellon Charitable Trust; the early public-health achievements of the Rocke- feller Foundation.

Because of these and other accomplishments, founda- tions cannot be dismissed as totally worthless, for any insti- tution that spends millions of dollars in half a century's time is bound to be noticed by society. The law of averages, if nothing else, would guarantee that some of the money was put to good use. Yet legitimate questions remain: Do these accomplishments justify the tax benefits gained by donors who create and control foundations; or the creation of a swelling corps of professional philanthropists with unlimited power to determine where their money is spent?

THE MONEY GIVERS is an attempt to sift through the myths and realities of foundation philanthropy—to tell what they do, and how and why; and also to explore the reason this peculiarly American institution found itself under attack, in the latter part of the 1960s, by the Con- gress, the public, and the press.

Oddly, for all their good works over half a century, foundations attracted little public attention until a fire- cracker string of controversies late in the decade: a $175,000 grant by Ford to the Cleveland chapter of the Congress of Racial Equality, part of which financed a voter registration drive in black wards at a time when Carl Stokes, a black, was running for mayor; New York businessman Frederick Richmond's use of funds from his personal foundation to campaign against the veteran Brooklyn Congressman, John Rooney, in a Democratic primary; a $20,000 grant to Su- preme Court Justice Abe Fortas by the family foundation of financier Louis Wolfson, who shortly thereafter went to prison for stock manipulations; travel-study grants by Ford to eight aides of the slain Senator Robert F. Kennedy, denounced as "severance pay" by critics, defended as the "right thing to do" by Bundy; and, finally, the deep involvement of Bundy, as citizen and as foundation officer, in the messy emotional fight over decentralization of control of New York public schools.

We shall have more to say about each of these episodes later. However, Cleveland brought into focus some questions which philanthropy and the public had never before faced: What are the proper functions of foundations? Are foundations an adjunct to government, or an equal, independent participant in public affairs? How much freedom of action should foundations enjoy? Should not the public and its elected representatives have the authority—even the responsibility—to control how and where foundations spend wealth that has been granted the privilege of tax exemption?

These questions were at the core of the fierce Congressional debate over "foundation tax reform" during the 1969 session. This debate contained a good deal of sham. Regardless of the banners held aloft, Congress's primary concern was *not* tax reform. Congress jumped on the foundations because of what anthropologist Robert Ardrey has called the territorial imperative—"the inward compulsion in animate beings to possess and defend . . . an area of space . . . which an animal or group of animals defends as an exclusive preserve." [11]

The Ford Foundation's financing of a voter registration drive and the Frederick W. Richmond Foundation's financing of "neighborhood study clubs" in Congressman Rooney's Brooklyn district were actions which violated Congress's territory. Furthermore, foundation activity in civil rights and in community action programs challenged the "established order" at every level of government.

A foundation executive who begged anonymity summarized the situation:

> Congressmen are like gladiators who are forced to go down into the arena once every two years and fight for their lives. Their helmet gives them a rather restricted field of vision, and they are wary of any new and unknown factors that are introduced into the battle. Foundation money was a new factor, and it scared the hell out of them. Everyone listened to old John Rooney when he waved his finger at the House Ways and Means Committee, told them of his experience with Richmond, and said: "This could happen to each of you—or to any other officeholder in the country."

That the world of foundation philanthropy reeks with business and tax abuses—many of them on the verge of criminality—was no secret to Congress. Beginning in May, 1961, Congressman Patman issued report upon report giving highly detailed (and also highly selective) accounts of foundation misdeeds. Congress and the public read Patman's reports—and yawned. But once Congress felt its own territory threatened, and the public discovered these mysterious foundations (and particularly Ford*) were involving themselves in the field of racial rights other than in the distant South, they fell upon foundations with righteous anger —and for the wrong reasons.

---

* "FORD GRANT AIDS NEGROES' MOVING," The Washington Post headlined on March 28, 1969, in reporting on a $300,000 Ford grant "to encourage Washington Negroes to move into white suburban neighborhoods at a rate ten times faster than they are doing now." The white-collar passengers on my Northern Virginia commuter bus the morning this story appeared reacted as if Ford had provided H. Rap Brown with two battalions of tanks and a wing of F-104 fighter-bombers, to be used in the leveling of Arlington.

Acutely illustrative of Congress's malevolent attitude was the attempt to ban foundations from making grants to individuals. Congress's true intent could have been expressed through a simple resolution: "Lots of us didn't like Bobby Kennedy, and we think the Ford Foundation made a mistake when it gave all that money to men from his staff." But in its malice Congress swung an axe that would have killed such programs as the Guggenheim and Woodrow Wilson fellowships. (Senator Russell Long, a macabre humorist, scheduled hearings on the bill on the first anniversary of Kennedy's assassination, giving witnesses sixteen hours' advance notice.)

Conversely, for almost two decades Congress found no cause for alarm in the fact that pseudophilanthropists used foundations to avoid thousands of dollars of taxes, to the detriment both of the U. S. Treasury and business competitors. Sharp dealing is a mode of behavior that Congressmen expect and accept from their constituencies.

CHAPTER 2

Founders and
Their Motives

A CLEAR MAJORITY of the big American foundations were created by rich men who had the good sense, late in their careers, to realize they were but one short step ahead of either outraged public opinion, their own uneasy consciences, or the tax collector. Piety and piracy are well-documented parallel characteristics of the American industrialist. Raymond B. Fosdick, who spent his life in service to the Rockefeller family, once wrote in an embarrassingly effusive "authorized" history of the Rockefeller Foundation that many of the great philanthropic fortunes were acquired "under conditions unique in the history of the country, and not infrequently by methods which, if permissible at the time, no longer accord with social conscience or the requirements of law." [1] What Fosdick was saying, in his gentle, roundabout style, is that much of the wealth controlled by American foundations was ruthlessly accumulated, with great accompanying human misery, by men who took full and knowing advantage of the casual, do-anything mores of the Robber Baron era of American business.

That they chose to rebate a portion of the loot through establishment of "charitable" foundations is to the credit of the big rich. But historical perspective demands that we keep in mind the source of the wealth and the motives which prompted the transfer of varying percentages of personal fortunes to foundations. John T. Jones, Jr., president of the Houston Endowment, once declared to fellow foundation executives: "I think we can all agree that foundations are originally created and endowed by men of more than normal wealth who wish to pass on this wealth for the public benefit." [2] Anyone who has circulated among the very rich—and especially the persons who help them decide how to spend "charity" dollars—could be expected to cough embarrassedly at such a claim, or perhaps to exchange a quick, incredulous wink with a friend. Thus, Jones added a saving qualifier to an assertion incapable of proof either by social scientist or metaphysician: "Whether this wish is motivated by pure virtue, a slightly-tarnished desire to see a name perpetuated beyond the grave, or nothing more than sheer animal hatred for the Federal government is not of concern to us."

Perhaps motive is irrelevant: certainly it is to the persons who depend upon foundations for support. The director of a medium-sized ($4,000,000 annual budget) research institute that is totally reliant upon foundation funds, responding to my question as to "why" certain persons gave him money, replied without hesitation: "That's a question that would require a research grant to find the answer, even if it's available. As the person responsible for raising money, I have a rather simplistic notion about motive. If someone wants to give it, and if blood isn't dripping from the check, I'll take it, and give the damnedest thank-you speech imaginable." Tick through a list of the big (and medium, and little) American foundations, and it isn't difficult to add other nonaltruistic motives to Jones' list:

— The hope of preserving a business, of achieving what one foundation official has called "corporate immortality." Putting control of a business in the hands of a foundation can protect it from dissipation by bumbling heirs and from destructive estate taxes. The founders of the Hormel Company, the meat packer, "greatly feared a takeover by industry giants" after their deaths; thus they put controlling interest of their firm in hands of the Hormel Foundation. Foundation trustees are required to "have their chief financial interests" in Hormel, Minnesota—a guarantee they won't sell the stock to outsiders who would trifle with the community's largest employer.[3]

— A means of paying conscience money to society for the depradations that created the fortune. (In this respect, Representative Wright Patman of Texas has called foundations a "strange creation of American folkways, a holdover from the conscience-stricken moments of the robber barons at the turn of the century.")

— A way of getting rid of the money when no acceptable heirs are available. Amherst H. Wilder, although never a household name even in his native Minnesota, built that state's first million-dollar fortune, from real estate, cattle, and Civil War government procurement contracts. Wilder's only daughter, Cornelia Day, was well-protected by the family, which equated suitor with gold-digger. The parents dispatched two early loves without record. Then Cornelia met a young eye special-ist, Dr. T. E. W. Villiers Appleby. A Wilder family his-tory states: "When the doctor proposed marriage to Day, Fanny Wilder [the mother] was sure the young doctor was primarily interested in her daughter's money." The Wilders consented to the marriage only after Dr. Appleby signed an agreement reserving to Day "full power and control over all her property." They married in 1897; both mother and daughter died in 1903. Appleby litigated the agreement for seven years, but ultimately had to content himself with an annual in-come of $10,000. The bulk of the Wilder estate—his late wife's money included—went to the Amherst H. Wilder Foundation, which by June 30, 1967, had a market value of $461,200,000, an increase of almost eighteen times the original value, and which during the half-cen-tury had spent $25,500,000 on "service to the poor, sick, aged, or otherwise needy people of St. Paul." [4]

— The purchase of social prestige, even at the White House level. Walter H. Annenberg, the Nixon adminis-tration's ambassador to the Court of St. James, is presi-dent of Triangle Publications, Inc. (*Morning Telegraph, Racing Form, TV Guide, Seventeen Magazine,* and assorted radio and television properties) and, until January 1, 1970, was publisher of the *Philadelphia Inquirer.* Old-line Philadelphia shunned Annenberg because the fortune he inherited came chiefly from the gambling wire serv-ice of his father, Moses L. (Mo) Annenberg, a raucous man, more at ease at the track than in a Main-Line par-lor. Donations of the Annenberg Foundation, whose assets consist chiefly of Triangle Publications stock, show a striking favoritism for organizations which are properly respectful of Walter H. Annenberg vis-à-vis honorific titles. During 1965–66 the Annenberg Foundation donated almost $120,000 to the University of Pennsylvania, which cheerfully welcomed Walter Annenberg to its board of trustees. The Annenberg Foundation donated almost $400,000 to the Peddie School, preparatory school attended by Walter Annenberg, which now includes Walter Annenberg on its board of incorporators. The list is seemingly indefinite: $4,000 to Villanova University, of which Walter Annenberg is a "member of the advisory board, lay trustee"; $7,268 to the Philadelphia Museum of Art, of which Walter Annenberg is a trustee; even $1,250 to the Navy League of the United States, of which Walter Annenberg is a "member, executive committee, Philadelphia Council." But Annenberg's most fruitful gift was the donation of a portrait of Benjamin Franklin to the Fine Arts Commission of the White House in 1962, during Jacqueline Kennedy's renovation program. The Annenberg Foundation purchased the painting from New York dealer M. Knoedler & Company for $160,000. Legally, of course, Walter H. Annenberg and the Annenberg Foundation are separate entities. Yet it was the former who received public credit for the gift (his *Philadelphia Inquirer* announcing it as being from "Mr. and Mrs. Walter H. Annenberg")— and an invitation to dine alone with the Kennedys at the White House. After he went to London as ambassador for his longtime friend President Nixon, Annenberg spent almost a million dollars of his foundation's funds refurbishing the U.S. Embassy.

— The construction of conspicuous marble monuments

in public places (what one foundation executive calls "the edifice complex"). The Charles A. Dana Foundation is the creation of a New England industrialist whose company, the Dana Corporation, is "one of the nation's largest independent manufacturers of components for the auto and truck industry, with more than 20,000 employees at 31 plants in eight states." [5]

The name Dana is also prominently before the eyes of students at an annually-increasing number of colleges: the Charles A. Dana Fine Arts Center at Agnes Scott College, Georgia; the Charles A. Dana Hall for Science and Engineering at Hartford College, Connecticut; the Dana Auditorium at the E. H. Little Fine Arts Center,* Queens College, North Carolina; the Charles A. Dana Hall at Colby College, Maine; the Charles A. Dana Auditorium of the Language Arts Center, Middlebury College, Vermont; the Dana Arts Center at Colgate University; the Charles A. Dana Law Library at Stetson Law Center, Florida; Dana Hall at Berry College, Virginia; the Dana Science Laboratory at Davidson College, North Carolina; the Dana Science Building at Indiana Technological College; the Charles A. Dana Auditorium at the University of Toledo; the Charles A. Dana Building of Science at the University of Bridgeport. In the medical field there are the Charles A. Dana Clinic and Hospital Diagnostic and Service

---

* By assigning donor names to sectors of a building, much as a butcher does to portions of a side of beef, the college can insure proper credit to all benefactors and increase the number of rich men willing to contribute to the project. The general rule is that the largest contributor gets his name on the overall building. There are exceptions: Homer C. Holland, a New York investments counselor and banker, gave Dickinson College $465,000 towards the construction of a student union building; the federal government, $2,000,000 (of a total cost of $2,500,000). Dickinson named the building for Holland.

Building of the Yale-New Haven Medical Center and
the Charles A. Dana Recovery Pavilion at the New
York Memorial Center for Cancer and Allied Diseases.
And, finally, there is Dana House in mid-Manhattan for
"unwed mothers and other troubled girls."

— A variety of tax and other business advantages, limited only by the imagination of the rich man's tax attorney, and so varied that they warrant an entire chapter.
There is strong evidence that taxes are the most important factor in much philanthropy. A foundation study
commission headed by Peter G. Peterson,* chairman
and president of Bell & Howell Company, in 1969 obtained the names of eighty-five persons whose *median* individual annual giving the last five years had been
$375,000. Peterson's group asked the following question:
"If there were no tax benefits at all; that is, if you gave
money to charitable organizations out of your after-tax
income, what effect would this have on your charitable
giving?" The median reduction was seventy-five percent; only four percent said they would continue to give
the same amount.[6]

AS FOUNDATION EXECUTIVES often and fondly re-
mind us, the philanthropic foundation has pre-Christian
roots. The Chinese and Egyptians of 4,000 years ago set
aside properties to support religious observances and to
maintain pyramids of the assorted Pharaohs. Plato directed
that income from his estate be used for perpetual support of
his academy. Plato's "foundation"—actually, successive
control of his properties by heirs who designated their suc-

* The Peterson Commission, in future references.

cessors—survived from his death in 347 B.C. until its suppression by the Emperor Justinian in A.D. 529 for "spreading pagan doctrines." In 1601, during the reign of Queen Elizabeth, a Statute of Charitable Uses was enacted, which recognized a charitable trust has a function that is at once public and private, and that monarchical and church participation were not essential. F. Emerson Andrews has called this statute "the cornerstone of Anglo-Saxon law concerning philanthropies." [7]

The foundation concept flourished early in the New World. Benjamin Franklin, in addition to endowing the American Philosophical Society, bequeathed 1,000 pounds sterling (worth around $4,445) each to Boston and Philadelphia for loans to "young married artificers of good character," and detailed a formula for accumulation of principal and interest for two centuries. In 1991, by Franklin's computations, each endowment would have grown to more than $18,000,000 to be spent on public works "of the most general utility." The first expenditures from the funds, permitted after the lapse of 100 years, resulted in construction of the Franklin Institute of Philadelphia and the Franklin Institute of Boston; the remainder of his bequest continues to accumulate.

An even earlier foundation was the Magdalen Society, formed in Philadelphia in 1800 to benefit "that class of female who have been unhappily seduced from the path of innocence and virtue and who at times seem desirous of a return thereto." The society failed: its clientele proved too insubordinate for counseling. The society became the White-Williams Foundation (named for two Episcopal bishops who devoted futile years to the reformation of prostitutes) and now gives assistance to needy Philadelphia schoolchildren.

There were numerous other nineteenth-century charities and "relief societies" devoted to aiding the poor which
were, in function, no more than institutionalized distributors of alms. But there were two innovations during that
century which are now recognizable as forerunners of the
modern "operating" foundation.

First was the Smithsonian Institution, created in 1846
by a $500,000 bequest from James Smithson, an English sci-
entist-inventor who apparently displayed absolutely no
other interest in America during his lifetime. Smithson had
no American friends, never traveled here, and never spoke
of the country to friends. His only "personal" connection
was so slim as to be meaningless: a half brother commanded
British troops at the Battle of Lexington. Nonetheless
Smithson left "the whole of my property . . . to the United
States of America, to found at Washington, under the name
to [sic] the Smithsonian institute, an establishment for the
increase & diffusion of Knowledge among men." Congress
was suspicious at taking the mysterious Englishman's
money, John C. Calhoun declaring it "beneath the dignity
of the country to accept such gifts from foreigners." The appeal of 105 bags of gold sovereigns outweighed such objec-
tions, although Congress was to wrangle another two decades before deciding exactly what the Smithsonian Institute
should do. It ultimately became a body that both produced
(through research) and distributed (through museums and
publications) new knowledge. Thus, the Smithsonian, although philanthropic in origin, had a noneleemosynary
character.

The second innovation was the creation of the Peabody
Education Fund in 1867 to assist the war-stricken South.
The donor, investment banker George Peabody, directed

that the foundation give a public accounting of its activities and expenditures, the first American foundation to do so. Warren Weaver, among other foundation historians, considers the Peabody Fund to be the "beginning of the foundation as we know it today." [8]

HOW DID THE HUGE FOUNDATIONS OF TODAY come into being? The previously-quoted Raymond Fosdick was always very touchy about insinuations that the various Rockefeller charities "were set up as a shield against public censure [to] . . . ward off the abuse to which over many years he [Rockefeller] was subjected." Fosdick, who was president of the Rockefeller Foundation from 1936 to 1948, and a trustee of six other Rockefeller philanthropies, displayed as Exhibit A a ledger Rockefeller kept during his teens when he held his first job, a $6-per-week clerkship. From this pittance Rockefeller gave six percent to his Sunday school and its religious missions. His gifts rose thereafter in proportion to income.

Furthermore, Rockefeller was a faithful churchgoer who apparently felt there was some divine cooperation in his construction of Standard Oil Company, which monopolized the United States petroleum industry beginning in 1872. "God gave me my money," he told an interviewer in 1915.[9] After financing establishment of the University of Chicago, Rockefeller told a campus meeting: "The good Lord gave me the money, and how could I withhold it from Chicago?" In his later years Rockefeller mused that his wealth was an "accident of history," possible only because of the peculiar business circumstances of oil and the nineteenth century, and that he was only its "trustee."

Fosdick feared Rockefeller's wealth, and he once wrote his benefactor: "Your fortune is rolling up, rolling up like an avalanche! You must keep up with it! You must distribute it faster than it grows! If you do not, it will crush you and your children and your children's children." Rockefeller was "hounded almost like a wild animal" by persons seeking gifts. According to Fosdick, the announcement of a bequest to a university or church would bring as many as 50,000 appeals in the next month's mail. Rockefeller complained to the *Philadelphia Public Ledger* in October, 1908:

> The good people who wanted me to help them out with their good work seemed to come in crowds. They brought their trunks and lived with me. I was glad to see them, too, for they were good people and earnest—they were all earnest. So they talked with me at the breakfast table and they rode downtown with me so as to miss no opportunity. When I left my office in the evening they were waiting to ride home with me. At dinner they talked to me, and after dinner . . . these good people would pull up their chairs and tell their stories . . .

The chore of dealing with these petitioners fell to a one-time Baptist minister, Frederick T. Gates, who shared with Rockefeller the feeling there was some special connection between Heaven and the amassing of the Standard Oil wealth. Gates joined Rockefeller in 1892 as an advisor on charitable giving and remained in his service until he retired from the foundation board in 1923 with a ringing peroration to his colleagues: "When you die and come to approach the judgment of Almighty God, what do you think He will demand of you? Do you for an instant presume to believe that He will inquire into your petty failures or your trivial virtues? No! He will ask just one question: *What did you do as a trustee of the Rockefeller Foundation?*" [10]

Both Gates and Rockefeller realized that ad hoc contributions would never dent the fortune. In the twelve-year period 1885–1897 Rockefeller received $60,000,000 from oil alone—the equivalent of a billion modern dollars. In the name of efficiency, Gates and Rockefeller experimented with institutionalized giving: the creation of the Rockefeller Institute for Medical Research, in 1901, with $200,000 to be spent over a decade; the General Education Board, in 1903, with a $1,000,000 endowment, to be spent over ten years for the improvement of schools "without distinction of sex, race or creed"; then the Rockefeller Sanitary Commission, in 1909, also with $1,000,000, charged with eradicating the hookworm in the South (to the outrage of Dixie, which denied both the existence and the debilitating effects of the intestinal parasite: "Where was this hookworm or lazy disease, when it took five Yankee soldiers to whip one Southerner?" demanded an Atlanta newspaper[11]). Despite such ungrateful bluster, the Rockefeller sanitary commission controlled the hookworm within two years.

These experiences convinced Gates that the most effective means of keeping Rockefeller's fortune within reasonable bounds was to assign chunks of it to independent bodies, governed by trustees with expertise in the area in question. Rockefeller biographer Allan Nevins has described Gates as "essentially a businessman with a talent for large affairs, a keen interest in the power of money, and a passion for seeing it expended with the greatest possible efficiency. He was, in short, a man after Rockefeller's own heart." [12] On June 3, 1905, Gates gave Rockefeller a format for the creation of a great foundation:

> I have lived with this great fortune of yours daily for fifteen years. To it, and especially its uses, I have given every thought. It has been impossible for me to ignore the great

question of what is to be the end use of all this wealth. You have not made me the confidant of your thoughts in this, which neither surprises nor grieves me. Nevertheless, I venture, after long hesitation, to lay my thoughts before you.

Two courses seem to me open. One is that you and your children, while living, should make final disposition of this great fortune in the form of permanent corporate philanthropies for the good of mankind. It seems to me that either you and those who live now must determine what shall be the ultimate uses of this vast fortune, or at the close of a few lives now in being it must simply pass into the unknown, like some other great fortunes, with unmeasured and perhaps sinister possibilities.[13]

Gates proposed that he and Rockefeller ascertain "the prominent lines of human need and human progress," whether men could be found who were "competent to administer these trusts now and in successive generations," and "what elements of human progress suggest themselves as of sufficient practical importance and practice as to invite specific legal endowment." Gates ticked off some possible purposes of such a "great fund":

— To promote a system of higher education in the United States.

— To promote the fine arts and "refinement of taste in the United States, and the development of a distinctive American art, just as the art of Greece represented Greek life."

— To promote scientific agriculture and the enrichment of American rural life.

— To promote Christian ethics and Christian civilization throughout the world.*

---

* Of the possible functions listed by Gates, this is the only one not now performed by the Rockefeller Foundation.

— To promote "intelligent citizenship and civic virtue in the United States."

Gates proposed that the funds "should be so large that to become a trustee of one of them would make a man at once a public character. They should be so large that their administration would be a matter of public concern, public inquiry and public criticism. They should be so large as to attract the attention and the intelligence of the world, and the administration of each would command the highest expert talent." Was such an undertaking possible? Gates didn't know, but "It is true that no historic personage has made benefactions so vast or so broad in scope as those here contemplated . . . nothing less would benefit the vastness of your fortune and the universality of its sources."

In 1909 Rockefeller proceeded with Gates's plan. He gave 72,569 shares of Standard Oil Company of New Jersey to a new trust, The Rockefeller Foundation, created "to promote the well-being and to advance the civilization of the peoples of the United States and its territories and possessions and of foreign lands in the acquisition and dissemination of knowledge, in the prevention and relief of suffering, and in the promotion of any and all of the elements of human progress." In March, 1910, following procedures used with his earlier charities, Rockefeller asked Congress to incorporate his foundation.*

If Rockefeller indeed was the stirring good fellow the approved histories would have us believe, the incorporation would have speedily passed. Between 1889 and 1907, thirty-

* The request was legally superfluous, for no such authorization was required. But Rockefeller's advisers felt the action would give a "public character" to the foundation.

four similar organizations had been incorporated by Congress, including the Carnegie Institution of Washington, an early philanthropy of steel magnate Andrew Carnegie, the American Academy in Rome, and the American Historical Association. But the angry response of Congress reveals most explicitly the public belief that regardless of the high esteem given Rockefeller by his advisers and benefactees, more than pure charity motivated his giving.

The trust-busting activities of President Theodore Roosevelt had signaled America's big rich that the era of industrial and financial freebooting was nearing an end. One requisite of becoming very rich is to sense social and political trends ahead of anyone else. To Rockefeller and fellow millionaires, the popular support given Roosevelt's crusade meant it was time for the rich to yield partially, and thus preserve the core of their fortunes, or to resist and risk losing all of them.

Rockefeller's major philanthropic acts had distinct chronological juxtaposition with Rockefeller's major business troubles and public embarrassments. The Rockefeller Institute for Medical Research was founded in 1901, when muckraker Ida Tarbell began interviewing Rockefeller associates for a series of articles on Standard Oil Company. The first of Miss Tarbell's articles appeared in McClure's Magazine of November, 1902, and a few months later Rockefeller formed the General Education Board. But chiefly because of Miss Tarbell, the nation now knew the source of the wealth which Rockefeller was distributing, and one of his gifts (of $100,000 to the American Board of Commissioners of Foreign Missions, a Congregational body) was preemptorily rejected as "tainted money." (The board later relented.) Miss Tarbell spelled out dramatically the

nature of the taint, beginning with the creation of Standard
Oil in 1872; she told how it "openly made warfare on business, and drove from the oil industry by any means it could
invent all who had the hardihood to enter it."

Miss Tarbell's indictment carried brutal detail:

> . . . he [Rockefeller] worked with the railroads to prevent
> other people getting oil to manufacture; or if they got it he
> worked with the railroads to prevent the shipment of the
> product. If it reached a dealer, he did his utmost to bully or
> wheedle him to countermand his order. If he failed in that, he
> undersold until the dealer, losing on his purchase, was glad
> enough to buy thereafter of Mr. Rockefeller. . . . There is no
> gambling table in the world where loaded dice are tolerated,
> not athletic field where men must not start fair. Yet Mr.
> Rockefeller has systematically played with loaded dice, and it
> is doubtful if there has ever been a time since 1872 when he
> has run a race with a competitor and started fair. Business
> played in this way loses all its sportsmanlike qualities. It is fit
> only for tricksters.

Of Rockefeller the churchman, she lamented that young
rate clerks learn "their first lessons on corporate morality"
by taking Standard Oil bribes to give information on ship-
ments of competitors; if one of these clerks "happens to sit
in Mr. Rockefeller's church on Sunday, through what sort
of haze will he receive the teachings?" [14]

After Miss Tarbell's articles, there were public troubles.
Judge Kenesaw Mountain Landis fined Standard Oil of Indiana $29,000,000 for antitrust violations. The Hearst news-
papers found correspondence in which Standard Oil vice
president John D. Archbold transmitted almost $100,000 to
Senator Joseph B. Foraker, with references to antimonopoly
legislation that "needs to be looked after." (President Roosevelt, a foe of Foraker, characterized the transaction as

"the purchase of a United States Senator to do the will of the Standard Oil Company.")

Finally, the request for Congressional incorporation came in the midst of a federal attempt—begun by Roosevelt, continued by President William Howard Taft—to force dissolution of the Standard Oil trust. Attorney General George W. Wickersham wrote Taft: "Is it appropriate that, at the moment when the United States through its courts is seeking in a measure to destroy the great combination of wealth which has been built up by Mr. Rockefeller . . . the Congress . . . should assist in the enactment of a law to create and perpetuate in his name an institution to hold and administer a large portion of this vast wealth? Never has there been submitted to . . . any legislative body such an indefinite scheme for perpetuating vast wealth as this." Taft responded: "I agree with your characterization of the proposed act to incorporate John D. Rockefeller."

Actually, the Rockefeller bill would have given Congress greater control over the Foundation than any legislation ever enacted. A Rockefeller representative, Starr Murphy, testified that Rockefeller was "perfectly content to leave this great foundation in the hands of Congress, that it may at any time in the future exercise its protecting power, not merely to protect his wishes, which are solely that this fund shall always be used for the public welfare and for no other purpose, but also that Congress may have the power, if at any time in the future this fund should get into the hands of men who might seek to use it for improper purposes, to exert its authority and bring this fund back again to the use for which it was intended."

To appease dubious Senators, Rockefeller accepted five

amendments: (1) total property to be limited to
$100,000,000; (2) income to be spent currently, and not ac-
cumulated; (3) principal to be distributed after fifty years
by vote of trustees, or after a hundred years by direction of
Congress; (4) new trustees to be approved by majority of
a board composed of the President of the United States, the
Chief Justice of the United States, the president of the Senate, the speaker of the House, and the presidents of Harvard, Yale, Columbia, Johns Hopkins, and Chicago; and
(5) investments to be limited to ten percent of any one corporation.

But Rockefeller's spokesmen could never define with
satisfactory precision exactly what the Foundation would
do. Murphy told a Senate committee: "It is impossible to do
so, because to attempt to define would be to impose a limitation, which is exactly what he [Rockefeller] seeks to avoid.
. . . He desires . . . to have a charter which will give to
him that . . . freedom of scope . . . that wherever there
arises a human need this board may be in a position to meet
it, if that shall seem wise." [15] Such imprecision, coupled
with public distrust of Rockefeller, doomed federal incorporation. "Fundamentally, it is not sound policy to concentrate and to tie up in the hands of a few men such a vast
sum of money for so long a time," said Senator Charles Cul-
bertson of Texas. Even Rockefeller's supporters were grudg-
ing. Senator Harry Lane of Oregon said that many people
believe "there is sweat and blood and grime and mothers'
tears on every penny of his money," but he added: "if he
wants to do any good, do not interpose a law that will prevent him from doing it." *The Arena*, a muckraking journal,
said: "There are worse men than John D. Rockefeller . . .
[but] there is probably not one, however, who in the public

mind so typifies the grave and startling menace to the social order." *The Arena* called him a "dissimulator and hypocrite by nature" and accused him "of giving to charity with one hand and collecting back the sum of his bounty from the poor by raising the price of kerosene."

The Rockefeller people, throughout the debate, kept making a point which Congress ignored: defeat of the bill would not prevent establishment of the foundation; it would merely prevent Congress from exercising any control over it. Congress haggled over the bill for four years; it passed the House in one session but never got out of committee in the Senate. In 1913 Rockefeller went to the New York legislature, which passed the desired incorporating act in two quiet months. The restricting amendments added by Congress were not in the New York version; thus, Rockefeller could set his own rules. And the statement of purpose had melted to a wondrously broad generality: "To promote the well-being of mankind throughout the world."

Almost immediately the contradiction of Rockefeller the philanthropist and Rockefeller the unfeeling financier was dramatically propelled into the public consciousness, this time with the new Rockefeller Foundation conspicuous in the foreground. The dispute involved a strike at the Colorado Fuel and Iron Company, at Ludlow, Colorado, of which Rockefeller and three Foundation trustees were directors. State militia summoned by the company invaded a strikers' camp and set fire to shacks and tents; more than a score of persons, many of them women and children, were burned to death; others were clubbed, shot, or deported from the state. The Ludlow Massacre, as the brutal event became known, sickened much of America. But Rockefeller, despite his investment in Colorado Fuel and Iron since 1902, professed to know nothing of the labor conditions which prompted the strike, much less the militia action. "It is not customary in any corporation that I have ever been connected with as director to receive regular information regarding labor matters," Rockefeller told an inquiring Congressional commission headed by Senator Frank Walsh of Montana. Thereupon, Walsh produced a letter which Rockefeller had written company officials after the massacre:

> You gentlemen cannot be more earnest in your desire for the best interests of the employees of your company than we are. We feel that what you have done is right and fair and that the position which you have taken in regard to the unionizing of the mines is in the interest of the employees of the company. . . . Whatever the outcome may be, we will stand by you to the end.

Senator Walsh was undisguisedly hostile to Rockefeller, asking him at one point: "Have you ever had a description prepared for you, Mr. Rockefeller, of what might have been accomplished if the sums which have been given through your benefactions of various kinds, had been given in increased wages or increased the conditions of labor and standards of living in the communities from which the investments of Mr. Rockefeller have drawn the profits?"

Rockefeller replied, "I have not."

Walsh asked, "Do you consider that 12 hours work in steel works in the rolling mills is a hardship to employees?"

Rockefeller said, "I am not familiar enough with the work to know."

At this same time, the Rockefeller Foundation was also engaging in what Walsh's commission considered to be suspicious if not outright reprehensible conduct. The president

of Colorado College and the dean of the College of Liberal
Arts at the University of Denver had recruited signers of a
"public manifesto" calling upon the strikers to return to
work, charging them with provoking violence and acting in
bad faith. Soon thereafter the General Education Board (a
Rockefeller group) and the Rockefeller Foundation gave
the two schools $100,000 each in unrestricted grants.

The Foundation also began a widely publicized study of
American industrial relations, to be conducted by Macken-
zie King of Canada, a recognized authority in the field, and
later his country's prime minister. King's study was supposed to be an objective survey of the causes of the Ludlow
and other strikes. Peculiarly, his "investigation" in Colorado didn't include interviews with the striking United
Mine Workers or the State Federation of Labor. Senator
Walsh accused Rockefeller of attempting to supplant the
work of his own commission and to perpetuate nineteenth-
century labor policies through the use of ostensibly charitable funds.

The Foundation embarrassedly halted King's survey,
and the Walsh Commission recommended that the Rockefeller Foundation be dissolved and its funds be spent to re-
lieve unemployment and to curb sickness and accidents.
The Foundation's assets, the commission charged, consisted
of money that should have gone to workers in the form of
wages: "These wages were withheld by means of economic
pressure, violation of law, cunning, violence practiced over
a series of years by the founder . . . and his business associates." Samuel Gompers, writing in the *American Federation-
ist* for November, 1914, said: "The one thing that the world
could gracefully accept from Mr. Rockefeller now would be
the establishment of a great endowment of research and ed-

ucation to help other people to see in time how they can keep from being like him." [16]

THAT ROCKEFELLER could spend money on churches and Chinese relief while militiamen acting in his name slaughtered workers striking one of his companies was a paradox Americans found hard to understand. But Henry Ford, who amassed a foundation fortune greater even than that of Rockefeller, posed no such puzzle. Dr. Samuel S. Marquis, first Ford's clergyman, then his employee, wrote in a friendly "interpretation" of the industrialist:

> Mr. Ford hates the word charity and all that it stands for. He gives generously to friends and employees, but it is in recognition of services rendered. He gives neither a stone nor money to the man who asks bread, but a job. . . . I have heard him say that the only man on whom he ever bestowed a charity was ruined by it. The amount given in this case was, as I recall it, about seventeen dollars. The investment of that seventeen dollars has saved him millions. Just another example of a wise use of money for which he has become famous.[17]

During his lifetime Ford was besieged by individual requests totaling as much as $6,000,000 a month; churches and other organizations asked for one, three, five, even fifty Ford sedans and trucks at a clip. All went away empty-handed. Marquis says that Ford had "his own ideas" on charity as on other subjects: "His theory . . . [was] that wealth should be amassed in a way that will not create poverty, and so make charity unnecessary; that the profits of industry are not so much of a private and personal affair as to justify any one man in making even a philanthropic distribution of them; that the proper disposition of such profits is to put them back into industry for the benefit of labor . . ." Ford himself has been quoted on the subject: "Why should there be any necessity for alms-giving in a civilized society?" [18]

Ford would not endow a foundation, although he listened with interest to the philanthropic views of his good friend and frequent traveling companion John D. Rockefeller, Jr. "Endowment is an opiate of the imagination, a drug to initiative," Ford said. "One of the greatest curses of the country today is the practice of endowing this and endowing that. . . . No, inertia, smug satisfaction, always follow endowments."

That Ford didn't commit his fortune to the propagation of his personal beliefs was in itself an act of charity, for during his last years he was caught up by a succession of bizarre ideas. Ford thought that illness, alcoholism, even crime were the result of poor dieting and that proper eating should be made "a part of religion." He saw no benefit in eating meat and looked forward eagerly to the happy day when reliance on the auto would make it possible for man to do away with the horse; also, "we could make milk commercially and get by without eating meat, so we could cut out these wasteful animals." Ford sponsored extensive research in the use of soybeans as a dietary staple. But not even his soybean desserts contained sugar, for Ford was convinced the granulated crystals cut the blood vessels and caused fatal internal bleeding.

Politically, Ford gave America of the 1920s a nasty dose of anti-Semitism with his support of the *Dearborn Independent*. The paper's constant theme was that an international clique of Jews was determined to gain control of world politics, business, and finance, even at the cost of deliberate provocation of war and revolution. High rents? "The Jewish landlord at work," answered Henry Ford's *Dearborn Independent.* Alcoholism? "The profits of spiritous liquors flow in large amounts to Jewish pockets." Flapper dresses? "All those thigh-high fashions came out of Jewish clothing concerns." Entertainment, movies, the stage? "Every such activity has been under the mastery of the Jews." A libel suit by a Jewish economist and attorney forced Ford to publish an apology: "Had I appreciated even the general nature, to say nothing of the details, of these utterances, I would have forbidden their circulation, without a moment's hesitation." (Yet, biographer Allan Nevins quotes Ford "associates" as stating the offensive remarks "were prompted largely by Mr. Ford," and that he "kept in touch with every phase" of the *Independent*'s operation.[19])

What, then, is the cause of the creation of the Ford Foundation—the world's largest, now worth $3,028,000,000 and growing—all from seed money earned by the noncharitable Henry Ford? The answer lies with two human instincts far more basic than charity and love for one's fellow man—power and money.

Henry and his son, Edsel, owned practically all the stock of Ford Motor Company. Since the company was privately owned, the Fords reported to no one and took in profits and earnings only the amount of money required to maintain their status among the very rich. Then in the mid-1930s, the Fords took a frightened look at the inheritance tax rates and realized something special must be done to retain family control of the company. Were the stock to pass directly to

Edsel's children, the legal heirs, most of it would have had to be sold to pay the taxes. The Ford lawyers got busy and in 1936 incorporated the Ford Foundation. It began operations with modest cash grants from the family, and for the next fifteen years concerned itself with local Michigan charities.

Edsel died in 1943; Henry, in 1947. In 1950, when both estates were finally settled, the values—and purpose—of the foundation became evident. The wills bequeathed ten percent of the Ford stock to heirs of Henry and Edsel—their respective wives and Edsel's four children. The remaining ninety percent went to the Ford Foundation. However, family control of the company was not affected in the least, for the shares given to the Foundation were nonvoting; the ten percent kept by the Fords was a voting class, and with it went domination of the company.

Had the Foundation not existed, the family's tax bill would have been $321,000,000, based on the conservative $135 per share value the government accepted in settling the estate. The Ford heirs, rich though they were, didn't have that sort of money readily available, and would have had to sell most of their holdings to satisfy the government. As lagniappe, the will provided that the bequests to the family be tax-free, thereby passing the burden of the inheritance tax, $42,063,725, to the Ford Foundation.

Henry Ford II, however, has insisted that more than avoidance of inheritance taxes was involved in creation of the Ford Foundation. Asked during 1952 Congressional hearings to comment on the allegation that "the whole scheme and plan of the Ford Foundation was a method whereby the Ford family could retain control of the Ford Motor Company," Ford responded:

My family had undertaken certain obligations . . . in the [Henry Ford] Hospital and in the Edison Institute [both local Michigan charities], that they felt they were obligated to keep up, and they were not sure just how that could be accomplished if the country were going to stay in the condition that it found itself in in 1933 and 1934.

I think that was one of the reasons they wanted to start this foundation; in other words, to carry on their obligations to charity, as they saw them.

Certainly, there may have been some other reasons, and far be it from me to say that some may not have been to get this stock in one's hands, that maybe with the possibility that they could still maintain a certain relationship between their stock and the operations of the company.[20]

THAT THE NONPHILANTHROPIC FORD'S name should endure in the title of the world's largest philanthropic enterprise is an irony, but by no means an isolated one. The personal spending habits of the very rich often prove 180 degrees removed from their attitude towards philanthropy. S. S. Kresge made more than $200,000,000 from his dime-store chain, but was penurious even to himself. His first wife, Anna, whom he married in 1897, divorced him in 1924 on grounds of "frugality and humiliation." Kresge boasted: "I've never spent more than 30 cents a day for lunch in my life and it hasn't killed me." Friends said Kresge was a poor golfer because he "spends too much time looking for lost balls." But Kresge began giving away his money in 1924, and by the time he died in 1966, he had endowed a foundation with assets now worth $350,000,000.

Russell Sage, the nineteenth-century financier, was also stingy with himself and family; contemporaries called him "the embodiment of the Yankee skinflint." Even at eighty-six, worth $100,000,000, Sage rode the trolley to business meetings, grumping that he couldn't afford a hack. When an office boy brought him a fifteen-cent sandwich for lunch, rather than the preferred nickel variety, Sage deducted a dime from the lad's pay. A young stockbroker was once in Sage's office when a madman entered and demanded money lest he explode a bomb. The broker, a Mr. Laidlaw, claimed Sage manuevered him into position as a shield and fled as the bomb detonated. Laidlaw's leg was maimed, and he sued Sage for damages. The proceedings dragged through four trials, with one jury awarding Laidlaw $40,000. But the appellate courts consistently backed Sage, who vowed publicly he would spend $100,000 if necessary fighting "an unjust suit." Although he won, biographer Paul Sarnoff adjudged: "To the world at large, he was guilty . . . of being the meanest, most miserly skinflint that ever lived." [21]

Sage didn't mind the abuse: "It is indeed hard to please. If you don't hold onto your money, you are a spendthrift. If you give your money to charity, you are doing it for show. If you spend it for pictures, you are taking bread from the needy. When you die . . . if you leave it to charity, you should have done it while alive." [22] When Sage's wife begged him to provide funds for a new building for her church, he replied: "If they want the church, they shall have it. I will be happy to lend them the money—if they have acceptable co-signers."

The wife took posthumous revenge on the old miser. Sage had been a shrewd stock-market speculator and money-lender who picked his way surefootedly through the financial debris strewn over America by Gould, Morgan, and Harriman. His estate was valued at $64,000,000, and, six months after his death, Mrs. Sage created the Russell Sage Foundation with part of the funds. One of its first projects was a blistering exposé of moneylenders and usurers, a study which caused the New York legislature to pass laws forbidding many of the practices through which Sage became rich.

To James Buchanan (Buck) Duke, a personal foundation served a dual purpose: preservation of a business and a thumb of his nose, from the grave, to persons who fought him in life. Farmers in Buck's native Carolina detested him; they considered his American Tobacco Company ("I taught the world how to smoke cigarettes!") a monopolistic devil responsible for low prices. Buck snorted at public opinion, but he did fear that "populist politicians and rabble-rousers" would smash the Duke Power Company, his second great empire, after he died. How, then, could he guarantee perpetuity and prosperity for Duke Power?

He decided that public attitudes towards business are determined primarily by three groups of people: lawyers, who dominate government; preachers, who dominate religion; and physicians, who have something to say about life and death. Buck and his lawyers spent ten years drafting an extraordinary indenture disposing of his estate in a manner designed to command the allegiance of all three groups. Not for him the sweeping generalities of the statement of purpose of the Rockefeller Foundation. Buck told his trustees exactly where the money should be spent, and how: Duke University, thirty-two percent of the income; hospitals in North and South Carolina, thirty-two percent; Davidson

THE MONEY GIVERS 47

College and Furman University, five percent each; Johnson
C. Smith University, four percent; Carolina orphanages,
ten percent; construction and maintenance of Methodist
churches in North Carolina hamlets of less than 1,500 population, ten percent; and "care and maintenance of needy
and deserving superannuated preachers" and their widows
and orphans, two percent.

Duke's logic was unshakable: Duke University would
have the South's outstanding law and medical schools, and
hard by would be a great school of theology. It was simple
enough. Here were the sources of public opinion. The University would take care of them. The endowment's health
programs would make it possible for the poor who work—
and vote—to have their health. And, finally, there were
those poor old worn-out preachers, for whom everybody
had sympathy, and the orphans. Would anyone be so cruel
as to meddle in a business that was taking care of them?

In a conversation with Carolina newspaperman Ben
Dixon MacNeill during the 1920s, Buck stated the premise
more bluntly: "People ought to be healthy. If they ain't
healthy they can't work, and if they don't work they ain't
healthy. And if they can't work there ain't no profit in
them." [23]

Not all Carolinians were happy with Buck's grand
scheme. Duke University was then Trinity College, a strug-
gling but proud little Methodist school, and one of its
trustees pointed out that the word "trinity" had certain special connotations to Methodism. He asked rhetorically if
Buck would be satisfied if the name were changed to "The
Father, Son, and James B. Duke University." However, the
Methodists took the money and changed the name as required.

As a further bind on the Duke Endowment trustees, Duke "recommended" the Southern Power System (Duke Power and its subsidiaries) as the prime investment, decreed that its stock not be sold except by unanimous vote of the board, and restricted investment of earnings to further purchases of Duke Power stock and to bonds of government units of more than 50,000 population which had not defaulted on interest payments since 1900. The will was written during the 1920s, and Buck didn't want his estate thrown away on speculative stocks. In 1962 the trustees decided the limitation was unduly restrictive and asked North Carolina courts for permission to buy stocks in companies other than Duke Power. One of them explained: "Mr. Duke's provision made a lot of sense in the 1920s, when there was no SEC and common stocks were pretty much of a gamble. But we thought a diversified portfolio would be safer, and return a better income for our beneficiaries." The North Carolina Supreme Court refused, saying that "Mr. Duke had as much right to name the securities in which the funds should be invested as he had to name the beneficiaries. . . . Past adherence to the provisions of the trust agreement has, as Mr. Duke wished, promoted the economic as well as the social welfare of this and our sister states." [24]

The decision wouldn't have surprised Buck Duke. He knew his power when he signed the indenture:

> I've got 'em fixed now so that they won't bother it after I'm gone. I'm the last Duke,* but I don't think anybody will bother this thing I'm leavin'. What I mean is that I've got 'em fixed now so there won't be any more meddling with it by legislatures and courts and newspapers like I've been bothered

---

* Buck apparently referred to the fact that he had no male heirs. Daughter Doris Duke was bequeathed enough of a nest egg to warrant establishment of her own foundation; she is also a board member of the Duke Endowment.

with all my life. But I've got 'em now and it's going on making profits. Not even Joe Dan'els [Josephus Daniels, editor of
the *Raleigh News & Observer*] will cuss me now.[25]

The Duke Endowment now has assets of more than
$614,000,000—a fortune with which North Carolina cannot
meddle, just as Buck Duke intended.

IN 1940 PRESIDENT ROOSEVELT'S temporary National Economic Commission, charged with exploring the
conditions that led to the Depression, identified thirteen
major "family-ownership" groups with controlling interest
in the two hundred largest nonfinancial corporations in the
country. As of mid-1959, each of the thirteen had at least
one foundation. Depending upon one's definition of "control" and "foundation," Ford dominates either ten or thirty-
three; the duPonts, ten; the Mellons, six; the Andrew Carnegie estate, five. The others are McCormick, Hartford,
Harkness, Duke, Pew, Clark, Reynolds, and Kress.

Fortunes put into foundations mellow with the passing
of years. Andrew Carnegie is not remembered as the ruthless steel manufacturer who enforced the twelve-hour day
with the lockout; he is the philanthropist whose foundations
initiated a national pension system for college professors
and scattered libraries around the land. Andrew W. Mellon
is no longer thought of as the scion of the family that rav-
aged Pittsburgh—economically and aesthetically—but as
the source of the dollars which purchased all those beautiful
paintings in the National Gallery of Art in Washington.
The duPonts are not the "merchants of death," whose gun-
powder has boomed on the battlefields of many wars; they

are the donors of the quiet rolling lawns and neatly-clipped greenery of the Winterthur estate near Wilmington, visited annually by scores of thousands of admiring tourists.

Respectability. Social responsibility. The magnanimity of voluntary giving. Family foundations have become as famed, in their own right, as the families themselves. Thus are images scrubbed clean. Insuring that the images *remain* clean is the function of two groups vital to foundation philanthropy—the trustees and the professional staffs.

CHAPTER **3**

Guardians of the Money— and the Status Quo

THE PROTOTYPAL FOUNDATION TRUSTEE is a man in his sixties who was graduated from a private college and either practices law or has a business in the immediate vicinity of his foundation's home base.[1] He is the personification of the WASP ethnos dominant in America in the second half of the twentieth century. His politics, if stated, are moderate Republican. His skin is white; few black faces are found in the board rooms of the twenty-five largest foundations. (One notable exception is Whitney N. Young, Jr., president of the National Urban League; he is a trustee of the Rockefeller Foundation. The Ford Foundation, despite its pioneering role in racial relations, had a board as white

51

as the membership committee of a Jackson, Mississippi, country club until the election of Dr. Vivian Henderson, president of Clark College, in Atlanta, Georgia, in early 1970.) His exception-to-the-prototype colleagues, when they exist, are educators of the subdued conventionality necessary for ascension to prominence through the bureaucracy of academia or 1940-vintage iconoclasts with heresies made respectable by the passage of time.

The characteristics of trustee rule have a distinctively monarchal cast: arbitrary decision; secrecy; nonaccountability for actions; lifetime tenure; hereditary succession (in that boards are self-perpetuating, with incumbent members choosing persons to fill vacancies); aloofness from public opinion, and at times more than a little disdain for it; the unbridled authority to satisfy personal whims in disbursing money or to reward social friends or institutions willing to reciprocate by glorification of his name or that of the foundation he represents; remoteness from the great mass of people beneath his social and economic station and unawareness of or contempt for their needs; suspicion of new ideas for philanthropic spending and of the persons advocating them; pride in conservation of the wealth entrusted to him, rather than innovation in spending it—in sum, a regal do-nothingism, nonmalicious in intent, but sorely wasteful of national resources through stifling passivity. Foundation boards are representative of *a* community, but not of *the* community. One looks in vain among directors of the twenty-five largest for a labor-union leader, a small merchant, a farmer who actually tills the soil. Instead, one finds, in seemingly unending procession, the banker, the corporation executive, the lawyer from a large firm, the nonteaching "educator," the social and the business friend of the foundation creator.

Put most cruelly, foundation trustees view the present with almost as much alarm and consternation as medieval kings did the future. Not unintelligent, these watchdogs of wealth have the uneasy feeling the world is changing ("You know something is happening but you don't know what it is, do you, Mr. Jones?" sums up folksinger Bob Dylan) and are not sure what to make of it. Their confusion is plainly visible in the "on-the-other-hand" and the "either-or" argumentative style of foundation annual-reportese. Here is a connoisseur's specimen from the 1968 annual report of the Alfred P. Sloan Foundation:

In facing these dilemmas [of what to do about domestic issues and turmoil in society] the Sloan Foundation can learn a great deal by examining its past, but it must do much more than this, for the history of our present society is not a simple extension of what has gone before. From that past, however, we find evidence overwhelmingly in support of the importance of investing in people—people of promise and commitment. Equally important, we find it is possible to strike a reasonable balance between ventures whose objectives are to be achieved in the short term and those whose objectives are long range. At the same time that we reaffirm many of the foundation's past concerns, we can modify and extend them in recognition of the radically changed nature of our times.

At another point, wondering whether the turmoil in American schools should be exploited by foundations which hope to improve the system, the Sloan Foundation declared: "Any foundation which is concerned with education must stay alert to such opportunities. At the same time, it is not necessary or desirable to throw overboard time-tested values and aspirations."

The Sloan trustees should well be cognizant of the

teachings of "past concerns," and eager to protect "time-
tested values and aspirations," for their ages and backgrounds make them veritable caricatures of the breed. Of
the eighteen directors whose names appeared in the 1968
annual report, four were seventy-five years old; one was seventy-seven; one was seventy-one. Five were in their sixties;
two, in their fifties; the youngest was forty-nine. The average age was 62.6 years. The professional backgrounds were
overwhelmingly big business and finance: two former executives, now directors, of the General Motors Corporation;
the president and a director of Morgan Guaranty Trust
Company of New York; a director of E. I. duPont de Ne-
mours & Company; a senior partner of Lehman Brothers,
the investments firm; the president of Bell Telephone Labo-
ratories; a former board chairman of New York Life Insurance Company; the chairman of the corporation of Massachusetts Institute of Technology; the chairmen of Dun &
Bradstreet, Inc., and Xerox Corporation; the vice chairman
of International Business Machines; the president of Wesleyan University (whose most recent prior employment was
as president of the American Stock Exchange); Laurance S.
Rockefeller; and five philanthropoids, four of whom worked
for the Foundation itself, the fifth the board chairman of the
Sloan-Kettering Institute for Cancer Research, which
draws major support from the Foundation.*

---

* Alfred P. Sloan, president of General Motors from 1923 to 1937 and chairman
through 1956, created the foundation in 1937 and served as its active chairman
until he died in 1966. He formed the Foundation one year after the Treasury Department caused him acute public embarrassment by revealing that he and Mrs.
Sloan had avoided $1,921,587 in income taxes over a three-year period in the
1920s by the use of personal holding companies for their GM stock. The device
was not illegal, but the disclosure stung Sloan into releasing a tax return showing
that of his 1936 annual income of $2,876,310, he paid $1,725,790 in taxes and divided the remainder between charity and personal expenses. Creation of the Foundation, with an initial endowment of $10,000,000, was overshadowed by a forty-
seven-day sitdown strike at GM because of Sloan's refusal to bargain with the
United Auto Workers.[2]

That one-third of the Sloan Foundation's trustees are over seventy is possible because the foundation's bylaws do not set a compulsory retirement age. At Ford, conversely, the retirement age is seventy. "As far as I know that has never been modified, never been broken in favor of any one individual," states President Bundy. In 1968 the trustees debated changing this rule, with several seeing some form of limitation as the only guarantee of a reasonable turnover, geriatric medicine being what it is, and others simply not wanting to lose the services of the redoubtable (but seventy-year-old) Eugene R. Black. The compromise decision (applied first to former defense secretary Robert S. McNamara, who was elected in 1968) was to make board terms for six years, with only one re-election permitted. Bundy thinks this procedure "may . . . give us a sense of freedom in getting younger men. One of the difficulties of looking at a man of 35, is that if you appoint him, you are going to have 35 years of him. Therefore, you wait and say, 'Let's get somebody who is more seasoned,' or there is a tendency that way." [3]

The twenty-five largest foundations share a suspicion of acquiring young men. The only "outsider" trustees of less than forty years among them are Bill D. Moyers, formerly assistant to President Johnson and ex-publisher of *Newsday,* who was thirty-five when elected to the Rockefeller Foundation board in the spring of 1969, and William Donaldson, a Wall Street broker, who was thirty-eight when elected to the Ford board in early 1970. The Moody Foundation includes among its trustees Shearn Moody, Jr., thirty-four years old, but he is a family member.

Although one hears murmurs from philanthropoids that there is not "an adequate variety of trustee experience with current problems of the society," as the Carnegie Corporation's Alan Pifer wrote in his 1968 President's Report, few are willing to take more than tentative steps toward broader representation. As Pifer notes, some foundations take the view that "trustees can best serve the general interest precisely by not being representative of special interests." Pifer was unhappy that boards are "largely drawn from the same social class, the same age group, the same professions, the same educational background, the same sex, and the same race." And, peculiarly, he appeared to be describing his own board, which as of the end of 1968 was composed of the following:

—Fifteen persons, the average age of whom was 59.9 years, ranging from Pifer's forty-eight years to sixty-seven for attorney Charles M. Spofford; nine were over sixty.

—Seven graduates of Harvard, six of Yale, two with degrees from both institutions. Only one man, Robert F. Bacher, provost of the California Institute of Technology, attended a public college (the University of Michigan).

—Three attorneys; four industrialists (Louis W. Cabot, president of the Cabot Corporation, a chemical firm; Aiken W. Fisher, board chairman of Fisher Scientific Company; Malcolm A. McIntyre, president of the chemical division of Martin Marietta Corporation; and David A. Shepard, retired executive of Standard Oil of New Jersey); a broker, Amyas Ames, chairman of the executive committee of Kidder, Peabody & Company, Inc.; a publishing executive, Harding F. Bancroft, executive vice president of the *New York Times*; an educator, Caryl P. Haskins, president of the Carnegie Institution of Washington; a banker, Walter B. Wriston, president of First National City Bank of New York; a family member, Mrs. Carnegie Miller, niece of Andrew Carnegie; a philanthropoid, Pifer; and Frederick B. Adams, Jr., director of the Pierpont Morgan Library.

—Easterners: Bacher lives in California; Fisher in Pittsburgh. The other thirteen directors live and work in the Boston-Washington axis.

In a critical *Harper's Magazine* article in January, 1966, Washington philanthropist Phillip Stern challenged the Ford Foundation to take advantage of pending retirements to broaden its board's makeup. Stern noted that the board contained two college presidents, but no educators; three editor/publishers, but no working newsmen or columnists; and a full complement of industrialists, bankers and lawyers.[4] Seven vacancies have occurred in the sixteen-member board since 1966, and five of them had been filled as of October, 1969. The replacements show the foundation's penchant for recruiting Establishment figure to replace Establishment figure.

One replacement was ex officio, Bundy for retiring president Henry T. Heald. The other retirees, all caught by the seventy-year rule, were John J. McCloy, the chairman, a partner in the New York law firm of Milbank, Tweed, Hadley & McCloy and former U.S. high commissioner to Germany; Donald K. David, a foundation executive; Mark F. Ethridge, the journalist and editor; Lawrence M. Gould, president emeritus of Carleton College; Eugene R. Black, the financier; and John Cowles, chairman of the Minneapolis Star and Tribune Company. The replacements were Kermit Gordon, president of the foundation-supported Brookings Institution of Washington and director of the budget under Presidents Kennedy and (briefly) Johnson; Alexander Heard, chancellor of Vanderbilt University in Nashville; John H. Loudon, board chairman of Royal

Dutch Petroleum Company, The Hague, Netherlands; and Robert S. McNamara, president of the International Bank for Reconstruction and Development (the World Bank, popularly), former secretary of defense, and also former Ford Motor Company president.

Gordon and McNamara are men of such catholic interests and talents that they defy categorization; yet both are institutional figures, and McNamara's position as World Bank president is as demanding as a cabinet post. Heard's presence was explained to me by a Ford officer: "In 1966 we went South. We gave more than a million bucks to the Southern Regional Council. We were going to be damned conspicuous there. We needed a sensible Southerner on the board. Heard." Loudon, a native and citizen of the Netherlands, was brought onto the board by Black, who is also a director of Royal Dutch Petroleum. No Ford officer would comment on the uncommonly long lag (more than ten months) in naming replacements for Black and Cowles, who retired as of January 1, 1969.

Thus, a nearly fifty percent turnover in Ford board members had a barely perceptible impact on its composition—or on its liking for senior citizens. In 1963 ten of the Ford directors were in their sixties, three in their fifties, two (brothers Henry and Benson Ford) in their forties; the average age was 60.5. In 1969, despite the infusion of younger blood into the foundation (Bundy is fifty; Heard, fifty-two; and McNamara, fifty-three) the average age had decreased only to 59.7 years.

MOST TRUSTEES of the twenty-five largest serve with little or no compensation, for an obvious reason: they are rich men, and accepting fees for administering a charitable organization would be extraordinarily poor public relations, both for themselves and for the foundation. The Carnegie Corporation at one time paid travel expenses of trustees' wives or daughters to meetings; now the trustees receive only their personal expenses. The trustees of the various Rockefeller charities receive nothing, as do those of the Commonwealth Fund, and the Longwood, Mott, Kellogg, or Lilly foundations. Paul Mellon and his sister Ailsa Mellon Bruce, received no trustee pay from the Avalon or Old Dominion foundations, created from their share of Andrew Mellon's fortune. Nonfamily trustees of the Avalon Foundation were each paid $5,000 annually, as was the president, Charles S. Hamilton, Jr. (who received an additional $40,000 in that capacity). Moody Foundation trustees received $5,000 each (family members included); Houston Endowment trustees, $2,000 each (three of them are also salaried officers).

Asked about Ford Foundation trustee pay by Representative Rogers C. B. Morton in 1969, McGeorge Bundy said: "It has been for many years $5,000 a year for members of the board, and I may say they earn it." [5] Bundy's answer was somewhat incomplete. According to the Ford Foundation's 1968 tax returns, the board chairman, Julius A. Stratton, was paid $45,000 salary in that capacity in addition to the $5,000 in trustee fees, as well as travel and other expenses of $19,698. Eugene R. Black received $20,000 extra as chairman of the finance committee. John H. Loudon commutes from The Hague for meetings, and thus ran up a travel expense tab of $10,494.92, which the Foundation paid. (Other travel expenses ranged from $486.25 for U. S. District Judge Charles E. Wyzanski Jr., who lives in Boston, to $1,830 for John Cowles, president of the Minneapolis

Star and Tribune Company. Henry Ford II got $1,403 for travel from Detroit.)

For these fees, the Ford directors gather four times annually for meetings which begin late Wednesday afternoon and adjourn after lunch on Friday. In addition, each member serves on committees, and Bundy says individuals "with special skills are often asked to make special inquiries into particular proposals or to join in consultations on large issues in policy." (Director Bethuel M. Webster, a New York lawyer, has a strong personal interest in conservation, for example, and is a persistent devil's advocate on any programs presented by the staff.) The Ford trustees work an average of eighteen to twenty-two days annually. Black, because of his chairmanship of the finance committee and his proximity to the Foundation offices, works perhaps more than any other single director. But, as one foundation executive has said, "With only a couple of exceptions, you are talking about men who earn $100,000 a year or more; they're not at Ford for the money."

Conversely, trustees of the Duke Endowment, the creation of North Carolina tobacco and power magnate James Buchanan Duke, are in the peculiar position of earning far more in fees than most of them do in their full-time occupations: $43,003 each in 1968, the last year for which federal tax returns are available. Under the indenture through which Duke established the Endowment, the fifteen trustees each receive one-fifteenth of three percent "of the income, revenues and profits" earned on the estate each year. The fees have risen dramatically along with the fortunes of Duke Power Company, the Endowment's major holding. In 1962, each trustee received $28,596; in 1965, $33,247; in 1966, $40,193.

Several trustees also held well-paying positions with the

Endowment and with Duke Power. Marshall I. Pickens
(now retired), the highest ranking professional staff member, received $43,003 as his share of trustee fees and another
$45,000 as supervisor of the Endowment's main office in
Charlotte, North Carolina, for a total of $88,003, making
him the best-paid foundation officer in the United States.
Pickens received another $6,300 in fees as a director of
Duke Power. William B. McGuire received $90,000 in di-
rect pay from the Duke Power Company, of which he was
president, plus retirement benefits worth $43,741, plus his
trustee pay, for total remuneration from the Duke interests
of $176,744. Thomas L. Perkins, chairman of the Endow-
ment board, also served Duke Power as a trustee, for which
he was paid $25,000. Other Endowment trustees who re-
ceived director fees in 1968 from Duke Power were Benjamin F. Few, former board chairman of Liggett & Myers
Tobacco Company, $6,300; Robert C. Edwards, president
of Clemson University, $6,300; and Kenneth C. Towe,
former president of American Cyanamid Company, $1,300
for two meetings he attended before retiring.

Although the trustee fees are provided in Duke's indenture, there is no obligation that they be accepted; indeed
Doris Duke, daughter of the founder, began waiving her
portion in 1965 (because of mild rumbles from Internal
Revenue Service, Pickens told me in a 1969 interview). The
indenture provides for ten trustee meetings per year; Pickens says special committees on hospital, education, and or-
phan affairs gather prior to each formal trustee meeting, "to
go over their share of the agenda." Also, he says, "there is
considerable correspondence and report reading; they must
come to the meetings prepared."

Yet, the Duke Endowment maintains a staff that is both
large and well-paid in comparison with other foundations:

five officers earn more than $20,000 a year; almost a dozen others earn from $14,000 to $20,000. The Endowment also retains the services of a professional investments advisory company, at a further cost of around $30,000 per year.

The trustee fees look even larger when put into juxtaposition with another stipulated beneficiary of the Duke estate—retired Methodist ministers and their widows and dependent families. In 1968 the Endowment distributed $250,000 to 257 ministers, 287 widows, and 49 children. The largest check was $887.37 for a minister with 48.5 years of service—less than the Duke Endowment trustees received for one of their meetings.

I asked each Duke trustee, by letter, "In view of the fact that Duke trusteeships are part-time positions, and that a professional staff is available for conduct of the Endowment's daily business, can acceptance of such a high fee be considered consistent with the intent of Mr. Duke's indenture?" Secretary R. B. Henney, replying for the entire board, wrote:

> While the Duke Endowment does have a small but dedicated professional staff to handle the daily operations of the endowment, the trustees, all of whom are members of various committees of trustees, are called upon to render substantial services which including holding ten board meetings and numerous committee meetings throughout the year to establish policy, review requests for grants, make recommendations to the full board and give general direction to the operations of the endowment. While the professional staff is very capable and very necessary, the responsibility, knowledge, skill and judgment of the trustees remain in the trustees and cannot be delegated to any other persons.

Trustee W. B. McGuire added that his salary as Duke Power Company president "is very considerably less than the salaries customarily paid to chief executives by companies the size of Duke Power Company. In fact, it is about the average salary paid by companies less than half the size of Duke Power Company."

What are the criteria for picking persons for these handsomely paid sinecures? "We look for good people," Pickens says simply. The indenture suggested—but did not require —that they be natives or residents of North or South Carolina. With the exception of two Duke Power executives who live in New York suburbs, all trustees are Carolinians. Persons drawn from outside the Endowment and power company include: Mrs. Mary Duke Biddle Trent Semans, Buck's niece, forty-nine years old, who describes herself in *Who's Who* as "clubwoman," and who is active in hospital, library and other civic affairs in Durham, North Carolina, of which she has been mayor pro tem; Amos R. Kearns, sixty-four, president of Crown Hosiery Mills, High Point, North Carolina, where he is a former mayor and Chamber of Commerce president; and Dr. Wilburt C. Davison, seventy-seven years old, retired dean and professor of pediatrics at the Duke University School of Medicine. The amount of remuneration received by these trustees is not common knowledge even in Charlotte, where its main offices are located. When one ranking citizen heard the fee, he exclaimed voluntarily: "Why, that's preposterous! —— [naming a trustee] is a senile old man and can barely find his way out of the house. You mean to tell me that he is paid $40,000 a year?"

Pickens says Duke Endowment board keeps Duke Power representatives on the board because "much of our resources come from their operations." So it is with other foundations whose assets are concentrated in a single company. The John A. Hartford Foundation, which owns $236,194,013 of stock (twenty-two percent) in the Great Atlantic and Pacific Tea Company, has three longtime A&P executives on its board: Harold D. Hoag, Melvin W. Allredge, and William F. Leach, employees since 1924, 1931 and 1915, respectively. The Hartford Foundation spends upwards of $16,000,000 a year on medical research; as of January 1, 1968, it was supporting 252 projects at 133 hospitals, medical schools, and other research facilities in sixty-four communities in the United States and Canada; yet not a single medical doctor is on its board.

The Lilly Endowment board can find a quorum in the offices of Eli Lilly & Company: Burton E. Beck is president of the Lilly Company; Eugene N. Beesley is board chairman; Byron P. Hollett is with the law firm of Baker & Daniels of Indianapolis, which represents the company; Thomas H. Lake is president of Lilly International; Nicholas H. Moyes is the retired financial vice president; Eli Lilly (son of founder Josiah Lilly) and his wife, Ruth, round out the board. There is not a single non-Lilly representative.

The W. K. Kellogg Foundation, which owns fifty-one percent of the stock of the Kellogg Company, valued at $409,000,000 (as of August 31, 1969) identifies only one Kellogg Company official among the nine active trustees in the frontispiece of its 1968 annual report (two other persons are carried as "honorary" trustees). This is Lyle C. Roll, chairman of the board of the Kellogg Company. Standard & Poor's *Directory of Corporate Executives and Directors,* however, reveals that three other trustees also serve as Kellogg Company directors: A. H. Aymond, Jr., chairman of the board of Consumers Power Company, Jackson, Michigan; John O. Snook, Chicago attorney; and Kenneth V. Zwiener, board chairman of Harris Trust and Savings Bank, Chicago. The three ranking Foundation executives also serve on the board, meaning that seven of the nine trustees are employees either of the Kellogg Company or the Foundation.

ENTIRE LEGAL RESPONSIBILITY for management of a foundation rests with the board of trustees, and, in a sense, they can be considered its "owners." They are charged with insuring that foundation funds are invested and spent properly and that the founder's wishes are obeyed, insofar as is possible under the law. The hiring of a professional staff to manage day-to-day operations is an explicit delegation of these responsibilities; yet the conduct of a foundation, ultimately, is that which the trustees desire it to be. In tightly controlled family foundations the professional staff is frequently nothing more than an instrument for carrying out the desires of the donor. The experience can be a pleasant one, if founder and philanthropoid are ideologically compatible. A former minister, long active in the civil rights movement, now staff director of a smaller Eastern foundation endowed by a stockbroker, told me: "Mr. —— gave me a broad mandate to provide seed money for community action projects and told me to work out the details as I saw best. I tell him everything I do and he could veto my ideas. But we are comfortable together, and we believe in the same things, and he trusts my judgment."

Conversely, another philanthropoid was asked to become chief executive of a large family foundation ("one whose name is in the paper, and, frequently, but let's not go into the identity") and had a preliminary meeting with the donor. The philanthropoid had known the family since childhood and considered them personal friends. The con-

versation was warm for several hours, with the philanthropoid understanding that he was to have a fair amount of autonomy in developing programs. Then came a jolt: "Very
casually this rich man dropped into his conversation the
sentence, 'Of course, now since this is *our* money, we'll tell
you how to spend it.' He couldn't have insulted me more if
he had kicked me in the face. He didn't want a foundation
executive, he wanted a figurehead. The salary he offered
was several times what I was earning, but so far as I was
concerned, the interview ended right then."

Fund-raisers dependent upon foundation largess recognize the advantage—and also the dangers—of dealing with
directors rather than staff. Richard H. Andres, executive director of the Corning Glass Works Foundation, warns, in
the foundations relations manual of the American College
Public Relations Association, that attempts to vault over
staff to trustee friends "may get you nothing except a ticket
to Ill-Will Land." [6] But consultant Jeanne Brewer stated in
the same forum that while personal connections might be
negligible in the large, well-staffed foundations, they are important when dealing with small family foundations which
are "unhampered by program or policy." Miss Brewer said:
"Most of them are having fun with their own money; having fun avoiding all those taxes, supporting any causes they
darned well want to support—some worthy, some not so
worthy. Friendship, flattery, influence, pressures—one or all
may work with these foundations if we regard them as
human beings, not as institutions." [7]

Charles A. Brecht, a vice president of John Price Jones,
Inc., one of the more prominent professional fund-raising
firms, once did an analysis of ten successful college grant applications. Only two were carried out without trustee-to-
trustee contacts between the foundation and the college.

Below $50,000, Brecht counsels, staff-to-staff might suffice. "But, again, if some trustee-to-trustee contact is also involved, the chances of success are greatly enhanced. . . . I would say that there are only a half dozen or so giant foundations . . . in which leadership, through a trustee-to-trustee-relationship, may not be able to bear influence or would be unwelcome." [8] The merits of the project, he concedes, "means a great deal."

Nonetheless, Brecht says: "I know of several gifts of some of these giants which would not have been made or would have been smaller, if a chat in an office, or at a social function, or at the golf course, or a phone call had not taken place between the opposite numbers on the trustee level of the institution and the foundation." Of foundations closely aligned with a single corporation, through stockholdings or overlapping directorates, or both, Brecht declares, ". . . these foundations must be treated as self-interested groups, without the lofty eleemosynary motives which guide the giving policies and operations of the philanthropic foundations."

As a professional fund-raiser, Brecht does not agree with the suggestion (chiefly from philanthropoids) that it is "not cricket" to bypass the staffs. "If we are to succumb to thinking of this kind, then we ought to do all our fund-raising via letters and pamphlets. Foundations are basically people, whether they are big, medium or small—and people give to people, not to robots, machines . . . or other inanimate objects . . ." He advised the college money raisers: "You ought to lead a crusade to prevent approaches to foundations from becoming so impersonalized that in the future your appeal might be accepted or rejected by inserting it in an electronic device such as Univac or some other giant brain."

But Brecht does suggest diplomatic discretion in making the trustee contacts. The approach should be made *before* anything is said to the foundation staff, lest the philanthropoid feel the supplicant is attempting to pressure him into accepting a project to which he is cold. If the staff man is presented with a project in which he knows his trustee has *already* expressed an interest, he won't automatically close his mind "because it is presented inarticulately or because the [college] president smokes a pipe, or because he never thought much of the institution before or didn't know anything about it." [9]

It is accepted practice for universities to recruit actively foundation directors and other rich men for their own boards with the admitted intention of wheedling funds from them. Arnaud C. Marts, president of Marts & Lundy, Inc., a professional fund-raiser for nonprofit organizations, was asked to serve as president of Bucknell University at a time of financial crisis: the main administration building had burned, and professional councils were threatening to withdraw accreditation for the engineering school unless new facilities were constructed. In his memoirs Marts relates that he "mentally canvassed the trustees and discovered that I could count on only two of the twenty-five whose generosity could or would reach five figures. . . . This lesson sank in deeply. . . . I . . . resolved that when the next emergency at Bucknell should arise requiring substantial generosity there would be at least twelve or fifteen members of the board of trustees who could do something far more than cast a vote authorizing me to go out and find someone else to provide the funds for doing it. I let it be known among alumni and parents that I would like to learn of men worthy in their own lives and spirits to be trustees of Bucknell University and who were generous to causes providing education for ambitious boys and girls." [10] Marts succeeded: when Bucknell needed $1,000,000 quickly a few years later, he raised it within his own board "with little public activity or notice." (Among his trustees was Pennsylvania oilman Michael L. Benedum, who had created a foundation honoring his son, Claude Worthington Benedum, who died of flu during World War I, while in the army. The foundation has assets of more than $40,000,000, and it has been a consistent supporter of Bucknell.)

Whatever the efficiency for raising money, the trustee-to-trustee dealings have inherent insidious features. Personal friendships and social credentials, and not the merits of projects, determine which institutions and individuals receive money. A vice president of a New York group which is dependent upon foundation support told me:

> I estimate that I spend sixty percent of my time on fund-raising. Because I do know quite a few of the really rich people in this country, it's worthwhile for me to circulate with them as much as possible. So I spend part of my summer in Newport, part of my winter in Palm Beach. You have to be discreet and subtle. If you are *asked* what you do, you say so, briefly. If you are *asked* from whence comes your support, you say so, briefly —that is, that we rely upon contributions from individuals and foundations. If you are *asked* for more information, you give it or arrange a meeting for some later date. But the fact that you are at these gatherings as a social equal gives you a headstart. Again, one of your trustees or consultants might have a small affair intended to put you with a potential benefactor. You pack the house with enough other people to fill up the party, but the rich man is the *pièce de résistance,* and late in the evening, when the plates are all cleared away and the brandy has been poured, the host says, "Oh, by the way, Mr. Guest, has —— ever told you about the exciting things they're doing over at ——?" Very general discussion, and the next

day you receive a phone call from the chap who runs Mr. Guest's foundation, and you have a leisurely lunch with him, and get down to the dollars and cents.

There is philanthropic incest: Charles A. ——, a trustee of the Good Works Foundation, is fund-raising chairman for the Save Our Elm Trees Committee. His friend, Frederick T. ——, a trustee of the Better Works Foundation, is fund-raising chairman of the Save Our Oak Trees Committee. You give to our cause this year, Fred tells Charlie, and my foundation will take care of your committee next year.

There are overlapping business interests. Foundation trustee Smith runs a supply firm which has a six-figure volume of business with the manufacturing company owned by university trustee Brown. The university needs $300,000 for a new Punic War research project. At a trustees' meeting, members scan board lists of prospective target foundations, searching for personal contacts. "Hey," exclaims Brown. "Here's Joe Smith; I'll be talking with him at my office tomorrow. Let's try his foundation first." When the men meet to discuss renewal of Smith's supply contract, Brown mentions, oh so casually, that Old Ivy University "is doing some interesting things in Punic War history. I'd like to get you together for lunch with their president at the club next week." Brown says not a word about the pending request for money, but Smith receives the university president not as just another educator but as someone in whom a vital business customer has a personal interest.

The foundation executive director, meantime, has spent several months with a community action group that wants a grant to run a half-way house for convicts. With the aid of consultants, he has drafted a comprehensive prospectus calling for the local group to furnish a staff and part of the financing. But when he begins making his presentation to the foundation board, Smith interrupts him: "I think we'd better hold that in abeyance for a few more meetings. I've come across some exciting new work that is being done in Punic War history, and we can take this field all for ourselves, for no other foundation has any projects there. Everybody's messing around in the slums today, being dogooders with the poor and the blacks. We're not going to make a name for ourselves for following the pack. Now this Punic War thing is innovative, because it's new, and it's a definite contribution to scholarship, because no significant work has been done in the field since the early 1900s, and . . ."

And the $300,000 goes to the university, and Smith's supply contract increases to seven figures, and over the course of the next decade the Punic War Studies Center produces two PhDs, both of whom choose to remain there as teachers and researchers.*

There are isolated foundations which vigorously resist trustee courtships. The Max C. Fleischmann Foundation states in its literature: "Personal interviews with the trustees should not be sought either before or after the filing of an application. If the formal application needs amplification, the trustees themselves will request it either orally or in writing. Experience has shown that it is much more satisfactory to have as much of the record as is possible in writing. Any discussions or indication of interest prior to or after submission of a written application shall not be construed as a commitment by the foundation in any way."

* Although presented in fictionalized form, this episode is *not* fiction, nor is it exaggerated. Details have been altered to protect the hide of the philanthropoid concerned, who swallowed much pride and remained at the foundation and who was still mad enough five years later to tell me the story.

Ford and Rockefeller trustees regularly forward "request" mail to the foundation offices, telling the supplicant they have referred his application to the appropriate staff member. Yet, a Ford executive told me:

> I'd be less than candid if I tried to tell you that our directors don't listen to personal appeals, especially on the larger projects. Each of them is a man of stature in his own right, and each of them circulates with university presidents and trustees as a matter of course. It's perfectly natural that they hear of new ideas, and pass them along to the staff, either via Bundy or directly. But I will say this: if the proposal is something way outside our scope, nothing is done with it; a trustee recommendation can't override established policy. If he feels strongly about it, he's always entitled to put it before the board personally.

FREDERICK P. KEPPEL, the head of the Carnegie Corporation from 1923 to 1941, once told a Congressional committee he believed foundations should "operate with glass pockets." Only through complete disclosure of their activities could the foundations gain public respect, Keppel believed. Furthermore, secrecy by one foundation tarnishes the reputation of all foundations. Here Keppel liked to quote St. Paul: ". . . whether one member suffer, all the members suffer with it; or one member be honored, all the members rejoice with it."

To the outsider, watching foundations is akin to watching a TV show without the sound track. You see interesting images, and get a sense of motion; through deduction, you might even manage to block out a fairly accurate story line. But why the people are doing what they are doing, and what they hope to accomplish, remains a mystery. And after

one watches the foundations awhile he realizes that, like the
TV viewer, he is seeing only what the foundations decide
should go on camera.

For dollars-and-cents matters, the basic source material
on foundations is Form 990-A, which they use to make their
annual report to the Internal Revenue Service. At the in-
sistence of Congressman Wright Patman, the IRS, since
1963, has made public all portions of the 990-As except the
names of contributors. The public information supposedly
includes the salaries paid each officer; the amount of holdings, both at book value and fair market value; the excess of
income over expenditures (or vice-versa); the name and address of grant recipients, the amount paid and the purpose
(medicine, education, and so forth); and, on stocks that represent more than a five-percent holding in a single business,
the date, manner, and cost of acquisition, the current fair
market value, the number of shares owned and the number
outstanding, and the amount of dividends returned. The
public portion of the 990-As may be inspected at the IRS
district office where they are filed, at the national IRS office
in Washington, or at central repositories operated by the
Foundation Center, a private, foundation-supported group,
in Washington and New York. (The Center also has repository libraries in Atlanta, Austin, Berkeley, Chicago, Cleveland, Kansas City, and Los Angeles, with regional collections of 990-As.)

The 990-As, because they are written by lawyers and
tax accountants for their opposite numbers in the government, are mysterious accumulations of numbers which,
standing alone, tell little of what a foundation does or how
it earns and spends its money. A $100,000 grant for "educa-
tional" purposes could be to erect a new mathematics building, to endow a department of free love, or to create a chair

to propagate the foundation's theories of taxation, government, or religion. A $100,000 medical grant could finance studies of a cure for gout—or of the dietary value of litchi nuts. A 990-A can show that Professor Blank has received $15,000 to continue his study of the sleeping habits of free-lance writers, without revealing that during seven previous grant-years he established only that some like pillows and others don't.

The itemization of investments is frequently no more revealing than the fact that the foundation owns seventy-five percent of the Acme Development Corporation, the nature and operations of which remain unstated. Nor does the 990-A reveal how much money the foundation donor received from the Acme Development Corporation through salary or dividends, information which would put the foundation's return from dividends into proper perspective. IRS justifies the withholding of the names of donors on the grounds that to make this information public would violate the taxpayer's personal privacy. Yet *because* these names are withheld, the public does not know the backers of such "educational" foundations as Freedoms Foundation at Valley Forge, Pennsylvania; nor does it know whether a foundation is taking donations from firms with which its controlling party does business.

Of the 30,242 foundations on the IRS list, only 140 issue printed public reports on an annual or biennial basis, ranging from the attractively bound hard-back volumes with gold lettering of the Richard King Mellon Foundation, through the hefty paperbound volumes of Ford, Rockefeller, Duke, and Sloan, down to pamphlets of lesser size. Only seven of the ten largest foundations publish such reports, the omissions being the Pew Memorial Trust, the Irvine Foundation, and the Charles Stewart Mott Foundation. About one-third of the 261 foundations with assets of over $10,000,000 publish reports, and the Foundation Center thinks "this is a scandal." The Center says: "Foundations are quasi-public institutions, and they have an obligation to make information on the activities readily available to the public. The fact that the overwhelming majority of foundations do not do so is clear evidence that their trustees regard them as essentially private. This is damaging the whole foundation field." [11]

To its chagrin, the Foundation Center found that many foundations "strongly resisted" even its printing of a nationwide directory (chiefly for the convenience of people who wanted grants but lacked a central starting point). These foundations wouldn't give the Center information, and some "strongly opposed publication" of facts that were in the public domain via the IRS 990-A forms. Resistance varied from "threats of suit if we dared publish even the facts available in the public record" to complaints that publicity brings in enough callers to be a "decided nuisance," said the Center in its 1964 annual report.

To test the validity of this latter complaint, the Center invented a foundation; gave it a bogus deceased donor, a modest endowment, and a mailing address at the home of a staff member; and listed it in the directory with the notation that it "was not in a position to entertain present appeals of any sort." The Center reported: "No flood of mail materialized." In twelve months the "foundation" received only ten letters from applicants (one a fervent plea addressed to the donor, who was listed in the directory as deceased) and twenty-one pieces of junk mail.

Why the secrecy? Can it all be attributed to the regal spirit of the rich men who control the foundations—a public-be-damned attitude toward accountability? A panel of foundation executives at a 1967 conference at New York University ticked off these reasons for "constraints on reporting":

— In foundations where the donor family plays a dominant role, "an attitude of private decision prevails; recipients of grants tend to be institutions of special interest to the founding family. Policy towards the distribution of funds is predetermined; requests for support outside the interests of the donor are not welcomed."

— Reporting inhibits trustees from undertaking imaginative and innovative projects; experimentation suffers from early exposure, and projects might be criticized before they have a chance to prove themselves. "Prudence, therefore, would seem to call for a policy of quiet action."

— Foundations fear that publicity studies "emphasizing alternatives to governmental action" might make them vulnerable to government countermeasures, particularly loss of tax-exemption. And scientists feel that publicizing of proposals for studies at variance with government policy might make it difficult for them to get future support.

—Trustees and staff alike are reluctant to be held accountable, by virtue of sponsorship, for controversial findings.

—There were additional, miscellaneous reasons. Reports attract the attention of grant-seekers, who flood the foundation office with mail. Reports are costly and time-consuming to prepare. Reports appear boastful, and foundations shouldn't be "publicity seekers." Reports invite government inquiry.[12]

Frederick W. Bolman, associate director of the Esso

Educational Foundation, financed and controlled by Standard Oil Company of New Jersey, questions the efficacy of "handsome annual reports explaining what . . . [foundations] are doing and why." Bolman asks: "But who reads them, except other foundation executives? The three editions of the Foundation Directory [published by the Foundation Center] reveal a great deal, but these volumes are read mostly by people seeking funds. There has been a false humility based on an equally false pride frequent in much foundation thinking . . ." [13]

Foundation annual reports are not stirring literature, and they contain more nonsensical and self-serving sentences per page than any other existent printed matter save, possibly, for the *Congressional Record.*

As autobiographies tend to be, foundation reports are positive in tone. If a foundation is burned badly in one area, it withdraws to another, either remaining silent about the experience or shielding retreat with verbiage about "redirecting our resources to another phase of human needs." In going through more than a thousand annual reports, some decades old, representing the output of more than a hundred foundations, I found only one foundation which candidly told which of its projects failed and why—the Louis W. and Maud Hill Foundation, of St. Paul, Minnesota. In 1966, for example, Hill gave $35,000 to four St. Paul hospitals to create a computerized central-records facility for patients. "It soon became clear that the project was launched prematurely although enough work was done to indicate the feasibility and practicability of the concept," Hill reported the next year. "The project was cancelled. . . ." In another instance, Hill termed "unsuccessful" an attempt to introduce televised freshman and sophomore courses at the

University of Minnesota. Although the course content was adjudged good, and the TV classes did well academically, "the small enrollment response . . . made it necessary to discontinue this particular effort to establish a 'College of the Air.'"

But at other foundations, millions of dollars can be dissipated without a trace. During the 1950s, for example, Ford created a $210,000,000 endowment to "raise faculty salaries" at 615 colleges over a period of years. Later someone computed each professor benefited by four dollars per week, and that such a light layer of spending was having absolutely no effect on higher education. Ford abandoned blanket grants. Again, in the early 1960s, Ford gave $1,100,000 to the Philadelphia Council for Community Advancement to "mount coordinated attacks on deprivation in jobs, education, housing and recreation." In 1964 *Philadelphia Magazine* called the project "dead" and said, "nobody will acknowledge responsibility for the corpse." [14] Ford simply moved on to another city, and one can search its voluminous annual reports in vain for evaluatory comment. Yet such an evaluation may have provided excellent guidance for other projects of this type.

Ford's stated policy is to "respond fully to requests from the press and other media for information regarding amounts and purposes of grants," to publish "interim reports showing the progress of work and ideas within the foundation"; and to furnish information, "which we are in a position to provide," that is requested by Congress and other arms of government and from local and national educational, civic, and philanthropic organizations.[15] Ford maintains a well-staffed press office (formally the Office of Reports) which promptly and cheerfully finds answers to almost any question that can be asked.

Pamphlets, program descriptions, reprints of speeches by Ford executives, and other matter flow incessantly from this office, and one eventually gets the idea that he is learning more about Ford than he really cares to know. Yet Ford does have its limits. It will not release information that it thinks invades grantee privacy, and it refers to the grantees questions about operations and details of what they are doing with Ford grant money. Ford retains outside consultants to evaluate large and experimental grants and write detailed reports. These reports Ford considers to be no one's business but its own, and outsiders may not read them. Ford officers will talk about projects—the flops as well as the successes—so long as the opinions they express are not attributed to them publicly.

At the other extreme are the foundations that carry secrecy to the point of rudeness, not even declining requests for information but simply ignoring them. The Pew Memorial Trust ($541,000,000 in assets) won't receive inquirers at its office in a Pew-owned trust company in downtown Philadelphia. The Charles Stewart Mott Foundation ($413,000,000) and the Houston Endowment ($214,-000,000) would not respond to repeated requests for copies of their annual reports. These three foundations are among the twenty-five largest. A listing of smaller foundations which would not answer specific questions about their operations would fill two pages of this book. Manning Pattillo of the Foundation Center says he once met a university president who sent letters to 150 foundations. Only two acknowledged his communiqué; the 148 remained absolutely silent. Pattillo says "common courtesy and good public relations" demand better conduct from foundations.[16]

CHAPTER 4

The Philanthropoids

HERBERT B. WEST, a gregarious, inquisitive Southerner who is director of the New York Community Trust, once got into a conversation with an officer of a small, family-controlled foundation. The New York Community Trust, among other things, administers the grants programs of several hundred foundations, trusts, and other charitable organizations. West, who has a keen interest in the mechanics of philanthropy, asked the man to explain his foundation's grants procedures, hoping to learn something he could use in his own work. West quotes the reply:

Well, we don't know much about what we're doing, but we sure have a nice time doing it. Every December the chairman invites all of us to dinner. We have a few drinks and a good meal and a lot of laughs. After dinner he tells us how much we have to give away, and we all pitch in with ideas on who to give it to.

I usually suggest my college. Somebody else will tell about his niece who's working for a charity. I've always liked the girl, so we include the charity. And of course somebody's wife is always on the board of something or other, so we include that. It doesn't take much time.[1]

The shocking feature about the man's recitation, West said in repeating it later, was that the process he described is not an isolated phenomenon in philanthropy; to the contrary, it is the norm rather than the exception, even at several foundations on the twenty-five largest list. The Foundation Center counts only about a thousand "professionals" in the nation's foundations, several hundred of them clustered at the philanthropic factories operated by Ford and Rockefeller. As a result, there is philanthropic overkill in some locales, a vacuum in others. The Rockefeller staff directory lists enough names to fill a forty-three-page booklet. When Ford made a $630,000 grant in 1968 to the Southwest Council of La Raza, a Mexican-American group, the distribution list for the basic grant paper called for fifty-eight copies to be passed to twenty-eight persons, all in-house, and each invited to submit "comments and suggestions" to the foundation secretary, Howard Dressner.

Conversely, the Lilly Endowment, with assets of $579,659,732 and expenditures of almost $7,000,000 a year, gets along with a general manager, an adviser on religious affairs, and two secretaries, making its staff per-capita spending more than $1,500,000 annually. Not infrequently, Lilly is literally a one-man foundation. John S. Lynn, Lilly's $32,400-a-year general manager, interrupted our interview in August, 1969, several times to answer the telephone, apologetically explaining: "I'm sorry, both the girls are out of the office this afternoon, and I'm it."

Eighty-four percent of the foundations surveyed by the Peterson Commission in its 1969 study had no professional staff; eleven percent, a part-time staff; only five percent had full-time administrators. Fifty-eight percent of the foundations with assets between $10,000,000 and $100,000,000 did not maintain full-time staffs.

The proliferation of small foundations created solely for tax and business purposes further tarnishes the professional image of "foundation management." In 1936 the average expenditure per foundation was $117,000; the comparable figure for 1967 was $65,000 per foundation (and in dollars whose value had drastically shrunk in three decades). The *median* expenditure for 1967 was much lower: $9,000 to $17,000, if one disregards the inactive no-assets foundations which exist only on paper pending their utilization in estate settlements; much less than $5,000 per year if all 30,242 on the IRS list are counted. That such "foundations" even use the name galls the philanthropoids. One of them complained to me: "It's as if any guy who ever argued with a cop about a traffic ticket called himself a lawyer." In Herbert West's opinion, "It is usually felt that a foundation must have several million dollars in assets to be able to afford a professional director and still have money left for a meaningful grant program." [2] Arithmetic explains why: $2,000,000 in assets, invested in stock that yields five percent annually, would produce an income of $100,000. A foundation executive with the wits and initiative to be more than a human check-writing machine commands a salary of at least $20,000 a year.* Logistical support—an office, a secretary, stationery, and miscellaneous expenses—consume another $12,000 to $15,000 (more if the foundation is based in New York, as some forty-five percent of them are). The $100,000 is now $65,000, which simply is not enough money to require the full-time attention of a professional grant administrator, even if he hand-delivered all the checks. Thus, there is considerable incentive for both the foundation directors and the Internal Revenue Service to ask: "Why pay thirty percent in overhead costs for such a piddling program? The foundation lawyer has tolerably good taste; hereafter, he should decide where to spend the money. He'll charge a $1,000 fee, and run it from his office with his secretary."

Lawyers have conflicting opinions on the desirability of such arrangements. A New York attorney complains:

When you help a client create a foundation for estate or tax-planning purposes, you'd best realize that you are going to be stuck with "management" of it. This works fine when the client sits down and draws up a sensible list of established, recognized charities, and tells what percentage should go to each. Once a year your girl writes out a batch of checks, and you sign them.

Then you go to the other extreme. I once set up a foundation for a sweet little old lady whom our firm had represented for years. There wasn't much money involved, maybe $15,000 a year. But from the attention she gave it you'd have thought she was John D. Rockefeller, and she couldn't make up her mind. One week she'd be all hot about the Girl Scouts. The next week she'd go walking in Central Park and decide she

---

* This is not to say that *every* foundation executive who is paid more than $20,000 a year is ipso facto more than a human check-writing machine.

wanted to pay for the planting and care of a bed of flowers in a particular location, or one of her friends would convince her that no charity was more deserving than cerebral palsy. She'd drive me batty. Finally, I got to the point where I'd actually lie to her—tell her we couldn't make any more donations for six months because of the tax laws—and I'd give her a reason in legalistic double-talk. I had to, for self-protection. Her foundation was keeping me busy four and six hours a week (you ever try to call the Parks Department to get permission to endow a flower bed?) and I could not, in good conscience, bill her for all this time.

Yet another attorney says:

It's all part of the practice, especially when you're in tax and estate things as your normal fare. I'll even give you a little trade secret. Having absolute control of a foundation, even when it's a client's money, can be very convenient personally. A lawyer who is fairly active in the community receives far more requests for donations than he can handle from his own pocket. But if you are empowered to give $25 to the YMCA on behalf of the Joe Doakes Foundation, the fund-raising chairman is satisfied. He couldn't care less about the actual source of the check. All he knows is that he sent you a letter of solicitation, and received money by return mail. He doesn't bother you again.

"What do foundations need the most? Foundations need armed guards at the door—or at least some real honest-to-goodness hard-nosed bastards who are permitted to be nasty and winnow down the number of applicants for money in a way they wouldn't bother us again for a while. That way the rest of us could get some work done." The speaker was a program officer for one of the twenty-five largest foundations, responsible for higher education, and his day had been arduous, in a negative sort of way. Between 9:15 a.m. and noon he had rejected, by phone, by letter, and in person, requests from (1) an Ivy League school that wanted the foundation to assume financial responsibility for a professorial chair, now bereft of funds, established some years earlier by an alumnus; (2) a California college that decided the most efficacious way to revitalize its business school was to have the foundation buy it a computer; (3) another California college whose medical school had just learned it would not be receiving expected money from the National Institutes of Health, a federal agency, and wondered if the foundation would care to send out some dollars to fill the chink in its budget; and (4) nine other institutions whose application acquired the fatal endorsement, "outside program scope," at a lower staff level within the foundation.

On such money-demanding mornings the men inside the major United States foundations see the people on the outside as a rapacious, selfish bunch with the acquisitive characteristics of Jean Lafitte. (Asked once what he liked about foundation work, Robert Hutchins snapped: "You meet such interested people.")

The major requirement of a philanthropoid is compatibility with the rich and near-rich. Essentially, he is a member of a service industry, and one in which his primary loyalty is to him who gives the gift, not him who receives it. Courtiers of the American Establishment, rather than accepted members, philanthropoids are responsible for perpetuating the culture which created and brought success to their masters. That they call their particular kind of service "the promotion of human welfare" or "the betterment of education" makes them no less the trusted agents of the me who really matter in America, economically and socially. And they are agents who remain in their positions of derivative power only so long as the masters are happy.

During 1968 American foundations disbursed $1,500,000,000 in grants, through decisions both subjective and objective, made by a variety of men for a variety of reasons. If spread equally over the nation, the $1,500,000,000 divides to about $7.50 per citizen, and cynics have suggested this form of distribution would be about as equitable and productive as any existent foundation-grant program. This is not to be done, of course, but, nonetheless, the spending ultimately does affect human lives. "The possession of funds carries with it power to establish trends and styles of intellectual endeavor," states an internal Rockefeller Foundation analysis. "With the best will in the world the trustees of a foundation may select unwisely or place an emphasis where it should not be placed or initiate movements which serve only to close men's eyes to more promising avenues. To guard against these evils requires critical judgment, common sense, wide understanding and eternal vigilance . . ." [3]

A philanthropoid of unusual sensitivity once discussed grant recipients with me:

> When I am trying to decide between applications from researchers in the same general field, both of whom have worthwhile proposals, and ones which should be done, I can't help feeling a little like God. Dammit, it shouldn't be that way, but I know that what I decide is going to have a profound effect upon this man and his family, not only for the grant year but for the rest of his professional life. I think back to my own university days, and what it would have meant to us to have had that $7,000 extra from a foundation or what have you. What I am deciding, really, is whether this guy's wife has to take a job teaching at an elementary school, and leave the kids with a sitter all day, so that he can afford the year, or whether they'll get our money and have fairly normal lives. Sometimes I feel most uneasy when we interview applicants, because I

look at these people as human beings, rather than projects, and I'm supposed to decide grants on the basis of the value of the project, not whether I like one man or don't like another.

Let me give you another example. A group of citizens in Baltimore puts together a damned impressive community improvement project and asks for some of our money. So does another group in Rochester. What we decide here determines whether one neighborhood is to revive and whether another is to deteriorate and vanish. Am I being overdramatic about all this? I mean, everything in life revolves around decisions; some you can control, some you can't. People here will give you a lot of crap about being "strictly objective" in grant-making, and acting on the basis of which grant "will maximize our program objectives." I know all those words, because God knows but I've written enough of the papers. But what I do here in one morning can make or break a man's career, the difference between him starting something that could bring him a Nobel or leaving him in the corner as an assistant professor of humanities.

Although foundation officers freely use the word "profession" in referring to themselves and their work, the requirements for entering the priesthood of philanthropy are loose. Backgrounds of the staff men of the operating foundations are heavily (but not unanimously) academic, simply because there is such a wide overlap of education and philanthropy. But in a not atypical week of interviews, I talked with foundation presidents or ranking executives whose former occupations were: a vice president of a drug company; a professional engineer who was director of research administration for a diversified corporation; a Wall Street attorney; a law professor; a public-relations director for a small manufacturing concern; an assistant director of the Job Corps, a War on Poverty agency; a vice president for labor relations of an oil company; a professional fund-raiser for a private agency with an international program; an advertising man; and a president of a small college.

"Professionalism," when found in a foundation, is more apt to be professionalism in the foundation's area of interest, not in philanthropy itself. The Rockefeller Foundation sniffs at professional staff applicants who do not have doctorates. Nineteen of the twenty members of its agricultural sciences division staff in New York are PhDs, as are eleven of fourteen persons in the division of humanities and social sciences. Twelve of thirteen persons in the medical and natural sciences divisions are PhDs or MDs.

"A doctorate is evidence of professional accomplishment and competence," explains Dr. Sterling Wortman, director of the division of agricultural sciences. "When we recruit, we look for people who want to sign aboard Rockefeller for life, and the PhD tells us that they are good." The Foundation states formally:

> The very nature of the foundation's programs requires a high level of professional quality and sustained effort toward defined goals. In order to achieve progress on an international scale in the fields of public health, education, food production, population stabilization, and the arts, work must be supported over long periods of time . . . Such programs require the long-term services of qualified professional staff dedicated to the foundation." [4]

Although Rockefeller contracts are renewable annually, a person hired there can assume he has lifetime employment. But Rockefeller avoids any formal promise of tenure, for to do so would commit it to remain in specific areas indefinitely. In the 1950s, for instance, the board decided to dismantle the Foundation's public-health division on the grounds that government spending made further involve-

ment there unnecessary. As a result, many long-time
employees were dismissed when their contracts expired—a
bloodless, logical, and necessary purge, but a purge nonetheless, and one still discussed in the quiet of Rockefeller
offices with whispers and more than a little trembling. (The
Commonwealth Fund, faced with an identical decision in
the same field, permitted the employees to continue until
retirement age, then closed its public health division when
the last one was gone.)

As befits a career organization, Rockefeller president
Dr. J. George Harrar is a career man, whose first assignment was to establish an agricultural research facility in
Mexico in 1942. (The Mexicans were suspicious of Harrar.
Foreign oil companies had been nationalized only in 1938,
and the local press speculated he was in their country as an
"agent of the Rockefeller oil interests.") Joining Rockefeller
is akin to enlisting in the diplomatic service—or the foreign
legion. As of December 31, 1968, the foundation maintained offices in Belém, Brazil; Kandy, Ceylon; Santiago,
Chile; Bogotá and Cali, Colombia; New Delhi and Hydera-
bad, India; Lake Como, Italy; Mguga and Nairobi, Kenya;
Mexico City; Ibadan, Nigeria; Quezon City and Los Banos,
the Philippines; Castries, St. Lucia; Dar-es-Salaam, Tanza-
nia; Bangkok, Thailand; Port-of-Spain, Trinidad; Tunis,
Tunisia; and Kampala, Uganda. "Home" is two floors of
the Time-Life Building in New York; other U.S. offices are
in Berkeley, California (virus research program); Lincoln,
Nebraska (agricultural sciences); Boston (medical and natural sciences); New Haven (virus research) and Charlottes-
ville, Virginia (humanities and social sciences). When it
began, the Rockefeller Foundation consisted of one person
who shared a cubicle at 26 Broadway, then the office of the

Rockefeller oil empire, with a secretary and a four-drawer file cabinet. The Foundation's administrative expenses are now more than $2,500,000 annually—for operation of its New York and other offices, and for salaries and travel expenses of staff members and consultants.

THE GUSH OF GRANT APPLICATIONS being what it is, the disappointed far outnumber the anointed. Ford approves only one of every twenty-five "serious" applications —that is, those within the program scope—submitted by persons or groups who appear to know what they are talking about, the "walking sane," one Ford man calls them. In addition to these twenty-five, another seventy-five applications are peremptorily rejected in the mailroom, over the telephone, by the receptionist who makes sure that no one passes her desk in the West 43d Street lobby without a firm appointment with someone upstairs. (In an era that was less security-conscious, supplicants would roam Ford, office to office, tailoring their oral applications to fit the specialty of whatever hapless officer they happened to corner.)

The scope of the requests is bounded only by the imaginations of the two hundred million Americans in Ford's constituency, and the range is from absurdity to zaniness.

Some examples from the recent past include: an about-to-be-released convict who wanted a $10,000 annual stipend to prove that criminal instincts can be suppressed by a person in comfortable means; separate persons who proposed to make fertile, through irrigation, the Sahara, the Sinai peninsula, and Death Valley (the latter applicant offered to put a real-estate development there to relieve population pressures in Los Angeles); uncountable writers who were only a few thousand words (and dollars) away from completing the Greatest American Novel; students who thought society would benefit were they to complete another year of graduate school at Ford's expense; someone who wanted to plant a mile-wide bed of flowers along the Suez Canal, to accomplish with beauty that which diplomacy had failed to do with words.

In pour the projects by the hundreds: new schemes for schools (one man wanted to try a twenty-four-hour classroom day three times weekly, using as subjects children volunteered by their parents); inventions, including "perpetual health machines"; peace ("Why not use your billions of dollars to buy up all the nuclear bombs and missiles and store them in a secret cave in Colorado?"); war (Ford could subsidize soldier pay, providing the incentive for a volunteer army; the decline in draftee inefficiency and disaffection would mean a swift victory in Vietnam); and the arts (Assemble a country music symphony and send it abroad to show the peoples of the world that "America speaks from the land").

Many of the correspondents display a somewhat garbled concept of what foundations are all about. A lady wrote the Carnegie Corporation offering at a fair price a "cookstove which is in good condition and bakes good." A man asked whether Carnegie wished to purchase his Stanley Steamer. Another man offered a wreath made of human hair. A correspondent from India said: "We have been informed that you are interested in the purchase, for import to the United States, of 100,000 monkeys yearly."

Other correspondents want information: "What would be the best fuel for a ship going to Mars?" asked a letter from New Zealand, penned in a youthful hand. And still other letters have what former Carnegie president John W.

Gardner has called "an other-world quality." A man from Michigan once wrote Gardner that he was in constant communication with "many spirits from beyond," including Andrew Carnegie, and that Carnegie endorsed his request for aid. Another claimed he himself was Andrew Carnegie. "It seems I have been in the fires of purgation for aeons," he commented.

Sorting through these offspring of fertile American imaginations requires intuition (a "feel" for what could work and what is so far-fetched as to be dismissed summarily); institutionalization (defined areas in which the foundation operates, such as conservation and mental health, and the category of applicants which it considers); and integrity. In the latter category, Warren Weaver, a staff member and officer of the Rockefeller and Alfred P. Sloan foundations for more than three decades, pictures a frequent danger: "The philanthropoid sits on one side of the desk, the applicant sits on the other. Money, and all that goes with it, sits beside the philanthropoid. . . . Sometimes there is a temptation to clink and clank the money bags a little, meanwhile expressing regret that the visitor is interested in the wrong things. 'Now, if you had happened to be interested in . . .' you might say, clanking the coins a little harder in your bottomless purse." Such a situation can become "disgraceful both intellectually and morally," Weaver thinks. A related sin is planting answers. The philanthropoid, "of all persons, must never start a question by saying, 'Don't you think?' " Weaver says.[5]

Because of intensive staff screening, Dean Rusk said, while president of the Rockefeller Foundation, that his trustees "very seldom enjoy the luxury of being able to turn down a really bad proposal." [6] Rusk's confidence isn't uni-

versal. Maurice Rosenberg, a Columbia University law professor who directs the Walter E. Meyer Research Institute
of Law, complains that the flow of applications to his office
is "brisk but not torrential . . . [and] if quality of submission is taken into account, the stream shrinks to a trickle."
Rosenberg complains that it is an "unhappy fact" that few
applicants are capable of the outside-the-library research—
systematic observation as well as disciplined speculation—
that the institute wants to sponsor. He puts the defects into
two broad categories:

> On the one hand, the two-thirds or so of the submissions
> that come from lawyers and law teachers betray for the
> greater part a vast ignorance or naïveté about the logistics,
> costs and limitations of field research . . . again and again
> they will propose "research plans" that literally consist of ob-
> taining "traveling and interviewing expenses" usually in such
> frontier outposts as Washington, New York, San Francisco
> and New Orleans. Many of this group give the impression
> they believe there is no more to field research than collecting
> as many responses as convenient and reporting the results as if
> they spoke for the whole country with pinpoint accuracy.
>
> On the other hand, the minority of applicants who are not
> law-trained, though more sophisticated and realistic about
> methods, often fall down badly in their understanding of ele-
> mentary principles of law or gross features of the legal system.
> Not uncommonly a behavioral scientist will propose research
> that calls for wholesale violation of the attorney-client privi-
> lege, or even of constitutional rights.[7]

The subjectivity involved in awarding grants disturbs
some of the philanthropoids. "Sometimes I wonder if we
give enough attention to the really kooky ones," a staff
officer told me. "Simply because the unusual request requires more staff time for analysis, and literally shouts out
the probability that you'll have trouble getting it past the

board, and administering it even if approved, you tend to shove it to the bottom of the pile or give it to your secretary for a rejection slip. What would we have done, for instance, had a sailor walked in here five centuries ago and asked for money to make a voyage to prove the world is round? No, you're wrong, I doubt if we would have rejected him out-of-hand. We would probably have financed a university study to survey all available evidence on whether the world could be round—and *then* turned him down, for his idea was contrary to existing knowledge." Ford once spent several months pursuing a proposal that Midwestern farmers "grow kids" rather than crops, that is, take in homeless slum children and give them whatever benefits there are in bucolic living. Paul Ylvisaker, a Ford staff officer at the time, says he was initially impressed with the idea, but found Midwesterners so negative that it was dropped.[8]

One filter that lessens the philanthropoids' volume of work is a requirement by many foundations that grants be made to or through institutions or other tax-exempt organizations, rather than to individuals. For foundations not eager to become involved in "operating" programs (that is, those conducted by in-house staff personnel) the "institution rule" shuffles responsibility for supervision of its spending to an organization that has the explicit blessing of the Internal Revenue Service.

The rule stems from something more substantive than administrative convenience. It is a direct product of the controversy that swirled around the Rockefeller Foundation because of its questionable activities immediately after the Ludlow mine strike disaster in 1914. With Congress clamoring for the breakup of his foundation, John D. Rockefeller and the men around him realized it must prove its "integrity as well as high purpose" to a skeptical public. The discussion evolved to the "appropriate methods and techniques to be used," and Raymond B. Fosdick tells the decision:

> Except for a narrow range of noncontroversial subjects, notably public health, medicine and agriculture, the foundation's participation in the areas it wished to assist must be limited to grants to outside agencies competently organized and staffed to carry on the work in question. In other words, the foundation must become primarily not an operating agency but a fund-dispensing agency. This new policy obviously did not imply that the foundation would avoid controversial questions. It meant that its approach to such questions would take the form of grants to agencies independent of foundation control. In no other way could the objectivity of research be established beyond cavil and the projects freed from suspicion of ulterior motive.[9]

The institution rule, perhaps more than any single other philanthropic "principle," has forced foundations into partnership with established, traditional organizations. It is responsible for many glaring anomalies in foundation operations.

The Alfred P. Sloan Foundation states in its 1968 annual report that "for the young academic scientist who has not yet 'made a name for himself,' even though he may show every prospect of doing so in time, federal research support is hard to come by." For this reason Sloan established a Program for Basic Research in the Physical Sciences, that between 1955 and 1967 assisted 596 "young research scientists." Yet, noninstitution scientists are excluded from the program. Nominations may be made only by college department chairmen, former Sloan fellows, and "others in a position to identify unusually promising young faculty scientists." To make sure everyone understands these rules, Sloan adds: "The foundation does not accept direct applications for fellowships." Except for a Foundation vice president, all members of the selection committee are university professors. Further, "the fellowship grant is paid to the Sloan Research Fellow's institution for his use in accordance with the policies of the institution."

These restrictions do not support Sloan's claim that its program "affords a measure of freedom to young scientists very early in their academic careers"; they *do* support a conclusion that an institution scientist who gets along well with the dean and his professors can obtain money for closely-supervised research. But at Sloan and elsewhere, the lone-wolf scientist—the individualist who prefers the freedom of noninstitutional research—is not welcome.

The institution rule is a stifling presence throughout foundation philanthropy. The Grant Foundation, formed from the five-and-dime store fortune, declares (in the words of Dr. Douglas M. Bond, its president) that progress in mental health "will be brought about by imaginative and sound individuals. It is to the end of discovering and supporting such individuals that we propose that this foundation work." [10] Yet the Grant Foundation gives money only to institutions—colleges, "study centers," associations, and other foundations. The foundation grants, of course, further dilute the Grant Foundation's responsibility for "discovering and supporting" individuals. During 1965–66, $1,000,000 (of total grants of $3,126,378) went to the Foundation's Fund for Research in Psychiatry.

Other foundations that consider individuals off-limits so declare without resort to euphemistic language about "helping individuals." The Charles Hayden Foundation states that it gives money to institutions and organizations which "are well-established, with recognized reputations and dem-

onstrated capabilities." The Max C. Fleischmann Foundation of Reno, Nevada (a creation of the Fleischmann yeast
fortune) contributes only to "organizations which are listed
as tax-exempt by the United States government, and no
grants are made to individuals." Fleischmann carries the institution rule a step further than most foundations by not
giving to organizations "which, in turn, distribute them to
ultimate beneficiaries of their own selection." The Sarah
Mellon Scaife Foundation, a $145,000,000 appendix of the
Mellon fortune, does not make grants to individuals "for
any purpose." A sibling foundation, the Richard King Mellon Foundation, says it is "inclined to aid those worthy organizations which are shown to have a specific goal in mind
and whose members have themselves expended significant
effort in getting the work well under way." The Charles A.
Dana Foundation, also all-institution, won't entertain requests for building funds from colleges with less than a thousand students; applicants must also have an endowment.[11]

Sheer girth compels Ford to seek out institutions
capable of carting away large quantities of its annual income (although Ford also makes individual grants). President McGeorge Bundy calls this practice "wholesaling," as
opposed to "retailing," or grants to small programs "which
seem to us particularly important," or individual travel and
study awards. Ford has even created what Representative
George Bush, a Texas Republican, calls "satellite foundations" to run programs too large to be handled in-house,
and so new that no organizations existed to administer them
to Ford's satisfaction.

Ford is a generous parent, and some of these offspring
have developed into sturdy organizations with power and
constituencies of their own. The Council on Library Re-

sources in Washington, D.C., has spent $18,000,000 in Ford money since 1956, and has done more than any other group to plan the libraries of the future. The Fund for Adult Education, Inc., spent $41,105,000 in its ten-year life, 1951–61, "to develop methods and opportunities in adult education"; the charter of the Fund for the Advancement of Education ($72,647,266 between 1951 and 1967) covered elementary and secondary schools. Ford's conservation programs are run by Resources for the Future, Inc., of Washington ($28,842,000 since 1953) which lobbies in Congress and elsewhere "to foster, encourage and conduct scientific research and study on the use and conservation of natural resources."

The Center for Applied Linguistics, also in Washington ($4,500,000 since 1958) is said by Ford to be the "leading authority on the applied aspects of teaching second languages." The Educational Facilities Laboratories ($19,500,000 since 1958) is deciding the design of school and college buildings of the future. National Educational Television ($60,037,390 since 1963) provides hundreds of hours of news, cultural, and educational programs annually to educational TV stations ("the Ford Foundation Network," it is called at Ford, jocularly and discreetly). The Woodrow Wilson National Fellowship Foundation, formed in 1945, became a Ford dependent in 1957, and has received $55,600,000 "to increase the supply and quality of college teachers." With the Carnegie Corporation, Ford supports the National Merit Scholarship Corporation ($46,600,000 since 1955) "to identify and assist outstanding high school students to attend college who would not otherwise be able to do so." In all, Ford lists nineteen such organizations to which it has given "substantial or all of their operating expenses and in which the foundation had a role to their coming into being." [12]

Bundy doesn't think the term "satellite foundation" is wholly accurate. In most cases, he told the House Ways and Means Committee in 1969, the organizations have "completely independent boards of trustees which often take positions which are very clearly of their own initiative . . . and which do not represent gravitational guidance of any sort from the Ford Foundation." [13] Yet Ford, as a matter of policy, does not guarantee grants for a period of more than five years, even to the adjunct foundations, and each grant carries a proviso that the funds must be used for a certain stated purpose. With these strictures, whether Ford keeps a constant hand on the apron strings is irrelevant; both Ford and the recipient organization know that the strings exist and that they will be tugged if Ford becomes unhappy.

A Ford official argued to me:

> Wholesaling is the only way we can operate without building a bureaucracy the size of HEW [the U.S. Department of Health, Education, and Welfare]. Dealing with an established program, like the Woodrow Wilson fellowships, takes less time than we spend with something like the fair-housing center in Denver, even though the comparative expenditures are much higher—$2,400,000 compared to around $300,000 a year. You make an annual appropriation to Woodrow Wilson and forget about it; the money is safe, and it will be wisely spent. This comes down to a definition of what is "safe," for any grant can go sour, but I would estimate that something more than half our $200,000,000 annual expenditures are in that category. I mean, the money goes out, and we never think about it again, except in the most perfunctory of ways. The wholesale grants bring our income down to a manageable level. If we had to process each individual grant that these other organizations make, we'd have a building three times larger than this one, and such a mob of people that we'd have to appoint a cabinet to help Bundy run things.

Another reason for wholesaling is that foundations are convinced it helps them to prevent wasting money. Abraham Flexner, longtime servant of the Rockefeller philanthropies, once wrote: "There is no way of estimating the competency of the institution to which or the individual to whom a small grant, running from one year to three years, is made; nor can their effects be evaluated. . . . It is impossible to make an estimate as to which have taken root and which are mere ripples on the surface." Flexner thought foundations erred gravely when they scattered their money thinly over American academia, giving a dab to any professor or university willing to stand in line for it. Flexner's favored horrible examples came from the General Education Board at a time when it was the largest single foundation supporter of education: $4,000 to Ohio State University "to create a scholarship in ceramic design applied to tableware"; and $2,500 to Cornell University "for the purchase of photographic equipment and supplies to be used in a study of eating behaviour to be carried on in the Nursery School of the College of Home Economics."

Flexner declared: "It is impossible for any man or group of men to administer intelligently funds so freely distributed to agencies, the competency of which no man and no group of men could possibly judge. . . . Millions have been wasted which, if lumped together, might have been employed in endowing an institution of genuinely scholarly and scientific character. . . . If, for example, in the South one or two white or one or two Negro universities had been generously endowed, their graduates would in a single generation have attacked . . . problems with energy and enthusiasm, and all other institutions would have been endeavoring to emulate their example in respect to both endowment and program." [14]

The Rockefeller Foundation's alternative to Ford's large institutional grants is large in-house operating programs, most conspicuously in agricultural improvement for underdeveloped nations. The largest single item listed in the seventeen pages of annual report required to detail Rockefeller's 1968 expenditures of $41,488,095 was $2,198,918 for its "Conquest of Hunger" field staff. But vast though it may be, the Rockefeller Foundation can still think in terms of pocket-change grants of the sort Abraham Flexner denounced so vehemently. A sampling from 1968 shows the following grants: $750 to the American Economic Association for expenses of participants in a meeting on international liquidity; $744 for the library fund of Tougaloo College, Mississippi; $552 to the Population Council for research; $389 for "summer assignments for faculty members" of Fisk University, Tennessee; $410 to the Ministry of Foreign Affairs of the newly-independent, small African state of Lesotho for "the purchase of a collection of basic works in international relations"; $201 for support of the British Committee on the Theory of International Politics at the University of Cambridge; and $96 for "support of research" at the Central Institute of Islamic Research in Pakistan.

The danger of institutional grants is that a foundation can work itself into the position where all its available income is committed to the same recipients indefinitely. This violates one of the frequently-cited "sound principles" of the philanthropoids, which is to be "always alert for the new and the innovative." Under this theory, institutional grants are safe because any organization touched by the magic wand of foundation philanthropy supposedly receives such an infusion of vigor that within a few years' time it becomes "self-reliant and a recognized element of the community" (that is, it finds someone other than the foundation to pay its bills). The highly visible flaw in this philanthropic formula is that most of the organizations that come to foundations for handouts couldn't become self-supporting unless they robbed banks.

"Institution building" simply increases the number of supplicants who tour the foundations seeking money. For example, the Center for Inter-American Relations was launched with major support from the Ford Foundation "to stimulate informed North American interest and participation in Western Hemisphere policy issues and cultural affairs, through meetings and study programs for businessmen, journalists, scholars, artists and other professionals." Ford contributed $500,000 to the center in 1968; the Rockefeller Brothers Fund gave $100,000 for renovation and furnishing of its New York headquarters building. Now the center is making direct-mail appeals for funds to keep alive, with letters that say, in effect, "Weren't we wonderful to start this project for the benefit of all you good people, and now shouldn't you kick in some money and take it off our hands?"

There is something disquieting about the tendency of rich men to start projects on the basis of a unilateral decision that they are needed and then to attempt to pressure the public to support something it isn't really sure it wants. A former center staff man once told me candidly: "We spent one hell of a lot of time trying to persuade people to come to our seminar meetings. The lack of enthusiasm for center programs among the banks and business firms with commercial interests in Latin America raised serious doubts in my mind as to whether anyone else shared our 'conviction' that we served a useful purpose."

Philanthropoids speak deridingly of the "pensioners" who rely upon the same foundation for lifelong support of research and other projects. At foundations that frown upon pensioners, three to five years is the maximum period for a grant. "Our foundation doesn't exist to support selected individuals," a grant officer stated. "Our obligation is to the field as a whole. I couldn't support this claim with firm statistical data, but I feel that a scientist or other researcher who comes back to the same foundation year after year, and always receives what he wants, gets into the psychological frame-of-mind that allows him to drag out his work indefinitely, to go off down promising rabbit trails rather than stick to the business at hand."

A foundation officer who does believe in long-term grants answers: "How can you impose a three-year limit on a search for a cure for cancer? A scientist who knows he must stop every two or three years and begin that awful search for money doesn't focus his full attention on his research. But I do admit that we look at a project very hard in the third year, and that it's considerably more difficult to get money to continue past that point than it is to receive the initial grant." He adds:

> Don't be misled by those high-sounding statements about "pensioners" and the like. Much of it results from the fact that grant officers have a low threshold of boredom. They see the same name come up a few times, and what really excited them two years ago now seems commonplace, and not nearly so worthwhile as what Professor B is doing over at Berkeley.
>
> Too, the foundation officers have to justify their existence. Once a foundation's grant program becomes static, and the money is tied up with persons who are to receive long-range support, the staff has more time on their hands than they know what to do with. So they start looking for new recipients.

Until a host of high-level retirements brought an abrupt change in policy, the Commonwealth Fund was famed among philanthropoids (and benefactees in the medical and academic community) for its fondness for long-term support. Some examples include:

— Dr. May G. Wilson, study of rheumatic fever at New York Hospital, 1929 to 1962.

— Child Research Council of Denver, study of growth and development, 1930 to 1962.

— Dr. Walter Bauer, study of arthritis at Harvard Medical School and Massachusetts General Hospital, 1937 to 1958.

— Dr. Max Lurie, study of resistance and susceptibility to tuberculosis, at the University of Pennsylvania, 1942 to 1957.

A CONSCIENTIOUS FOUNDATION'S CONCERN for its grant money continues even after it leaves the premises; this brings us to one of the touchiest challenges of philanthropy —the relationship between benefactor and recipient. If the grant is made to a tax-exempt organization for a purpose permitted by the tax code, the foundation is not legally responsible for how it is spent. But foundations that are serious about their business want to know not only how the money was spent, but whether the intended purpose was achieved. Some foundations are satisfied with an occasional letter report from the recipient and do not make an on-site inspection to verify its claims. Leonard C. Cottrell, Jr., secretary of the Russell Sage Foundation, says this laissez-faire attitude "may be due to a delicacy of feeling that a giver should not embarrass the recipient by showing a concern in

the fate of the gift, or because of lack of staff and administrative and professional competence" [15]—or because of
sheer laziness or naïveté.

According to a story told often enough by philanthropoids, and with such consistent detail that it has the ring of
truth, the Rockefeller's General Education Board granted
$10,000 to an organization in the 1930s after negotiations
that were conducted entirely through the mails. The organization bore a ponderously impressive and authentic name,
and no one thought any more of the grant until a piece of
routine correspondence was returned by the post office,
stamped "addressee unknown." Who received the money,
and what was done with it, remains unknown, and current
Rockefeller staffers plead ignorance of the subject.

Another often-heard yarn (this one totally unconfirma-
ble) is of a crafty graduate student who was doing research
in an area in which one of the twenty-five largest foundations announced an interest. Through voluminous forgeries,
the student submitted a grant application that appeared to
have the endorsement of his university's development office.
He received $19,000, chiefly for "equipment purchases,"
payable through a special bank account specified in one of
the forged letters. Not a dime of the money was spent on research, and the deception didn't come to light for seven
years, when the foundation and university stumbled upon it
by accident. An official of the supposed victim foundation
would neither deny nor confirm that the fraud occurred. He
said, in effect, "If you will point to a specific grant and ask
whether it was what it purported to be, I will consult our
law firm and see what, if anything, we should say about it.
But in answer to your general question, I prefer to say nothing."

Another philanthropoid has said: "Statistical averages

and student ingenuity being what they are, I wouldn't be surprised if a million bucks or so of foundation grant money was spent on motorcycles and blondes a year. I'm not particularly larcenous by nature, but I could tell you half a dozen ways you could slip a phony application through our office and have a fair chance of receiving some money. I'm not going to, though."

Such whispers of scandal, of course, are so rare as not to worry the average philanthropoid. And because philanthropy is, by definition, a gentle business, the administrator must be skilled at doing what is required to keep the spending of grant money within proper bounds without offending the recipient.

This is not to say that foundations are not capable of showing people that philanthropic money has as much power as do other varieties of money. Yorke Allen, Jr., of the Rockefeller Brothers Fund, tells of an instance where the Fund gave money to a "well-known national organization" (he won't name it) for a project and specified how it was to be spent: "When the person chosen to carry out the project failed to follow the plan, and took an opposite course of action, we had to put sufficient pressure on the donee to fire the man before all the money was wasted." [16]

John E. Booth, formerly of the 20th Century Fund, remembers a case when a sponsoring foundation told a civic theater, "You must not pay an actor a thousand dollars a week." The artistic director resisted, saying the actor was a requisite for the kinds of plays he was directing, and offering to cut other expenses. Booth says: "He didn't get his man. The season went on and was not a success. Regardless of whatever factors were involved, the man had been denied the possibility of artistic success." Similarly, Booth cites an incident where a foundation objected when a symphony which it supported wanted to hire a first violinist at what it considered to be an unduly high salary. The director insisted the right man "could spell the difference between a first-rate orchestra and a mediocre one," Booth says.[17]

The Russell Sage Foundation's Leonard Cottrell thinks there are subtle ways a foundation can pressure a recipient without offending its officers or invading their prerogative in hiring and firing of staff. Consider the foundation officer who wants to warn a recipient institution not to include a particular academic figure in a project which the foundation wants to sponsor. The philanthropoid is much too polite to tell the university officer that although Professor X might have tenure and many learned degrees, the foundation wants nothing to do with him. When the man's name is mentioned, the philanthropoid says casually, "Oh, yes, I know Professor X, but his name would not have occurred to me in this connection." Translation: "We wouldn't take him on a bet."

The polite and alert recipient should be prepared to acknowledge that he received (and will heed) the message. As he is leaving, therefore, the foundation officer says, "Oh, by the way, give my regards to Professor X when you see or write him." The recipient answers, with equal casualness, "Well, I probably won't run into him anytime soon—probably not until our next annual meeting." The men shake hands, and Professor X is subtly eased out of the project.[18]

Dr. John Heyman, president of the New York Foundation, suggests that the amount of supervision required is comparable to that an investment bank gives various portfolio holdings: minimal if it buys AT&T or General Motors; maximum if it buys heavily into a small, beginning enterprise. Heyman explains: "Obviously, a grant of $2,000 to the American Red Cross should call for nothing more in the supervisory line than the reading of reports. On the other hand, if a foundation has made a major grant to a new experimental agency, it will be appropriate to become involved in other ways besides just the granting of money." [19]

The Research Corporation tries to make clear its desire to avoid interference in internal university affairs. Sam C. Smith, vice president in charge of the grant program, sends grantees a form letter:

> The grant is intended as a contribution to the academic and scientific program of the institution. It carries no connotation of an agreement whereby the institution or the personnel who may participate in the research undertake responsibilities to the Research Council. There should be complete freedom to make changes in the emphasis or direction of the work as it progresses, including changes in budget and time schedule.

To individual grantees, Smith advises that the Research Corporation requires or expects neither "formal, elaborate progress reports nor . . . a detailed accounting of expenditures. We shall, however, look forward to learning the results of your study, and an occasional brief letter whenever results warrant will be welcome." Smith holds that while a foundation "is entitled to satisfactory evidence that its funds have been used with propriety in attaining, or at least in approaching as closely as possible, the desired purpose . . . it does not, by awarding a grant, buy the rights to call all the shots." [20]

THESE ARE THE BASIC TECHNIQUES of the men responsible for the day-to-day operations of American foundations. As once-removed representatives of the rich men who created the foundations, the philanthropoids speak only with delegated authority. When the donor is still living, his whims and preferences can be a daily influence—for good and for evil—on the way his foundation's business is conducted. And even a donor's death does not necessarily dash his control over a foundation. Through carefully chosen trustees who are empowered by law to select their successors, a rich man can hold the reins of power from the grave. As an ancient adage says, "The only thing harder to change than a woman's mind is a rich man's will." And foundation programs, with few exceptions, are those which its trustees and its officers feel would be palatable to the donor.

CHAPTER **5**

Spending the Money I: Professors and Physicians

DURING THE CENTURY in which it grew into one of America's foremost industrial cities—with the Mellons as its foremost financial, cultural, and civic family—Pittsburgh degenerated into a vast industrial slum bounded by the abysmal misery of the western Pennsylvania coal fields. A social workers' survey issued in the early 1900s noted that manufacturers of steel and other goods preferred to hire Slavs and Italians "because of their docility, their habit of silent submission . . . and their willingness to work long hours and overtime without a murmur . . . in intense heat, the din of machinery and the noise of escaping steam." Laborers' slums clustered around the big industrial plants like the cottages of serfs in feudal times, with the manorial lord caring naught for the food they ate, the water they drank, the children they tried to raise in poverty and hunger.

When Andrew Carnegie purchased the Painter's Mill steel works, he renovated the mill but left untouched the notorious "Painter's Row" which housed its work force—five hundred humans "living in back-to-back houses, without ventilation, having cellar kitchens, dark, overcrowded sleeping quarters, no drinking water whatsoever, and no sanitary accommodations worth the name." [1]

Just how many of these wretched souls died annually in accidents because of their ignorance of the English language and modern machinery is an unrecorded statistic, but the social workers' report quoted a Pittsburgh priest as saying of one plant: "Oh, that is the slaughterhouse; they kill them there every day." The infamous "iron and coal police," literally a private army reinforced by Pennsylvania state troopers, smashed attempts of Mellon and Carnegie workers to unionize. In at least two instances, "special officers" of the Mellon-owned Pittsburgh Coal Company were convicted of murdering workers involved in strikes.

Conditions had not improved noticeably in 1947, when George Sessions Perry, in his landmark series on American cities for the *Saturday Evening Post,* adjudged Pittsburgh to be as dim, dank, and decaying as anything found in medieval Europe: "The multiple scuttles of soot one must devour per annum as part of the price of living in Pittsburgh is no laughing matter. Instead, they are a hellish, tormenting, disease-abetting and spirit-wilting thing."

The agony of Pittsburgh and western Pennsylvania, however, did not deter the Mellons from accumulating one of the truly big American fortunes: "Mellon's Millions," the headline writers called the dollars when Andrew W. was secretary of the treasury under Presidents Harding, Coolidge, and Hoover. As bankers, the Mellons furnished the capital with which Carnegie, Frick, and other, now-forgotten, steel and coal barons seized control of the nation's two basic industries. As investors, the Mellons put their profits into aluminum (the Aluminum Company of America was a prototype monopoly from birth); into oil (Gulf Oil has more assets than Ford Motor Company, and its record of economic imperialism in Latin America rivals that of United Fruit Company; yet it is but a mere fragment of the Mellon fortune); into railroads, electrical and gas utilities, glass, the multiplicity of enterprises upon which both business and public consumers are dependent.

And, finally, as "philanthropists," the Mellons created five separate foundations whose interests and accomplishments are a resounding demonstration of the detachment of the Big Rich from the social problems which their avarice and business greed did so much to create. The Mellon record is so much a caricature of what is wrong with American foundations that one would be hesitant to present it in fictionalized form. The Mellon foundations are not conscience money, because the family, through successive generations, retained the attribute which biographer Harvey O'Connor found in scion Judge Thomas Mellon: "Neither the medieval nor the Twentieth Century American notions of charity fitted in with his hard Knoxian theology, in which every man stood on his own two legs, asking no charity, and giving little . . ." Like Carnegie and the other Pittsburgh rich, Thomas Mellon "believed charity weakened the moral fiber of the recipients and added little luster to the donor." [2]

The A. W. Mellon Educational and Charitable Trust was created in 1930 by Andrew W. Mellon, when Americans were beginning to realize the severity of the price they were to pay for the economic arrogance of the men who owned their nation. As citizens stood in bread lines and peddled apples to stay alive, the secretary of the treasury looked about the country to see how he could put his charitable dollars to use. One place he did *not* look was the western Pennsylvania coal towns dominated by his family businesses, where conditions "sank to appalling depths," according to biographer O'Connor, a Pittsburgh labor journalist at the time. "In camps where men were working, charity organizations found it necessary to eke out the meager wages with relief. Hundreds of strikers, evicted, lived in pitiful tent colonies through the winter of 1931–32. Their kitchens closed for lack of soup meat and potatoes. Miners roamed through the suburbs of Pittsburgh asking for bread." [3]

Pennsylvania governor Gifford Pinchot went to Washington that dire winter and, while awaiting his audience with Mellon, admired the paintings which an underling proudly announced the secretary of the treasury had purchased from the Czars' Hermitage art gallery in Leningrad for $1,700,000. A few minutes later Mellon curtly rejected Pinchot's request for a $1,000,000 loan at four percent from a Mellon bank for state relief of the poor.

No, philanthropist Mellon had something else in mind of even greater urgency—a magnificent marble-walled art gallery in Washington to house his multimillion-dollar collection of Old Master paintings. Construction of this edifice, at a cost listed in foundation records at $79,000,000, was the A. W. Mellon Educational and Charitable Trust's act of charity during the Great Depression.*

---

* The Treasury Department, once the Roosevelt administration began, challenged Mellon's claimed tax deduction of $16,215,590 for paintings which he "donated" to his foundation before any specific plans were made for the National Gallery. Mellon kept the paintings in his private apartment, which meant that they could be viewed only by a handful of personal friends. By the time the case came to trial, however, the National Gallery was under construction. The Board of Tax Appeals permitted him to keep the paintings in his private gallery—and to take the tax deduction—until the National Gallery was completed. [4]

Another major beneficiary of the A. W. Mellon "foundation" was the Mellon Institute of Industrial Research (now simply the Mellon Institute), much of whose work was devoted to solving technical problems for such Mellon companies as Gulf Oil and Alcoa. One early project was a study to refute charges that use of aluminum cooking utensils harmed humans (a quirkish notion of a Toledo dentist who directed the Anti Cancer Club of America).

Andrew's son, Paul, is involved in two foundations: the Bollingen Foundation, of which he is founder and president; and the Andrew W. Mellon Foundation, product of a merger, on June 30, 1969, of the Old Dominion Foundation, which he controlled, and the Avalon Foundation, which was the domain of his sister, Mrs. Ailsa Mellon Bruce. (Mrs. Bruce was critically ill at the time of the merger and she died two months later.) By putting the two organizations under one roof, the trustees created a foundation with assets of $272,936,934, based on market values as of December 31, 1968. They also insured that the wealth would remain under tight family control, for the newly-constituted board is dominated by persons who served on the Old Dominion board.

The Bollingen Foundation is Paul Mellon's personal project, and its undertakings are of negligible interest—and even less value—to anyone in the western Pennsylvania steel mills and coal fields. The Foundation is named for the small village in Switzerland where Carl Gustav Jung, the founder of analytical psychology, had his rural retreat. Paul Mellon's first wife, Mary Conover Mellon, suffered from asthma for many years. According to Paul, "She felt that her affliction had at least partly a psychological basis," and felt that "somewhere . . . [Jung's ideas] held an answer for her."

The Mellons stayed with Jung at Bollingen during the

winter of 1939–40. "The association with Jung was an exciting experience for us both," Mellon has written, "and we felt we had been in the presence of one of the most extraordinary fertile and profound minds of this century. The lofty and sometimes obscure written expression of his thoughts and observations became more understandable and practical as we participated in his seminars . . . or talked privately with the man himself. In addition, we both developed a real affection and deep respect for him as a warm friend and wise counselor." The Mellons decided to sponsor a collected edition of Jung's works as a token of their respect, and they created the Bollingen Foundation for this purpose immediately after the war. Mrs. Mellon died in 1946, but the Foundation continued and, in Paul Mellon's words, "became gradually a far more comprehensive and catholic endeavor covering many other fields of learning and creativity." [5]

As Congressman Wright Patman discovered with much outrage, that original definition of purpose is extraordinarily broad. Patman's favorite (as horrible examples) Bollingen "research grants" were put before the House Ways and Means Committee in its 1969 hearings:

— The works of Hugo von Hofmannsthal.
— The phenomenology of the Iranian religious consciousness.
— The origin and significance of the decorative types of medieval tombstones in Bosnia and Herzegovina.
Patman thundered:

Congress certainly cannot complain if the entire Mellon banking family assembles in one of their Pittsburgh mansions each evening for a roundtable discussion on the origin and significance of the decorative types of medieval tombstones in Bosnia and Herzegovina. If the Mellons are more interested in medieval tombstones than in Pittsburgh poverty, and care to spend their money studying 12th and 13th Century church construction, that is the Mellons' affair. However, there is no obligation upon either the Congress or the American citizenry to give the Mellons tax-free dollars to finance their exotic interests.[6] *

The Avalon and Old Dominion foundations, before their merger, made most of their contributions (which totaled $10,837,944 in 1968) in the form of "safe grants" to established universities, medical centers, and art galleries: $500,000 to the American Council of Learned Societies; $150,000 to Harvard for enlargement of the Widener Library; $159,000 to Princeton for the acquisition of materials in European and British history; $150,000 to the University of Pennsylvania for enlargement of the University Museum; and $250,000 each to the New York Botanical Garden and the New York Zoological Society. On a more personal level, the Old Dominion Foundation each year found considerable money ($170,932 in 1967 and $145,476 in 1968) to pass on to the Paul Mellon Foundation for British Arts, which was established "to advance knowledge of British painting, sculpture, and graphic arts."

In partial and attempted rebuttal to Congressman Pat-

---

* Paul Mellon declined the author's request for rebuttal to Patman's oration. The Foundation's major activity, according to its annual reports, is publishing scholarly books "which would probably not be undertaken by other publishers because of exacting and necessarily costly editorial and manufacturing requirements." Some 261 libraries receive free copies of the volumes as they are published. Some recent titles include *Jewish Symbols in the Greco-Roman Period; The Shrines of Tut-Ankh-Amon; Archaic Techniques of Ecstasy;* and *A Study of the Ritual Disposition of Chinese Paintings with a Translation of the Chieh Tzu Yuan Hua Chuan (Mustard Seed Garden Manual of Painting).*

man, an officer of one of the "East Coast Mellons" foundations, during a 1969 interview, pointed to the record of yet
another institution, the Richard King Mellon Foundation,
which is dominated by what he called "the Pittsburgh
wing" of the family. Richard King Mellon was a Pittsbur-
gher, a tweedy, open-faced man of regal demeanor and signature, regularly bestowed that awed newspaper sobriquet,
"civic leader." When Richard returned to Pittsburgh after
the Second World War (he rose to the rank of lieutenant
general while seated in a Washington office, and the Foundation's 1947–62 report volume pictures him in full dress
uniform), he apparently realized that the city was sliding
into financial oblivion and that some of the Mellon fortune
could go with it. Neighboring communities dumped raw
sewage into the Monongahela and Allegheny rivers, which
come together in downtown Pittsburgh to form the Ohio.
No major expressways had been built or designed, and the
330 acres of the downtown business district were blighted.
More seriously, "major corporations were talking of leaving,
and some had leased space in other cities," as the Richard
King Mellon Foundation lamented in one of its reports.
The Mellon National Bank and Trust Company could not
tolerate any such exodus.

So Richard King Mellon developed an interest in Pittsburgh, one which a Foundation publication describes as
"typical of his family tradition and of his own sense of loyalty to his birthplace and his community." [7] With other
civic leaders, he sponsored a plan for the rejuvenation of
Pittsburgh, putting several hundreds of thousands of dollars
of his Foundation's money into the Allegheny Conference
on Community Development, which was the overall coordi-
nator. (Contemporary Pittsburghers also mention the role of
one David Lawrence, a Democrat who was elected mayor

in 1946, and who had the nerve to tell the Mellons and the other big rich: either make Pittsburgh livable for its citizens, or I'll make Pittsburgh unlivable for you. But Lawrence, a mere mayor, and a Democrat at that, goes unmentioned in the Foundation's account of how Richard King Mellon and his friends cleansed Pittsburgh.)

The Richard King Mellon Foundation's spending *has* been concentrated in Pittsburgh and western Pennsylvania —eighty-five percent of the $40,378,216 in grants paid between its creation in 1947 and the end of 1968, ranging from $110.40 to transport orphans to Forbes Field for a circus to $2,500,000 to local universities for "programs in pure science and basic research." Yet by no means have all—or even the bulk—of these funds gone to Pittsburgh redevelopment. Like his cousin Paul, Richard King had a plethora of personal interests which he pursued with Foundation funds. For example, he spent more on restoration of Fort Ligonier, a relic of the French and Indian War, than he did on the Allegheny Conference, the redevelopment agency.

Another group which the Foundation singles out as a "guiding force" in redevelopment is ACTION-Housing, Inc., a private nonprofit group which works for better housing. Between 1966 and 1968 the Foundation paid $62,500 to ACTION-Housing—and $200,000 to the marine research program of the Oceanic Foundation, Waimanalo, Hawaii. On second look, the marine grant is not foreign to the Mellon interests. Explaining the reasons for the grant in its 1966–68 report, the Mellon Foundation stated there were "untold and virtually untapped riches" which the Hawaii group was attempting to exploit. The report continues: "There are oil and gas. Some 15 percent of the world's production now comes from offshore wells; oil reserves in the

United States Continental Shelf are estimated conservatively at 2.5 trillion barrels—more than all U.S. land reserves."

For the Mellons, helping the Oceanic Foundation find a means of extracting these petroleum riches has business as well as philanthropic appeal. The Richard King Mellon Foundation's major holding is Gulf Oil stock ($97,041,514 of total assets of $160,560,654 as of December 31, 1968). Gulf Oil is also a major item in the investment portfolios of the individual Mellons, their banks, and their holding companies. Thus, the use of tax-exempt funds to finance research in which a very rich family has a very keen financial interest.

IN ANY CASE, the Mellons have spent enough money in Pittsburgh, endowed enough chairs and buildings at the nation's universities, supported enough medical research and university professors and community health centers to permit the family name to be said publicly in western Pennsylvania without evoking hisses and catcalls from persons who remember them as the silent, unseen general staff of the coal and iron police. The Mellons' money—more than $600,000,000 of it is now within the tax-free sanctity of foundations, with, of course, commensurate tax deductions —has put a few pieces of gauze on society's clawed, scratched face. But the Mellons' money, like most foundation money, is timid, and the people who control it rarely spend a dime on the reformation of institutions which are demonstrably outmoded. Here are some frames of reference:

— If one is satisfied with the present American university system, with its emphasis on research and publication, rather than classroom teaching, its requirement of a doctorate as proof of professional competence, its ability to mass-produce graduates, and its coincident possession of costly buildings and not-so-costly professors, then the foundations have succeeded.

— If one is satisfied with the present American medical system, with its emphasis on research and experimentation rather than on basic patient care, its determination to limit as severely as possible the number of persons permitted to practice, its increasing centralization of professional services in lavish facilities that are more factory than clinic, its incessant increase in costs that is inexorably carrying treatment beyond the grasp of the ordinary citizen, and its tenacious clutch on conservative political concepts, then foundations have succeeded.

— If one is satisfied with a gradualistic approach to problems of social injustice and economic imbalance and believes that the fundamental goodness of man will bring the black and the poor of America to equality, and that institutionalized control of communities and schools is superior to less efficient personalistic human control, then the foundations have succeeded.

— If one is satisfied that spending millions of dollars to increase foreign farm output is a wiser use of foundation funds than a challenge to the entrenched, reactionary forces which control domestic agricultural politics and contribute to the hunger of twenty million American citizens, then foundations have succeeded.

But are these questions properly put to the foundations? Are the foundations responsible for the priorities that have guided their spending during the half-century of institutionalized philanthropy in America?

"The foundations give the American people what the majority of the American people want," a former Ford official told me. "If there was any great grass-roots sentiment for wiser foundation spending, it would have been heard. But a 'grass root' by definition has its nose buried in the dirt, and instinctively reaches out for nourishment. Hell, everyone in 'formal' medicine and education in the whole country has a vested interest in continuing the present system. They've got their own heads stuck in the dirt, and they're getting nourishment—and by that I mean dollars—from the foundations. Why should they get involved in cabalistic plots to kill the most golden of geese?"

Another philanthropoid, late of the education division of one of the twenty-five largest, and now elsewhere, remarked: "Despite a lot of high-sounding talk about academic freedom and the independent spirit of inquiry, most university people are basically whores. Flash a big enough check at a college president, and he'll be panting and sitting in your lap. For a smaller check, he'll practically order his best friend to leave a department chairmanship and go to Wallawallowoo for five years to run a foundation research project, provided there are a few bucks in it for the university."

In a statement that could apply to most serious foundations, McGeorge Bundy wrote in the 1968 Ford Foundation report: "The oldest and strongest of the ties that connect this foundation to other parts of society are those that bind us to the world of education. We depend on learned men for advice and special study on nearly every subject we take up. More deeply still, we have supposed, from our very beginning, that the health and strength of American education was in and of itself an area of central importance to the na-

tional well-being." [8] (To this end, foundations gave
$2,087,871,802 to U.S. colleges and universities during the
eight years ending December 31, 1968.[9])

Then Bundy proceeded to indict an educational system
which foundations did much to create, and to imply that
the approximately $2,000,000,000 could have been better
spent. The current crisis of educational authority, Bundy
wrote, stems from "the disillusionment produced by visibly
poor performance on the part of men as highly honored as
the modern professorate. The traditional pattern of learning
has been ripe for reform since 1900 at least, and the best
efforts of the best committees have seldom done more than
nibble at its edges. . . . Today the average course of study
in the average university of the first rank is, in a quite fundamental sense, unaccountable. . . . *It is far more the product
of guild traditions than of a rational effort to make learning happen* . . ."

Guild traditions. The modern professorate. The traditional pattern of learning. All are foundation products, and
they are so claimed, and enthusiastically, in the formal autobiographies of foundation philanthropy.

When steel baron and philanthropist Andrew
Carnegie became a trustee of Cornell University, "he
began," says the Carnegie Foundation for the Advancement
of Teaching, "to appreciate at first hand [sic] the low economic status of college and university faculty members and
the hardship most of them faced in retirement. He regarded
this as a severe injustice, and he determined to use a portion
of his fortune to rectify this flaw in American academic
life." [10] (Carnegie didn't notice the steelworkers on Painter's
Row in Pittsburgh and their brethren elsewhere, who did

not have to retire to face hardship; they faced it daily on Carnegie's wages.)

Carnegie realized he could not finance personally a pension system but felt one solution would be a moderate endowment, the income of which would be used to provide free pensions. He recruited Henry Pritchett, then president of the Massachusetts Institute of Technology, and, in the space of three months in early 1905, he organized his foundation, gave it a $15,000,000 endowment, and recruited a board of trustees. Ninety-two private and nonsectarian colleges, universities, and technical schools were deemed qualified academically to participate.

But Pritchett wasn't satisfied. After surveying the benefactee institutions, he concluded that American higher education was a mess, that there was no real definition of a college or what it should teach or what professional standards its staff should meet. Many of these early twentieth-century institutions undoubtedly were diploma mills, operated to satisfy the financial or egotistical yearnings of professors. But there was also great diversity: community colleges, which met peculiar local needs; religious colleges, which espoused the beliefs of their sponsoring sects; private colleges, at which teachers could test their personal techniques and offer their personal interpretations of what the world is all about to anyone who would sit in a classroom and listen.

To Pritchett, a scientist who was a product of the formalistic, tightly-structured German university system, such free-form education simply would not do. He told Carnegie that "some criterion would have to be introduced as to what constituted a college." Thereupon, the Foundation (Pritchett, more accurately) announced its own definition of "college." To be eligible for Carnegie pensions, a college would have to have at least a $200,000 endowment ($500,000, several years later) or an annual income of $100,000 if it were a state university. It must inaugurate entrance requirements keyed to a high-school credit system recommended by Carnegie. And they must have at least eight academic departments, each headed by a professor with a doctorate.

Despite the surface plausibility of the last requirement—after all, did not possession of a doctorate set a professor apart from the mass of his fellows and signify serious professional accomplishment?—it thrust education under a stultifying blanket from which, in all likelihood, it shall not emerge for generations. After codification of the Carnegie requirements, the PhD was the passport to academic success, and a passport to be acquired only through completion of the dissertation—a work of increasingly marginal utility, cursed so pithily by academicians that one can pick and choose among the billingsgate for the most stinging quotation (my ultimate choice is the one of William Arrowsmith of the University of Texas; he called the dissertations "those immense Teutonic encyclopedias in which every known fact is embalmed").

The professors themselves realized what is required for "making it" in American universities. A 1964 survey of members of the American Political Science Association asked what factors they considered important in getting ahead in the teaching profession. Volume of publication ranked first; teaching ability, tenth.[11] *

The disquieting factor about the Carnegie "reforms"—and those of the Rockefellers' General Education Board,

---

* Factors two through nine, in order, were: school at which doctorate was taken; right connections; ability to get research support; quality of publication; textbook authorship; luck or chance; school of first full-time appointment; and self-promotion.

which soon was imposing *its* "minimum standards of eligibility" for its supplicants—was that they were never presented as such. Carnegie and the GEB never posed directly this question: "Do you gentlemen, as allegedly professional educators, think that the fundamental changes we want are good for the universities?" What Carnegie and GEB did was to tell the colleges: "This is what *we* think you should do, and if you are willing to do it, look at all the money we have for you."

The universities acquiesced, without recorded exception, for Carnegie and the General Education Board, together, made grants amounting to around twenty percent of the total annual income available to all colleges and universities in the nation. Education historian Ernest V. Hollis has written: "By this indirection the university was being importuned to do what President Pritchett most wished, and what he probably could not have accomplished by any amount of direct grants. . . . Both the logic of the situation and the desire for the money caused colleges to seek the scrutiny of the foundations." [12]

Because the Carnegie plan made pension rights transferable from one institution to another, professors learned to avoid nonaccredited universities, further incentive for administrators to submit to the foundations. The lure of the Carnegie money was so attractive that Wesleyan, Drury, Drake, and Brown severed their religious connections to partake of it. The Walsh Commission* concluded in 1916: "It would seem conclusive that if an institution would willingly abandon its religious affiliations through the influence of these foundations, it will even more easily conform to

---

* Formally, the U. S. Commission on Industrial Relations, 1914–15, chaired by Senator Frank Walsh of Montana.

their will in any other part of its organization or teaching." [13]

The pension plan soon evolved into a contributory, self-supporting system (the Teachers Insurance and Annuity Association) to which Carnegie made no further payments. But the foundations and the universities had found one another, and education consistently has been the largest single area of foundation giving. A 1968 survey by the Foundation Center, restricted to grants of $10,000 or more, found that forty-one percent of foundation money went to education. Because of the $10,000 minimum, this study covered only half of total foundation giving ($753,000,000 of annual grants of $1,500,000,000), but philanthropoids seem satisfied that the smaller grants follow much the same statistical pattern. [14]

In dollar amounts, foundation spending runs considerably below the annual budget of the U.S. Office of Education and other federal agencies.* But to many academicians foundation spending is of inestimable value whether, as Indiana University chancellor Herman B. Wells says, the grants are "large enough to elevate the quality of the institutions or merely the little, extra amount that meant the difference between launching a project and abandoning it when almost in reach." [15]

The listing of claimed accomplishments can (and has) filled many books. As physical evidence, the philanthropoids can point to campus canyons ringed by buildings constructed with foundation funds; to library shelves creaking

* According to the National Science Foundation, a government agency, total federal support to institutions of higher learning amounted to $3,367,000,000 in fiscal 1968, $2,212,000,000 of it from the Department of Health, Education, and Welfare.

under the weight of studies (most of them "seminal" or "watermark" or "pacesetting") financed by foundation funds; to the airliners which carry professors from conference to symposium to workshop (and occasionally home overnight for fresh laundry and a classroom lecture), at foundation expense; to the "imaginative, creative, boundary-stretching, even revolutionary undertakings which not only have produced enormous immediate and potential benefits but have enlarged the possibilities for higher education in the future," as stated by Chancellor Wells.[16]

The foundations indeed have "enlarged the possibilities for higher education"; and that is exactly why much of what foundations are doing on American campuses is misguided, unproductive—academically or otherwise—even harmful. For example, it is fashionable for foundations to be interested in urban affairs, yet few of them have the in-house staff to work up comprehensive programs, even of research. Hence they turn to the universities, using as bait the attractively-dangled coin purse. The bait works, and universities find themselves responsible for improving housing and rehabilitating skid-row derelicts.

Columbia University, because of its physical proximity to the New York-based foundations, hears the clank of money more frequently than any other university. During 1968 alone Columbia was involved in this array of Ford Foundation interests: research in American liberties, $200,000; criminal law and criminology training and research, $274,500; journalism training, research, studies, and education on urban and regional problems, $4,340,000; and "development," $9,368,153. Other Ford grants to Stanford were for studies and experiments in university "governance and innovation," $1,000,000; faculty research fellowships in economics, political science, and sociology, $48,120; development of school curricula, $20,000; advanced field training in archaeology, $45,000; research and training on China, $127,464, and Korea, $75,000; international studies program, $714,286; international urban studies, $66,667; and advancement of foreign journalism, $89,781.

Collectively, this is enough money to invigorate the pulse rate of a university development officer; separately, the pieces represent a staggering diversion of faculty time and energies from the classroom, especially in light of the highly-visible Columbia student discontent because of professors' extracurricular activities. Jacques Barzun, Columbia's iconoclast-in-residence, is critical of nonteaching projects foisted upon (eager) universities by foundations: "No one can cavil at the motives of good will and courage behind such departures from central university work, but no one will deny that they are improvisations, fraught with the great danger of social projects, the 'rathole phenomenon,' by which money is spent, honorably but without result." [17]

But universities find it impractical, if not impossible, to discourage foundations from forcing riches upon them. Once a foundation gets a toe hold in a university department with an initial grant, its division heads quickly find common ground with ambitious and aggressive faculty members. The university administration, even if wary of overinvolvement in foundation projects unrelated to its basic mission of education, is bracketed by pressures from within (the grant-seeking department) and without (the grant-giving foundation). Barzun says again: "The quickest way to alienate a scholar or scientist from his university is for an administrator to look askance at a grant which is well on the way to acceptance in the foundation hierarchy." Nor will a cease-and-desist order from the university dissuade a determined grant hog from sniffing out a foundation trough at which to dine. Barzun says: "All devices so far tried will not prevent an able man and an alert foundation prospector from lunching together; and at that lunch the university goes into debt just as surely as if the treasurer had signed a promissory note."

Faculty members become expert at packaging projects to make them attractive to foundations. The following is a slightly-disguised example of a recent grant grab. A small college in the Middle Atlantic states found wide student interest in courses in business uses of computers. Because of its limited finances, the college could not purchase a demonstration computer outright; because of its small enrollment, the college could not persuade a computer manufacturer to give it one as a gift. The development officer also quickly discovered that no foundation was willing to make a capital grant for the purchase of a computer.

Fortunately, a college faculty member formerly had worked for one of the twenty-five largest foundations and knew something of how philanthropoids' minds work. In a weekend of vigorous work he wrote a prospectus for an "experimentative" program in which a computer would be used not only for classroom work but also for keeping track of student records and college payrolls and other data. The professor had a friend, principal of the local high school, who was happy to avow interest in a shared-time arrangement for his own records. As a fillip, the professor added a crash course in programming for faculty and staff members who would be feeding raw material into the computer. When he had finished, what had begun as a simple request for a computer had mushroomed into a project calling for more than $3,500,000 to be spent over three years. Expenses included the full-time services of two new faculty members to be hired directly from industry, one to handle the classroom phase, the other the administrative; and consultant fees for the high school principal and business manager.

A major foundation approved the expanded grant request within six weeks. The faculty member who did the padding received a $2,000 raise and tenure a year ahead of schedule. Furthermore, the program, in its second year as of this writing, is receiving glowing progress reports.

Save for Barzun, one hears little open criticism of foundations from university sources. McGeorge Bundy, just before leaving his Harvard deanship for government, did assert that some university departments "are dangerously influenced by the market place of contract funds. . . . Some men build foolish empires; some spread themselves too thin in conferences and consultations; some are indeed remittance men abroad."

But such public heresies are rare. In private, comments are both blistering and derisive. They are blistering because foundations "are pushy bastards who tell you how to run your business," in the words of a Washington academician who had a sad experience with Ford; they are derisive because the foundations "are so damned stupid about how they throw their money around that you'd think they were sailors in the sixth hour of shore leave."

Foundation News, the bimonthly publication of the Foundation Center, was forced to resort to anonymous quotations a few years ago to obtain enough articles for a modest symposium on foundation-university relations.[18] One criticism was that a foundation, merely by expressing interest in an area and inquiring if a university had ever thought of doing work there, "motivates professors to take new directions." A professor with no true desire to know anything about country X perks his ears when he is asked whether he would like to oversee a $200,000 project there, including funds for faculty travel. (Finding work to occupy those long summers, be it makeshift or real, is a chronic worry of professors who don't want to sit home for three months.) One symposium contributor thought that when a foundation endows a project of no value, "it actually weakens the university, keeping faculty abroad, swelling the ranks of a single department far out of proportion, and creating a bulge in the university's planning."

Foundation grants are seldom "free" in the sense that the university receives thousands of dollars for nothing. Barzun cites the example of a university administration that watched a $34,000 grant to start a subbranch of science research ultimately grow until it cost half a million dollars during the five years after the expiration of the grant period. As Parkinson recorded, bureaucracies—academic or governmental—multiply spontaneously. Stopping the growth of a well-nourished research project is as difficult as rooting out crab grass.

Because foundation money is "seed money," the university is supposed to meet overhead charges not directly related to the project and to assume responsibility for its continuance after the grant ends. Barzun comments: "In short, by taking a grant the university has incurred present and future expenses of indefinite amount—an amount bound to increase, for overhead rises by inflation, and all salaries go up with length of service." Another irritating foundation habit is to make sabbatical grants of $5,000 to $7,000 less than the recipient's salary; the university, to show its gratitude, is expected to make up the difference, hire a replacement, and continue paying fringe benefits (such as medical insurance and retirement) that average eighteen to twenty percent of the typical faculty salary. And when fellowships are granted to faculty members, administrative costs fall on the university.

Despite this, there is no dearth of universities willing to submit to these indignities to pride, pocketbook, and autonomy in return for a grant. Manning M. Pattillo of the Foundation Center, while with the Danforth Foundation of St. Louis, complained in *Foundation News*:

> There is a tendency, particularly in the larger universities, to turn to foundations uncritically whenever any faculty member would like to launch something new. Every university has a few men who are almost professional "grant-seekers," spending a good fraction of their time "dreaming up" projects to attract foundation money. Undoubtedly, a reduction in this activity would be advantageous all along the line. It would save valuable faculty time, cut down on the torrent of paper flowing into foundation offices, and eliminate unnecessary projects that might, somehow, actually find support.[19]

Much of this research is sheer waste, according to the testimony of the academicians themselves. Kenneth W. Mildenberger, an official of the Modern Language Association of America, states: "Excessive duplication of local studies and surveys occurs constantly in American education. Some of these studies are valuable, others quite worthless." A primary reason, according to Mildenberger, is "the inability in American education to communicate adequately the findings of research and studies." [20]

And Francis Keppel, while U.S. Commissioner of Education, complained: "The most common form of educational research has been and is still the small, easily-managed research project. Focusing on miniature, obscure and noncontroversial issues, such projects are seldom worth the serious attention of administrators or teachers. . . . Most serious approaches to educational development have centered and still center on providing more of what already exists—more classrooms, more books, more courses, more visual aids, and more teachers, most of whom are not using what we already know as the result of research." [21]

Maurice B. Mitchell, a specialist in "educational technology" for *Encyclopaedia Britannica*, looked at what foundations had been doing in education, and he told a House subcommittee in 1966:

> For a long time I have had the suspicion that one of the most useful pieces of research we could do in education would be a study to determine why nobody ever uses the research that is already here. . . . [Mitchell asserted that education research] tends to be very superficial . . . [and] a great deal of it follows the fads of the moment. If it becomes fashionable to say that the curriculum is out of date, everyone rushes out to study curriculum change; then they rush off to study teaching methods, the computer, and other new attractions. The product of this is . . . a kind of spastic, unconstructive groping which gives us unrelated chunks of data that seem to have value but which are not created as part of any long-range plan designed to help direct us to where we want to go in the future. . . .
>
> Much of the research that we see today is not really research at all. A great deal of the foundation-supported research is essentially a demonstration of what the foundations have made up their minds about in advance. Many foundations use grants to promote ideas, rather than prove them. And the foundation grant is all around us, as a modern status symbol. . . . The net result of some of this loose use of grants for research is that while we have the use of foundation funds, they are actually buying tacit recommendations for philosophies of education which the boards or the membership or the staffs of the foundations themselves have decided to support.[22]

The conventional foundation wisdom is that grant money can create "new centers of excellence." The philanthropoids' reasoning is reminiscent of the oil-stain theory of rural pacification once prevalent in the Vietnam War: create a showcase village (university) in the midst of war (academic chaos) and it will be so admired by other villages (universities) that they will emulate it. The "centers of excellence" idea is more often fulfilled in annual reports than in fact. A research scientist, who lived and worked on foundation money for almost a decade while the focal point of a "center of excellence" in a biological science, told me: "You get to the point where you hope that your research doesn't attract too much attention, for the foundations and other universities start pirating your staff, hoping they can carve out a piece of the action. When an assistant has worked for you for two or three years, he naturally becomes restless and would like to branch off on his own. An extra grant might give us the equipment and staff we need for a breakthrough push. But more likely, your associate will find it easier to get the money and start a 'new' but very similar shop elsewhere."

Foundations have an affinity for servicing institutions that are rich in their own right. A 1967 survey by the Boston Fund showed seventy colleges reporting total endowment funds of $6,551,647,563.[23] Harvard was highest, with an endowment of $1,038,098,479—almost one-sixth the total—and an annual income of $40,365,132. Yale was second with $504,806,750 in principal; Princeton third with $350,942,192. Each of these institutions boasts alumni who are, man for man, the wealthiest college graduates in America.

Yet here is precisely where foundations choose to spend much of their money. The Carnegie Corporation (six of whose fifteen trustees are Harvard men) bestowed $1,003,394 on that school in the three years from 1966 through 1968. Yale got $307,000 from Carnegie; Princeton a meager, but intriguing, $37,500: $22,500 for a "study of social and psychological factors in fertility"; and $15,000 for studies of its decision to admit women students. The Alfred P. Sloan Foundation authorized grants to Harvard of $395,000 in 1967–68; Ford gave $7,186,636 in 1968 alone, in a diversity of categories from journalism training to archaeological research and studies of de facto school segregation.

Ford also had $5,000,000 for Yale in 1968 "to establish a planning and educational improvement fund." One portion of the gift will test "approaches to gift-giving in which projects or faculty chairs are immediately financed on the assurance of later support from a donor." (Hopefully, this will prevent Old Blues from establishing "chairs" named in their honor with the expectation that university funds will keep their memories alive in perpetuity.) For Princeton, there was $798,534, making the grand total for these Big Three $12,985,169, more than one-fourth of Ford's total expenditures for education and research.

Grants to Harvard, Yale, and Princeton are as safe a way to spend a foundation's money as dropping dollar bills into a church collection plate. But the nature of foundation courage is best shown in how it approaches the controversial, not the safe. And a classic case of foundation cowardice revolves around the ill-fated Institute of Hispanic American Studies.

Professor Ronald Hilton, a scholar of unblinking objectivity, formed this institute at Stanford University in 1944 and built it into the nation's most respected center for Latin-American studies. Although considerable amounts of foundation money were available for foreign-affairs research in the immediate postwar years (Rockefeller and Carnegie spent $34,000,000 on "area studies" between 1945 and 1948), Hilton neither sought nor received foundation support. A major sideline of the Institute was the *Hispanic American Report*, the only scholarly journal in the field for students of the Spanish- and Portuguese-speaking nations of the Western Hemisphere. The *Report* was frequently and keenly critical of U.S. policies in Latin America; it did not share, or publish, the popular alarm that Fidel Castro threatened to convert Latin America into a communist prison: it suggested that Latin nations were evolving their own forms of nationalistic regimes, and that the U.S. should be prepared to accept Latin-American solutions, rather than attempt to impose its own. The *Report* built a quiet but influential reputation as a journal that could be trusted as an independent source of information on Latin-American affairs—all the more valuable because of the paucity of coverage of Latin America in the U.S. mass media.

Then, in 1959–60, there was trouble, under circumstances that gave the Ford Foundation several clear choices between scholarship and servility to interests which sought to stifle discussion of unpopular ideas.

In 1959 Ford offered Stanford a $25,000,000 grant on condition that it raise an additional $75,000,000 in matching funds. Stanford managed to find the money but discovered an unusual amount of benefactor discontent with Professor Hilton and the *Hispanic American Report*. Such companies as the Standard Oil Company of California, which has extensive oil investments in Latin America, asked university officials why they should give money to support a man "who is trying to destroy us."

Hilton has said: "It was suggested that I avoid offending

powerful fund raisers; a key member of the administration
demanded that, even in editorials bearing my signature, I
cease expressing controversial opinions . . . and that, while
no attention was paid to the Institute's two advisory boards
who gave me every support, the administration proposed to
appoint two secret committees to keep an eye on the *Report*." [24] Hilton's troubles with the Stanford administration
were so well-known on the Palo Alto campus that they
could not help reaching the ears of the Ford Foundation
officers responsible for administering the matching grant.
But Ford said nothing to deter its funds from being linked
with an attempt to stifle Hilton.

Then, in late 1960, by compiling facts that were common knowledge in Central America and among Cuban ref-
ugees and intelligence agencies, the *Report* detailed how the
Central Intelligence Agency was training Cubans at a re-
mote Guatemalan base for an invasion of Cuba. When the
Bay of Pigs invasion ignobly failed a few months later, Hilton was widely criticized for "endangering national security"—by printing information that was about as secret as
street corner gossip. (One of the men offended was Richard
Bissell, who had been with the Ford Foundation before joining the CIA, and who had operational responsibility for the
Bay of Pigs misadventure. He lost his job because of its failure.)

Hilton's butchery was swift, and Ford helped pass out
the knives with which the job was done. In 1961, when Hilton was at the height of his controversiality, Ford announced its intention to spend $42,000,000 at selected uni-
versities to strengthen international studies. Each institution
was permitted to work up its own prospectus. At Stanford
the task fell to Dean Carl Spaeth of the law school, one-time
assistant to Nelson Rockefeller in the Bureau of American

Republics Affairs at the State Department, later director of Ford's division of overseas activities. When Ford made its initial grant to Stanford in 1962, it stipulated that Spaeth's committee decide where the funds should be spent, but it specifically barred any expenditures on Latin America, pending further study. The "study" included a series of meetings of Latin-American scholars from which Hilton was excluded, even though he was the one man at Stanford who would be most affected by the decision.

The Spaeth committee soon concluded there was no way to conduct a Latin-American program at Stanford without including Hilton's Institute, lest the entire university be branded publicly as a fool. With Ford obviously unwilling to spend money on anything with which Hilton connected, Hilton must go. Since he would not leave voluntarily, he must be humiliated. Stanford informed Hilton that doctoral candidates were being withdrawn from his Institute and that he must thereafter concentrate on "practical instruction" at the master's level. Hilton resigned. Stanford suspended publication of the *Hispanic American Report*.

Two weeks later, Ford Foundation granted Stanford $550,000 for Latin-American studies.

With scant exception, Latin-American "scholars" choose to stare past the Hilton affair into the distance, where the shine of foundation funds is a more pleasant sight than the wrecked career of a single colleague. Their current trade union, the Latin American Studies Association, begun with a $100,000 Ford grant, is headed by Dr. Kalman Silvert, listed in the 1968 Ford annual report as a "program advisor" for Latin America.

To the foundations' somewhat outraged surprise, American universities did not rush to their defense : 1969, when the House of Representatives included in its punitive legislation a proviso that tax-exempt organizations be required to spend an amount equivalent to five percent of their assets annually. Foundation officials I interviewed that summer professed to be at a loss as to why the universities cared so little for the plight of their longtime friends and benefactors. (When a coordinated foundation group went before the Senate Finance Committee in the fall to argue against the legislation, the headline academic witness was President Theodore H. Hesburgh of Notre Dame, who is also a trustee of the Rockefeller Foundation.) Their consensus answer to my question "Why?" was as follows: "The universities are greedy. They think that the five percent rule will force us to pay out more money, and they want every cent they can get. Also, for every grant we make, we reject ten or twenty. So the dissatisfied far outnumber the satisfied."

One can draw two conclusions from the philanthropoids' own answers: universities consider foundations to be money bags, not equal partners in education; universities don't want the foundations on their campuses, only the foundations' money. One of the *Foundation News* symposium contributors stated:

> The best thing might be to liquidate foundations. Allow them to choose a couple of universities as donees and dispose of all their assets. The next best thing is surely to insist on more unrestricted grants, given to institutions for whatever purposes they, in their good judgment, saw fit. Just as they corrupt the individual scholar by offering him money to do something he would not freely choose to do himself, so foundations corrupt universities, unbalancing them. Foundation projects are constantly soaking up free funds that are crucially needed to finance areas where the universities need strength-

ening. If foundations judge universities to be incompetent, they should spend their money elsewhere. But if they think universities are competent, then the universities should be left to run their own house.[25]

A third alternative apparently never occurred to this anonymous philanthropoid: foundations might recognize the entire educational system as incompetent and give it a to-the-roots jolt. The universities tolerated mild foundation irritants (such as the encouraging of grant hogs) and good-humoredly accepted whatever funds the foundations offered. But the universities never listened seriously to foundation statements about "educational reform" until a single foundation—Ford—showed, at a lower academic level, that reform was possible. To this point we shall return in due course.

ALMOST SIMULTANEOUS with Dr. Henry Pritchett's glum assessment of American universities in 1910, another Carnegie agent, Abraham Flexner, wrote a failing report card for American medical schools. Working with a modest $10,000 grant from the Carnegie Foundation for the Advancement of Teaching, Flexner surveyed the 155 institutions which purported to train physicians. Many were proprietary outfits which produced quasi-literate butchers; few had any university affiliation or academic responsibility. And even those with links to formal universities were so loosely run that a medical degree meant only that a student had appeared more or less regularly at class and had not offended the professor. Flexner's report, published in 1910, has been called a "classic chapter" and a "significant milestone" in American medical education because it emphasized the importance of greater university influence, the value of the full-time system (both for professors and students), the need for research as a complement to teaching, and the lack of adequate facilities.[26]

Flexner had the ideas, Rockefeller and Carnegie had the money, and their marriage was spectacular. The Rockefeller Institute for Medical Research (an older and smaller brother of the Rockefeller Foundation, formed in 1901, and no longer a dispenser of grants) and the General Education Board showered money on tolerably respectable schools and on professors who expressed interest in research. "It was a vast pump-priming operation, geared to an ambitious idea," in the words of old Rockefeller hand Raymond B. Fosdick.[27] "The hundred million dollars contributed by the . . . Rockefeller boards, matched many times over by the generosity of scores of citizens like Rosenwald in Chicago, Eastman in Rochester, and Harkness in New York, took the teaching of medicine in the United States from the discreditable position it occupied in 1910 and gave it a status it shares with only a few countries in the world." And Dr. Luther Terry, when Surgeon General of the U.S. Bureau of Public Health, said that foundations "profoundly influenced the development of the nation's medical education system and provided the basis for present levels of achievement . . ."[28]

Flexner's report and the resulting foundation spending did succeed in eliminating the diploma mills, to the indisputable advantage of any American who has ever suffered anything from a bellyache to tuberculosis. But the reform has proven to be almost as much a menace to the citizen as the evil it cured. State licensing regulation prompted by the Flexner report put control of medical education firmly in the hands of the American Medical Association. Becoming a physician in the United States today requires a diploma from a school accredited by the AMA's adjunct, the Council on Medical Education.

This is bad. This is bad because, as Adam Smith once said about guilds, be they of doctors or of tailors, "People of the same trade seldom meet together, even for merriment and diversion, but the conversation ends in a conspiracy against the public or in some contrivance to raise prices." The AMA's contrivance happens to be what we could call professional family planning: keep the number of physicians low, and everyone will profit.

In 1910 4,400 persons were graduated from medical schools. A decade later, with the diploma mills shuttered, the number dropped to 3,047. By 1940 the curve was rising again, to 4,097—117 less than were graduated in 1900. In 1968 graduates totaled 8,000. Man for man, the physicians are better trained; but not even the AMA can offer cogent arguments for why a decrease in the number of medical graduates per capita from one per 14,468 in 1900 to one per 25,000 in 1968 should be considered a gain for American health services. Flexner deserves much credit for divesting us of the quacks; the foundations deserve much blame for not exploiting the initiative once it was seized. "We are importing about 1,000 practicing physicians every year, and yet from the standpoint of our international responsibilities we should be educating more medical and dental students than we need in order that some could be made available for less fortunate countries. It is a serious situation, sir," Dr. Terry told a House subcommittee in 1961.[29]

But not so serious as to prompt the foundations to attempt a reformation. Instead the philanthropoids are content to continue financing a restrictive, discriminatory medical educational system. A researcher who wants $20,000 to trace the source of an obscure toe itch that afflicts sixty-nine-year-old members of a Connecticut country club can find, through patient shopping, an interested foundation. But American foundations have never summoned the nerve to suggest to the AMA-dominated medical schools that they need more students, not scholastic apartheid.

If the foundations chose to speak, their voice would resound with the solid clang of the cash register. Their expenditures on health and hospitals totaled more than a half-billion dollars between 1964 and 1968, according to a compilation by the American Association of Fund-Raising Counsel.[30] But the foundations' "innovative money" goes for research, not for the production of doctors who treat human beings. Medical schools, realizing this, paint their faces the hue desired by their customers. Social critic David Hapgood has asserted: "The medical school curriculum and its entrance requirements are geared to the highly academic student who is headed for research. In the increasingly desperate struggle for admission, these academically talented students are crowding out those who want to practice medicine." [31]

Academic medicine and specialization are stressed, to the detriment of patient care. A student can go through his first two years in many American medical schools without laying his eyes, much less his hands, upon a single patient. A hospital can find the six-figure grant for the lavish equipment required for open-heart surgery—a prestige item, even if used only three times annually—but black ward orderlies and practical nurses struggle along at wages giving them a life scarcely better than the slavery of their ancestors. But what foundation wishes to subsidize a semi-skilled black who empties bedpans and dispenses pills? Better to endow a pavilion that can be named after the rich man who created the foundation. What foundation would have the cheek to inform the AMA: "Unless you relax your foolishly high standards for admission to medical schools, we intend to spend our funds elsewhere."

Crass, yes, but the AMA is a crass union, and its ears are demonstrably and notoriously deaf to purely humanistic arguments. But the medical profession does quiver excitedly when it hears the fast riffle of thousand dollar bills. Since Ford began nationwide operations in 1950, it has spent more than a third of a billion dollars on medical schools and hospitals, including $100,000,000 with a single scratch of the pen in 1956, when its sale of Ford Motor Company stock brought in an embarrassing amount of money. Had Ford paused and asked knowledgeable men, "What is wrong with medicine, and what sort of cure can we effect with this money?," the $100,000,000 would have constituted a club to clear out a selective group of medical schools, whose main business would be the training of doctors, not the support of marginally-valuable research. Medicine indeed needs research; even more, however, it needs physicians who can put new knowledge to practical use by actually treating patients—which is, after all, what medicine is all about.

Ironically, foundation philanthropy's most conspicuous medical achievements came *outside* the United States. The Rockefeller Foundation's international health division at one time worked in seventy-five nations, and combated, with varying degrees of success, twenty-one diseases or health problems, including tuberculosis, yaws, rabies, influenza, typhus, amebiasis, undulant fever, dysentery, typhoid fever, hepatitis, hookworm disease, malaria, and yellow fever. The Foundation spent almost $100,000,000 on international health between 1913 and 1950, when the division was disbanded.

The most dramatic result, among many, was in Ceylon, where campaigns against malaria and hookworm reduced the 1940 crude death rate from 20.1 per 1,000 (twice that of advanced countries) to 9.1 per 1,000 in 1960, less than the rate of the United States. The Rockefeller public health pioneers suffered personal hardships (at least three of them died in the line of duty) and wrestled with local superstitions (workers in Ceylon thought vermifuge capsules given them for hookworm were small bombs that would burst and kill them in case of a German occupation, so that no one could tend the British plantations). What Rockefeller did *not* encounter, however, was any entrenched medical hierarchy comparable to the AMA; thus, its programs worked.[32] *

Foundations rebut criticism of their research fetish by trotting out Nobel Prize winners to whom they have given money over the years. It is an impressive group. Thirty-two Nobel Prize winners at one time in their careers had fellowships from the Rockefellers' foundation complex; seventy-three other Nobel winners received lesser Rockefeller support (funds for travel, laboratory equipment, and so forth).

* In 1969 the Rockefeller staff was ordered to begin studies on what the foundation could do to improve the supply of and availability of physicians in the United States. The reason: a Rockefeller vice president became ill one Sunday afternoon at his home in Scarsdale, New York, and was unable to find a doctor who would attend him. After several frustrating hours he telephoned a vice president of Presbyterian Hospital in Manhattan, who produced a physician. Henry Romney, the Foundation's information officer, told me: "If an officer of the Rockefeller Foundation, which had been identified with medical affairs for fifty years, could not obtain a doctor without going to such extremes, you can imagine what it's like for other persons in New York."[33] No specific Foundation plans to rectify the situation had materialized as of this writing.

The conclusion drawn is that, because of this record, research spending is, ipso facto, good.

Or is it?

Because foundations reserve the right to evaluate their own accomplishments and to keep secret any findings they choose, objective data on the efficacy of medical grants is scarce. A scientist who squanders $100,000 on a search for a cure for cancer by soaking Irish potato peels in Kentucky bourbon and spreading the residue on crickets can avow, with total honesty, "Jones didn't find cancer either, and he had $37,800 more and six months longer." But should Smith have been given the $100,000 at all? Should not proper screening stop the frivolous and inane? A House investigative subcommittee report issued in 1967 challenged the notion that all medical research is necessary and worthwhile. The report, which reflects upon three major foundations, came about as follows.

The Sloan-Kettering Institute for Cancer Research, in New York, has long been a major supplicant of the National Institutes of Health, a federal agency. But during 1964–66 NIH suddenly got tough with Sloan-Kettering and began bouncing grant applications with alarming frequency. Of thirty-four applications submitted during the two years, only twenty were approved. Thereupon, Sloan-Kettering changed its approach. No longer did it submit individual grants for approval. Instead, a five-year lump sum contract was obtained, calling for minimum NIH appropriations of $22,600,000, or 47.3 percent of its operating budget. Escalator clauses on research costs protected Sloan-Kettering against inflation.

Although the House subcommittee recognized Sloan-Kettering as a "leading cancer research institution," it was disturbed that its grant applications "will no longer be

subject to the established scientific review process, thereby
depriving the grantee [NIH] of an objective, outside judgment on its individual research proposals." Such independent review was sorely needed, the subcommittee said, and as
evidence it cited these excerpts from evaluation reports in
which NIH rejected Sloan-Kettering applications:

> This unimaginative proposal plans to do studies which
> have become almost routine in institutions with active hema-
> tology and radioisotope services. There is no research support
> warranted for this plain data-gathering exercise.
>
> . . . .
>
> Disapproval is recommended. The conceptual approach
> and experimental plan are remarkably unsophisticated.
> There is nothing in the application to inspire confidence that
> continuation of this work would add to the understanding of
> the mechanism of action of antitumor agents.
>
> . . . .
>
> There is nothing in this proposal to indicate that the ap-
> plicants are in a position to contribute significantly to this
> heavily worked area.
>
> . . . .
>
> Results of this program have been disappointing, and on
> the basis of the application and information obtained through
> the site visit, there is no reason to expect that marked progress
> or significant results will be forthcoming in the future.[34]

The Alfred P. Sloan Foundation, the Sloan-Kettering
Institute's major private benefactor, makes its $400,000-a-
year payments in the form of "unrestricted support"—that
is, Institute officers decide which research projects are to be
financed. Similarly, the Rockefeller Brothers Fund contributes $120,000 a year "for the expansion and improvement
of facilities and for research and teaching programs." Recurring, fixed-amount grants with no project review might
have disturbed the House of Representatives, but most phi-

lanthropoids defend the procedure. "With a blue-ribbon recipient like Sloan-Kettering, the last thing a foundation
should do is question research projects," one of them told
me. "If you can't accept S-K's judgment on cancer research,
go spend your money elsewhere."

The faith of this philanthropoid—and others—does not
detract from the central fact that the evaluators of NIH had
labeled as worthless more than forty percent of the research
projects proposed in one year by America's premier foundation-supported cancer research institution.

Foundations are popular with the medical establishment because they do so much to preserve it. A well-en-
dowed regional foundation—Kellogg in Michigan, Moody
in Texas, Lilly in Indiana—can be as influential in hospital
affairs as is the state medical association, through grants for
construction, operating expenses, and research. By tradition, however, the foundations are partners, not competitors, of the medical associations, and they permit the physicians to dictate local practices.

The most striking example of foundation influence in
medicine is the Duke Endowment's gentle but pervasive
dominance of hospitals in North and South Carolina: rigor-
ous in such noncontroversial areas as bookkeeping procedures and the operation of switchboards; oblivious to the de
facto segregation that gives one quality of medical care to
white Carolinians, a lesser one to the blacks. James Buchanan Duke's indenture provided for payments of one dollar a day for each charity patient treated by "properly-
operated" community hospitals, which in the 1920s represented one-third the cost. The Endowment took upon itself
the task of prescribing minimum standards for eligibility—
in records keeping, in staff, in methods of treatment. Duke

also persuaded physicians who operated one-man proprietary hospitals to sell them to community groups and become eligible for aid.

Marshall I. Pickens, longtime Duke officer, recollected that several doctors considered community ownership "some form of socialism." [35] Duke reassured them by insuring that communities paid a fair price. "For years these country and small town doctors had provided the only medical services available to their areas," Pickens said, "and they deserved consideration. We got them out of a financial bind. Here you'd have a doctor whose entire assets consisted of a hospital built around his talents. That wasn't much of an estate to leave his widow." Between 1924 and 1968 Duke spent $70,883,301 on hospital subsidies and research for improving administrative services. In 1968 alone 188 hospitals in 157 Carolina towns received help from Duke.

Save for administrative projects, Duke does not support medical research, for, as Pickens puts it, physicians are "too tied" to universities. "They don't get out and practice," he said. "Professors pick off the brightest students and steer them towards specialties. We are interested in getting medical service out where the people are." Duke will help a community organize a hospital building campaign (its contribution always comes last, to encourage local initiative), design the physical structure, staff it (Duke's Charlotte office is an unofficial hiring office for hospital administrators), and operate it. And its popularity in Carolina medicine was demonstrated in 1968 when the citizens of Greenville, South Carolina, who had worked for a hospital system for some three decades, named the first completed building in honor of Marshall I. Pickens.

But there are Carolinians who think the Duke Endowment is something less than goodness institutionalized.

Prominent among them is Dr. Raymond K. Wheeler of Charlotte, a physician, a longtime civil liberties activist, and a director of the Southern Regional Council, a group active in voter registration and other civil rights work. Wheeler's pique arises from Duke's role in development of Charlotte hospitals and can be summarized this way: "For decades, Charlotte blacks have been forced to rely upon the antiquated, inadequate facilities of Good Samaritan Hospital, in an industrial-ghetto area. It's a dirty, smelly, ill-equipped place where white Charlotte sends its chauffeurs and cooks for treatment, and expects you [the doctor] to go there and care for them as a community service. One of the first things I did when I arrived in Charlotte in 1948 was to press for its closing." [36]

Charlotte's Social Planning Council, a broad-based community group, agreed with Wheeler in the mid-1950s, and recommended that Good Samaritan be closed, and that Charlotte Memorial, the leading white hospital, be integrated. The medical establishment's answer was to propose modernization and integration of Good Samaritan.

Dr. Wheeler reports: "The Duke Endowment—that is to say, Marshall Pickens—brought in another consultant to resurvey the situation, and, most predictably, he recommended a bond issue to renovate Good Samaritan and keep it open for the blacks. There was a full-blown campaign on its behalf—this is basically a prejudiced community anyway—and the issue passed. The federal government wouldn't match the funds [for Good Samaritan renovation], so we gave away a million dollars to keep that outdated old place open."

Wheeler does not charge that there is a conscious racist taint to the Duke Endowment. (Yet there is a discernible paternalism, as exemplified by officer Robert J. Sailstad's casual reference to Johnson C. Smith College, one of the institutions named as a beneficiary in the Duke will, as "our Negro college." [37]) But Wheeler does assert: "The Duke Endowment has tremendous influence on the medical affairs of this community. That power and influence has been, in the past, and still is, colored by the mores of the southern region in which they [the officers] operate. And this background influences their decisions. In that respect, this influence is not good for the community."

The hospital dispute is now shifting to another area in which Duke's influence—and its tolerance of segregated medicine—is even more visible. In 1966 Charlotte's Health and Hospital Council said a fourth general hospital would be needed in the city by 1980, and recommended that it be planned for the inner-city, adjacent to the existing facilities of the Charlotte Memorial Hospital complex. In the face of this recommendation, Duke gave the local county commissioners $250,000 of $500,000 needed to buy an eighty-acre site in a white, affluent suburban section of Charlotte, inaccessible to inner-city blacks who are most in need of care. "The Duke Endowment has no concern for the basic economic problems of the community," asserts Wheeler. "A downtown hospital would be a boon for a decaying area of Charlotte. But Duke—they're interested in erecting a beautiful hospital on a beautiful tract of land on the fringes of town, not available either to the poor or the doctors willing to treat them, only to the white doctors and their private white patients. I don't think that's particularly good medicine."

YORKE ALLEN, JR., a longtime executive of the Rockefeller Foundation, once remarked he had a "blunderbuss" question for grant applicants: "What would be the result if your project were undertaken? What would it prove?" [38] Allen's implication was that Rockefeller did not support research to satisfy a scientist's narrow whim or to add a meaningless footnote to an established body of fact. Under the Allen theory, although a foundation may support a diversity of projects, each should point toward a specific goal.

Unfortunately for foundation philanthropy, many philanthropists use the blunderbuss itself, rather than the blunderbuss question, in making their grants. Rather than isolating and attacking a clearly definable problem, these foundations fire sporadic broadsides at an entire field. Individuals may accomplish a minor goal or two, but few gains of any significance are ever made. The grantees plod on from year to year, interrupting themselves annually while the sponsoring foundation boasts of the multiplicity and curiosity of projects in which they have invested since the last inventory.

The Foundations' Fund for Research in Psychiatry, funded by a consortium of four foundations,* was formed in 1952 for research "into why people become mentally and emotionally ill, why they get well, how best to help them get well, and how best to prevent their becoming mentally and emotionally ill." [39] A frequent worrier about its role as competitor with well-funded researchers of the federal government and larger foundations, FFRP said in its 1967–68 annual report that it intended to spend its half million dollars of annual income on "new and unusual but promising research areas . . . [and] young or unknown investigators." Here are some specimens:

* The Social Research Foundation, the Ford Foundation, the Grant Foundation, Inc., and the van Ameringen Foundation, Inc.

— $6,500 to a Detroit teacher to study the "response of Greek mothers to low academic achievement" of their children.

— $25,000 to a man-and-wife anthropologist team to look into "peculiarities" of the culture of the Dani, a New Guinean tribe, including "reports of extremely low sex drives in these people."

— $30,000 to a woman researcher for a three-year study of the "relationships between the internal vicissitudes of a creative person and those of the society which molds him," based upon the "microscopic examination of all available data pertaining to the life an individual . . . [including] diaries, correspondence, notes, manuscripts and other writings . . . as well as interviews."

— $27,274 for the "Development of New Methods for the Analysis of Animal Vocalization." ("More specifically, the project is concerned with artificial syntheses of bird sounds, behavior in the system producing the sounds, and physiology of mechanisms resulting in the sounds.")

Bird sounds. The libido of primitive New Guineans. Greek mothers' worries about Junior's report card. $30,000 and three years to poke through a genius's papers and then to guess why he is one. FFRP is not alone in off-beat interests. The Grant Foundation spent $84,000 developing an "extra-mural activities program" for Atlantic College in southern Wales, Great Britain, which prepares students for coast rescue service work "along a dangerous and much used stretch of sea, cliff and beach" in England. Grant stated: "The purpose is to help young men discover and develop their own abilities, and to satisfy youth's desire for adventure, social significance, and humanitarian service.

From service comes a concern for others; from hardship and danger—self-reliance; from adventure and excitement—a new interest in life. The physical challenges to which the students are exposed may be overcome through conditioning and disciplined planning . . ." [40]

For guaranteed perpetuity and lack of measurable accomplishment, the Carnegie Endowment for International Peace ($45,540,269 in assets as of June 30, 1968; expenditures of $1,300,000 to $1,400,000 annually) is in a class by itself. Andrew Carnegie formed the foundation in 1910, with an endowment of $10,000,000, and told the trustees "the one view they shall keep unceasingly in view until it is attain, is the speedy abolition of international war between so-cald civilized nations." *

Carnegie continued:

> When civilized nations enter into such treaties as named, and war is discarded as disgraceful to civilized men, as personal war (duelling) and man selling and buying (slavery) hav been discarded within the wide boundaries of our English-speaking race, the Trustees will pleas then consider what is the next most degrading evil or evils whose banishment—what new elevating element or elements if introduced or fosterd, or both combined—would most advance the progress, elevation and happiness of man, and so on from century to century without end. . . . Let my Trustees therefore ask themselves from time to time, from age to age how they can help man in his glorious ascent onward and upward and to this end devote this fund. [41]

The trustees gloomily conceded in a fiftieth anniversary "statement of rededication" that they could "no longer

* Carnegie's spelling reflected his Scottish nativity.

share . . . [Carnegie's] degree of optimism" that war would be "discarded as disgraceful to civilized man." Said the trustees: "We do firmly believe that substantial progress toward a world in which nations no longer resort to armed conflict as a means of settling disputes is imperative and possible in practice. But peace, when it exists, is like health in that it can never be taken for granted; the threat of armed conflict, like illness, is a constant challenge . . ." [42] Thus, the trustees recognized that the Endowment was engaged in "an endless activity."

The "endless activity" occupies the full-time efforts of fifty-eight staff members, in New York and Europe. The Endowment publishes pamphlets, books, and other papers; it underwrites conference after conference; it gives money to other foundations and organizations to support their programs. "Our product is equal quantities of paper and hot air," a Carnegie Endowment officer told me in 1969, several months before he resigned. "Doing work towards such illusionary goals requires either a high degree of dedication or a high degree of self-delusion. I don't have either."

"I suppose that in someone's mind or judgment almost everything that man might do could have some educational significance, even in any day-to-day activities," Representative John W. Byrnes, a Republican from Wisconsin, mused during the 1969 tax reform hearings.[43] McGeorge Bundy of the Ford Foundation, who was testifying, agreed: "What is attractive to one professor seems like nonsense to another and what seems like an extremely promising line of activity to one university seems like a waste of money to another. You have heard testimony about the supposed unwisdom of certain kinds of grants from the Bollingen Foundation. In other parts of this city you can be told with conviction that it is the most imaginative and fruitful philanthropic institution there is. People who tell you that are people whose interests fall into that area."

This is, of course, a perfectly human situation, for children don't criticize the candy they have just been handed, or question the motives of the person who gave it to them. If asked, they are apt to say he is a fine fellow indeed and encourage him to give again. Similarly, philanthropoids hear little but the sycophantic, soothing voices of their own supplicants, who, when asked, reply that the foundations are doing exactly what is right for the world and should continue.

This happy, incestuous state of affairs marked foundation-supplicant relations for a full half-century. Proven accomplishments during the period are as much the result of the law of averages as of philanthropic skills. Proven failures are as few, for so much of the foundation work was done in that gray area of esotericism where success is nigh indistinguishable from dignified silliness.

In one area, however, foundations have a better performance record—as vehicles for espousing the philosophical and political views of the persons who control them.

CHAPTER **6**

Spending the Money II: Philosophies Right and Left

FOUNDATION FUNDS flow in uneven driblets to both the Right and Left of the American political spectrum as grants for "educational," study, and community-action projects. The Institute for Policy Studies (IPS), a New Left think tank in Washington, has received funds from the Ford Foundation (briefly), the Stern Family Fund, the Samuel Rubin Foundation, the Milbank Foundation, the Field Foundation and the Janss Foundation. The institute's co-director, writer Marcus Raskin, was the chairman of the Committee for the Formation of a New Party, which ran the presidential campaign of black comedian Dick Gregory

159

in 1968; he was also a codefendant in the Spock draft conspiracy trial.

An IPS associate fellow, Richard Kaufman, is a staff member of the Joint Economic Committee of Congress; his studies at IPS helped alert Congressmen to wasteful cost overruns in military spending and prompted the acrimonious challenges to defense appropriations in the 1969 session. Another IPS senior fellow, Arthur I. Waskow, helped organize the demonstrations at the 1968 Democratic National Convention in Chicago. Ivy covers the front of IPS' building in northwest Washington, but there is no other resemblance to formal academia: its staff practices, not preaches, social activism.

IPS receives its share of abuse. Senator Strom Thurmond, angered about its defense spending studies, charged IPS with "developing broad changes in our social structure without reference to the political structure upon which our nation is based. Its members seek to override the republican form of government and to institute those changes which they, as an elite, feel will be beneficial without reference to the desires of the American people, or the federal and state governments. . . . In effect, our tax policy is subsidizing the revolutionary policy of the IPS." [1]

The Stern Family Fund, most adventuresome of the liberal/Left-oriented foundations, has given IPS as much as $50,000 a year (toward an annual budget of $400,000) "to research, analyze, criticize and propose public policy." Stern has also made numerous special purpose grants to IPS: $500 for workshops for persons from Mississippi, Alabama, and Georgia active in civil rights; $3,000 for development of a neighborhood foundation in a Lutheran church in Columbus, Ohio; $10,000 for forming community cooperative warehouses in Washington. "It is planned to extend the effort to other cities and to establish marketing relationships with southern Negro producers and a proposed food processing plant at Mound Bayou, Mississippi," states a program summary.

Stern has also given money to the Students for a Democratic Society ($4,849 for a conference of persons working in community development in northern cities and Appalachia) and to the League for Industrial Democracy ($32,500 for training civil rights and community development workers). In 1968 Stern gave $10,000 to Business Executives Move for a Vietnam Peace, a vociferously active antiwar group, and $10,000 to the United States Youth Council for a program whose participants included the College Young Democrats, the Campus Americans for Democratic Action, and the Young People's Socialist League, among others.

As a change of pace, Stern has as a partner in another project none other than the United States Army. In 1968 Stern gave $18,000 to the Metropolitan Community Aid Council of Washington for a pilot project to rehabilitate housing and train ghetto youths in construction trades "with the technical assistance of the U.S. Army." Stern states: "The idea arose from the desire of some of the citizens of Washington to search for an appropriate positive role for the army in the ghetto beyond restoring uneasy peace." The army is providing "supervisory personnel skilled in construction"; the program's area is that which army troops occupied during the April, 1968, riots in Washington.

The Field Foundation, which was brave long before Ford (but without enough resources to attract attention to itself), has concentrated on helping southern blacks. Grants during its fiscal year ending September 30, 1968, included $5,000 toward legal costs of student militants expelled from

Grambling College, Louisiana; $30,000 for the Committee on the March of Equality, which was supporting the garbage workers' strike in Memphis, Tennessee; and $25,000 for a series of "experimental conferences" with young militants. Field also gave $10,000 to the defense of thirty-five South-West Africans "being prosecuted under the South African Terrorism Act." Between 1964 and 1967 Field gave more than $100,000 to the Highlander Research and Education Center in Nashville for voter registration. Southern segregationists consider Highlander to the left of the Kremlin, and state and local officials have subjected the center to continuing harassment.

Still farther to the Left is the Louis M. Rabinowitz Foundation of New York, founded in 1944 by a rags-to-riches manufacturer of hooks and eyes for the garment industry. Until Louis Rabinowitz died in 1957, the Foundation's chief interest was research into "Jewish contributions to American life." It financed archaeological expeditions and gave generously to universities and established charities; it was indistinguishable in function from hundreds of humdrum foundations.

Then control of the Foundation passed to Rabinowitz's son, Victor, a New York lawyer with an affinity for left-wing causes of varying respectability. Victor Rabinowitz was at one time a registered agent for Fidel Castro's Cuban government. He has defended literally scores of witnesses accused of communist sympathies before Congressional committees, and he was active in the Fair Play for Cuba Committee. Under Victor Rabinowitz' guidance Foundation programs have taken an abrupt turn to the Left.

— The Louis M. Rabinowitz Foundation has granted tens of thousands of dollars to writers for "research on socialism," which has resulted in articles for *Monthly Re-*

view, self-described as an "independent Marxist" journal, and in books published by International Publishers, the Communist Party's U.S. publishing house.

— The Foundation has sponsored two Socialist Scholars Conferences in New York, papers for which were prepared by persons working with Rabinowitz grants.

— The Foundation gave more than $37,000 to black separatist James Forman during the period he was attempting to lead the Student Non-Violent Coordinating Committee into the Black Panther organization.

— The Foundation funded research that produced articles portraying Cheddi Jagan, one-time leader of British Guyana, as a popular hero. Victor Rabinowitz' wife, Marcia, who is Foundation secretary-treasurer, at the time was an officer of Friends of British Guyana. Voters later turned out Jagan.

Other grant recipients, while less controversial, were, nonetheless, politically oriented. In 1967, for instance, the Rabinowitz Foundation gave $1,500 to Clergy and Laymen Concerned About Vietnam, which states in its literature, "We act to influence public and legislative opinion from our pulpits, in the courts, at draft boards, in the streets." And the Foundation also helped finance the New Left journal, *Studies on the Left*.

Right-wingers, such as Senator Thurmond, charged that because such foundations have tax-exemption, "the taxpayers are paying for attacks upon themselves whether they like it or not."

LIKE IT OR NOT, taxpayers are also paying for right-wing projects supported with foundation funds. The

Lilly Endowment has given money to the far-out "Christian Anti-Communist Crusade" to distribute "anti-Communist books" in Brazil. Sun Oil millionaire J. Howard Pew, who controls the Pew Memorial Trust, is a faithful supporter of the Far Right. One of his favorite charities is the Christian Freedoms Foundation, whose president, Howard Kershner, speaks to the nation for fifteen minutes nightly over some 150 radio stations on "the Christian religion and education in the field of economics."

The Pew foundation also supports the Intercollegiate Studies Institute of Philadelphia, a clearing house for intellectual conservatives. Another Pew foundation, the Glenmede Trust of Philadelphia, is a benefactor of the Christian Anti-Communist Crusade. Dr. Fred Schwartz, chieftain of this scare outfit, sets the tone for its programs: "Christians! To arms! The enemy is at the gate! Buckle on the armor of the Christian and go forth to the battle! When they come for you, as they have for many others, and on a dark night in a dank cellar, they take a wide-bore revolver with a soft-nose bullet, and they place it at the nape of your neck . . ." [2]

The Economic and Business Foundation of New Wilmington, Pennsylvania, in the Pittsburgh industrial area, supports "economic education programs" at which teachers and middle-management employees of supporting firms are subjected to Birchite nonsense which would draw hoots and jeers from noncaptive audiences. At a 1964 meeting a speaker told three hundred high-school teachers: "We have attained a high level of material well-being, but what else do we have to crow about, now that our constitutional form of limited government is on the verge of going down the drain and a large part of our structure and liberty and freedom to assume responsibility and make decisions have been washed away by the tide of socialist intervention?"

A few years later Martin Gainsbrugh, a vice president of the National Industrial Conference Board, in another seminar sponsored by the Economic and Business Foundation, gave a revisionist view of the robber barons: "The lean reward to labor under early capitalism . . . was far more a result of restricted capacity to produce and the low state of science than of capitalistic exploitation."

Business supporters rely upon the Economic and Business Foundation to "condition" teachers and employees to be friendly to capitalism, and the Foundation apparently succeeds. The Foundation's annual reports feature supposedly "unsolicited" letters from teachers praising its programs. (Oddly, most are written in the last week of the school term, and are similar in format.) Typical is one from Don A. Yanessa, of Aliquippa, Pennsylvania: "Being that I come from a steel producing family (labor class) I had previously to this course had a prejudiced viewpoint against big business and profit. However, I have come to appreciate management's point of view in a light which I didn't think I would be capable of appreciating or sympathizing with previously . . ."

For sustained and profitable nonsense, however, Freedoms Foundation towers over other right-wing organizations like a flag-draped colossus. Freedoms Foundation's product is its version of the American Way of Life (a phrase invariably capitalized in the Foundation's abundant literature), embodied in the American Credo, a document so important that it is carved into marble on a monument amid the neo-Colonial buildings clustered on its hundred-odd acres of land abutting Valley Forge National Park. The

American Credo firmly supports the "Right to Work in Callings and Localities of Our Choice"; the "Right to Go into Business, Compete, Make a Profit"; the "Right to Freedom from Arbitrary Government Regulation and Control"; the "Right to Own Private Property"; and the "Right to Bargain for Goods and Services in a Free Market." These rights are highly important to the business community which supports Freedoms Foundation. But the American Credo doesn't concern itself with certain "Rights" which other Americans might consider important —the right to attend an integrated school, or to buy a home in the neighborhood of one's choice, or to achieve quality education.

Freedoms Foundation's emphasis on "Rights" for corporations rather than human beings is natural, for it is the personal creation of a Los Angeles advertising man, Don Belding, whose firm long represented West Coast industrial and business interests. The Foundation's chief function is to collect money from rich corporations and decide which individuals, journalists, educators, ministers, and school children are the Best Americans. Evaluating other people's Americanism consumes almost all of the $1,000,000 income that Freedoms Foundation reaps each year. And this million dollars is really what the Foundation is all about.

The Foundation's own story of its inception is stirring. The way it is told in Foundation literature,[3] one Sunday in 1948 Belding and his wife were visiting Mr. and Mrs. Kenneth D. Wells and their sons, Kenneth, then 17, and Dick, 11, at the Wells' "modest home" near Bedford Village, New York. Wells was a labor management man for Union Oil Company of California; a charismatic salesman, if you happen to find his vehement view of the twentieth century cred-

ible; and a Midwesterner who views the East Coast with
deep suspicion.

The conversation that Sunday concerned the Beldings'
recent trip to Europe, and how Belding had described the
American Way of Life to persons he met abroad. The Foundation history relates:

" 'Mr. Belding,' spoke up 11-year-old Dick, 'what did
you say it is? What is the American Way of Life?' Don
Belding stopped short. There was a puzzled, thoughtful expression on his face as he looked at the youth. For a moment there was silence. 'Dick,' he said, 'I'm a little embar-
rassed. We keep talking about the American Way of Life.
But what is it? Really?' 'That's what I'd like to know,' Dick
answered."

Thereupon, Belding took out a pencil and began scrawl-
ing on the white linen tablecloth. " 'First,' he said, 'we have
a constitutional government . . .' " The discussion lasted
all afternoon, Belding gradually filling the cloth. "Outside
evening shadows began to gather. . . . Hours passed . . .
[by] late that night the group . . . had drafted the basis of
the American Credo. 'Now,' said Dick, 'I understand what
the American Way of Life is.' 'So do I,' Kenny answered.
. . . But Belding and Wells wondered, 'How many Americans know what the American Way of Life is? How many
merely take their rights and freedoms for granted, not
knowing what they are, how they were purchased and what
they cost? The more they thought about it, the more they
realized they should do something about it.

" 'I think we've got something,' Belding said after the
boys had retired.' " Indeed they had. Belding had already
tried to sell the National Association of Manufacturers on
an anti-Communist advertising campaign. The NAM said
no. Belding had persuaded the fundamentalist Harding

College, in Searcy, Arkansas, to create an "Americanism" course for businessmen, but not enough money materialized to make it worthwhile. The American Credo turned out to be more marketable merchandise. DeWitt Wallace, publisher of the *Reader's Digest,* helped Belding rework the table-cloth document, and published it in his magazine in March, 1949. The exposure was invaluable for Wells and Belding. But, as the Foundation history recognizes, they "realized that an organization would be needed to promote [sic] the American Credo."

Digest tearsheets in hand, Wells went to former President Herbert Hoover and Dwight D. Eisenhower, then president of Columbia University. Both men agreed to lend their names to the idea, Hoover as honorary president, Ike as honorary chairman. Belding next visited and convinced Edward F. Hutton, the New York stockbroker and longtime patron of rightist causes (during the 1930s he financed the American Liberty League and the Crusaders, formed to fight President Roosevelt and the New Deal). Next, Belding found a fifty-three-acre dairy farm at Valley Forge ("It just seems as though the whole heart of America started here," Wells said, according to Foundation literature).

Hutton bought the place and rented it to the Foundation for a dollar a year. The Foundation offices moved into an old barn heated with a cast iron pot-bellied stove. Wells quit Union Oil and moved into the sprawling farmhouse (rent free) as president of the Foundation. Then they got down to serious business—persuading rich men and corporations to donate money to support the American Way of Life, as written on the tablecloth and as blessed by the *Reader's Digest* and Messrs. Hoover and Eisenhower.

The heart of Freedoms Foundation's "program" is its awards to persons and organizations which contribute "toward the understanding and propagation of the American Way of Life," as defined by the Foundation. The judging is done by a jury, one-third of which is composed of justices of state supreme courts; the remainder, "heads of national veteran, patriotic and service organizations." Wells announced publicly during the first awards year that the prizes would be greater than the Nobel and Pulitzer committees together. They weren't, but the Foundation did give $84,000 cash to some 600 winners. Prizes for "services against socialism" went to an interesting grouping of Americans: Senator Robert Taft, for pushing the antilabor Taft-Hartley Act through Congress; Hearst columnist George E. Sokolsky, for a speech condemning the "welfare state"; Harold Gray, author of the comic strip "Little Orphan Annie," for an unnamed deed, although Daddy Warbucks would be comfortable at Valley Forge; and baseball player Jackie Robinson, not for breaking the color line in baseball but for testimony before the House Un-American Activities Committee in which he criticized singer Paul Robeson for saying the Negro in America was in trouble. ("Silly and untrue," said Jackie.)

The cash outlay was too much for the Foundation promoters. What's the use of raising money only to give it away again? They have explained in Foundation pamphlets: "We learned . . . that Americans are not as much interested in the money as they are in the recognition they get." The Freedoms Foundation therefore has not repeated the mistake of the first year. During the year ended June 30, 1968, the Foundation received contributions of $1,040,594 and disbursed only $27,150 in cash awards, and medals and certificates valued at $18,839. Another $17,167 went for "pilgrimages," not described further in tax returns, for a total of $63,156.

Selecting the award winners cost the Foundation no less than $512,783. Raising the million dollars which kept the Foundation alive cost another $275,794, or about one-fourth the total take. Wells, as Foundation president, drew a salary of $35,000 and expenses of $6,702. His son, Kenneth Wells II, a veteran of the tablecloth document, was paid $11,750 in salary and $2,498 expenses as "Senior Vice President, Awards." Officer compensation totaled $157,625; other salaries, $187,314.

The Foundation's "principal award" in 1968—the George Washington Award, worth $5,000—went to General Harold K. Johnson, the retiring Army chief of staff. Other featured winners included: Dr. Leon Sullivan, for bringing black capitalism to Philadelphia ghettos; J. Howard Wood, the rightist Chicago publisher; baseball star Stan Musial "for his vital, strong, personal example to American youth, of integrity, sportsmanlike conduct, self-reliance and patriotism. . . . God bless Stan Musial!"; Lawrence Welk "for his extensive, quiet, conscientious endeavors to emphasize fundamental ideals of the American Credo through his life in television entertainment; for his entertaining, inspiring and artistic blending of musical selections and patriot salutes by invited guests to remind his viewers of the blessings of our Republic under God";* George Putnam, the right-wing Los Angeles TV commentator; and Alice Widener, the columnist, "for her courageous life of superior scholarship and strenuous personal endeavor that the tyranny of Marx-Leninism and anarchism be fully reported and understood for its dangers to our Republic and our democratic methods."

* A Foundation officer confirmed that this citation indeed did refer to Welk's Saturday night television show.

Freedoms Foundation also gives awards for public addresses, sermons, letters to editors, community programs, cartoons, editorials, essays, published articles, "governmental unit activities" (won by the FBI because the *Law Enforcement Bulletin* and the "articulate and profound" statement of director J. Edgar Hoover to the Kerner Commission alerted Americans "to serious problems facing our nation . . ."); and letters from armed forces personnel (won by Lieutenant Colonel William R. Ellis, who penned, "The time has come for all Americans, who respect our laws and are loyal to the Constitution, to stand up and be counted as our forefathers have done before us").

Two $100 winners in the public address category show the general tone of entries, which flood the Foundation's office as entry deadline approaches. Cartoonist Al Capp declared: "We have failed our young campus activists. . . . We've granted them everything they've demanded except the only thing they need to straighten them out . . . and that is a swift kick in the pants." And C. D. DeLoach, then number three man in the FBI, got $100 for these lines: "America and her Flag have been slandered for fighting for freedom abroad. . . . She is being rebuked for protecting her law-abiding citizens. . . . She is being censured for her refusal to become a welfare state, and few are openly defending her."

Officers testily dispute charges that the Foundation is right-wing or even conservative. "We're Americans," says W. C. (Tom) Sawyer, who ran the Americanism program of the American Legion before joining the Foundation as a senior vice president for education, at a salary of $16,000, plus expenses of $3,749. Yet, the Foundation has attracted a sizable grouping of vociferous patriots and reactionaries: Charles R. Hook, chairman of Armco Steel and a sponsor of the Birchite Manion Forum; Mrs. J. Howard Pew, wife of the Sun Oil president, whose foundation is a generous supporter; retired Admiral Felix B. Stump, a headline orator for the Christian Anti-Communist Crusade; Dean Clarence A. Manion, member of the national council of the John Birch Society, adviser to the Rev. Billy Hargis' Christian Crusade, and founder of the Manion Forum; and Mrs. James B. Patton, former president-general of the Daughters of the American Revolution. There are also some surprises —Walter Cronkite, the CBS commentator, for example. Why does Cronkite keep such company? "I was invited by Eisenhower, and I didn't feel I could turn him down," he told *Philadelphia Magazine* writer Greg Walter. "I told him that I wasn't too clear about the aims and ideals of the Freedoms Foundation but that if he wanted me to, I would serve . . ." Cronkite dropped out after a year because "I didn't have the time . . ." [4]

It would seem, however, that, anomalies such as Cronkite aside, the Freedoms Foundation's choice of officers betrays its true, if veiled, character. In 1967 it selected Howard (Bo) Callaway, the one-time Georgia Republican Congressman, as chairman of its board of trustees, succeeding the retiring General Eisenhower. Callaway is an avowed segregationist who managed to get to the right of even Lester Maddox in a Georgia gubernatorial race.

Callaway felt at home at Valley Forge, for at the same time he was elected, the board named Associate Justice Tom P. Brady of the Mississippi Supreme Court as one of its seven new trustees. The South knows Brady as the man who, in a book called *Black Monday,* wrote that Negroes are "inherently inferior" to whites and that the U.S. Supreme Court's 1954 decision on school segregation was "unconstitutional" and part of a communist conspiracy. Brady says

in his book: "Whenever and wherever the white man has
drunk the cup of black hemlock, whenever and wherever
his blood has been infused with the blood of the negro [sic],
the white man, his intellect and his culture have died." Negroes are little better than the chimpanzee, in the opinion of
this learned judge:

> You can dress a chimpanzee, housebreak him, and teach him
> to use a knife and fork, but it will take countless generations of
> evolutionary development, if ever, before you can convince
> him that a caterpillar or a cockroach is not a delicacy. Like-
> wise the social, political, economical and religious preferences
> of the negro remain close to the caterpillar and the cockroach.
> This is not stated to ridicule or abuse the negro. There is noth-
> ing fundamentally wrong with the caterpillar or the cock-
> roach. It is merely a matter of taste. A cockroach remains
> proper food for a chimpanzee.[5]

That Freedoms Foundation accepted the author of such
insulting racism as a "trustee" tells much of Freedoms
Foundation. Its success in attracting prestigious names,
however, is not affected. Those whom it honors are eager for
publicity, and the Eisenhower respectability lingers. "Editors like to get these awards," Vice President Sawyer told
me during an interview.[6]

The people at Freedoms Foundation are not totally stupid. They realized that although Justice Brady is a folk hero
in Dixie—he helped organize the "citizens councils" to battle integration—his presence on the board could be an embarrassment, and affect corporate donations. So, coincident
with his election, the Foundation created "The George
Washington Carver Library on the Contribution of the
Negro to American Culture."

Its name takes about as much space as the library.
When I visited Valley Forge, my tour guide took me into a

basement of the Martha Washington Building of the American Freedoms Center, the Foundation's main office building. As we walked past stacks of scrapbooks and assorted "patriotic displays" submitted by schoolchildren, the young lady informed me: "Some of these are pretty interesting. We even get maps of the United States made out of red, white and blue rice." Next we came to the Richard W. Sears Library on Free Enterprise, advertised in Foundation literature as a collection of "volumes on economic theory . . . [and] histories of successful American businesses and industries . . . [that] illustrate the operation of our free economic system." The Sears Library, upon examination, proves to be a collection of less than three hundred books— including accounting texts and laudatory puff biographies of businessmen—which fill seven small shelves.

We walked on and came to the Carver Library—a cubicle reminiscent of a display booth at a country fair, ten feet wide, perhaps twenty feet deep. Spread on one shelf is a display of assorted products derived from the peanut—jars of peanut butter, cosmetics, paints, plastics. Why the peanut? Well, Dr. Carver devoted his life to the peanut, and the Foundation has a mimeographed list with which the guide supplied me. A retired Negro educator is "curator" of the library. He opened a file cabinet and pulled out a folder. "We keep clippings and other material on Negroes who are prominent," he told me. "We are also compiling a card file listing every Negro who has made contributions to American life." Perhaps twenty-five books are stacked on one of the tables crammed into the booth. Pictures of prominent Negroes, cut from magazines, cover most of one of the walls. The tour guide found another brochure: "Emphasis is given in the Carver Project to early and little-known contributions of the Negro towards establishing our American Way of Life and to the positive things which have built this nation, rather than to negative forces which divide and fragmentize Our Country."

Thus, the Freedoms Foundation pays penance for its racist trustee.

THE "EDUCATIONAL" FOUNDATIONS of the Left and Right give the rich an opportunity to espouse their ideological beliefs at reduced cost. Foundations are also convenient for the "philanthropist" who wants to pursue a hobby with tax-exempt funds.

Governor Winthrop Rockefeller is an antique car buff, a man who appreciates a 1907 Stevens Duryea touring car or a 1910 Speedwell Raceabout. In addition to his interest in the Rockefeller Brothers Fund, Winthrop Rockefeller also maintains what he calls his "Arkansas foundation," the Rockwin Fund. Cars, not charity, is a major activity of this Fund.

In 1960 the Rockwin Fund purchased an antique auto collection known as "Autorama" from singer James Melton for $200,000, borrowing $150,000 of the purchase price from the Rockefeller family's Chase Manhattan Bank. After the purchase, it was discovered that the federal government had a $92,952 tax lien on the collection, plus interest and penalties of $14,000. The Rockwin Fund paid these deficiencies, only to be handed another bill for $25,126 to clear other liens. The Fund then paid for hauling the old cars to Rockefeller's mountaintop ranch near Petit Jean, Arkansas, and put them on display to the public. Other purchases and miscellaneous costs increased the Autorama costs by another $62,467 within a year. A year later the

Rockwin Fund sold the collection to the Governor for a loss of $24,710.

Rich men who invest in antique autos have the same interest in reducing their tax bills as do rich men who invest in stocks and bonds. But when one attempts to donate appreciated property to charity it is considerably easier to dispose of a hundred shares of AT&T than of a 1923 Stutz. The government doesn't permit tax deductions for contributions to private collectors, and an antique car is not the sort of thing one offers to the local United Fund. Once again, the utility of the Rockwin Fund was proved. In 1962 Dr. Samuel Scher of New York, a friend of Winthrop Rockefeller, donated two antique cars valued at $30,000 to the Rockwin Fund. Two years later the Fund sold them to Petit Jean Attractions, a Rockefeller-owned firm which by now had title to the Autorama collection, for the same price. Dr. Scher received his tax deduction. The Rockwin Fund received its $30,000 by selling them to Petit Jean. And Petit Jean Attractions got two new display items. The Rockwin Fund has provided the same courtesy to several other collectors.

For the late James H. Rand, Jr., former president of Remington-Rand Corporation (now Sperry-Rand), control of a foundation meant a startling diversity of personal and business advantages—everything from the purchase of specially-built "air mass" beds for $225; to the granting, through a conduit foundation, of $650,000 to three business associates and their wives to study "the advancement of human welfare"; to the payment of Rand's household expenses. Rand died June 3, 1968, during the midst of an attempt by the Internal Revenue Service to collect $17,600,000 in taxes and fraud penalties from the Public

Health Foundation for Cancer and Blood Pressure Research, Inc., of Stuart, Florida, which he founded and controlled.[7] According to IRS briefs, between 1955 and 1962 the Foundation made contributions of $4,197,242, of which $3,146,644 were illegal for one reason or another. Although Rand made "substantial" contributions to the Foundation, IRS said: "he benefited by a deduction . . . on his individual tax returns, which were in an 80 to 90 percent bracket." One contribution of $100,100 in 1955 resulted in a deduction of $96,414.

Listed below are some of the things that happened to the money according to IRS charges:

— The Foundation bought Rand's forty-one-acre estate in Darien, Connecticut, for $231,462, ostensibly for "research purposes and to house visiting scientists." Rand rented it back for $2,400 a year and continued living there, with the Foundation paying household expenses and servants' salaries.

— The Foundation constructed a so-called research laboratory in Florida for $159,196. "The principal use of the lab was to grow hydroponic vegetables free of toxic insecticides and of utmost nutritional value, such as tomatoes, celery, green beans, squash, cucumbers, and other vegetables for the personal use of . . . Rand and a few of his friends."

— The Foundation gave grants of $10,000 and $15,000, respectively, to two of Rand's longtime business associates for "achievement in charitable endeavors." These two men, their wives, and another couple, later received grants of $200,000, $250,000, and $200,000 to spend for the "advancement of human welfare. They were not accountable to anyone for their distribution of the income or corpus, and had the right to name a successor manager." IRS said that "the whole transaction was merely a scheme by . . . Rand to reward them for their loyal service to him."

— The Foundation made low- or no-interest loans to Rand's friends, gave jobs to them and relatives, and purchased their properties at inflated values.

The Foundation's attorneys entered general denials to the IRS claims; in addition, they claimed IRS agents got most of their evidence through an illegal raid on the office of one of Rand's attorneys in Fort Erie, Canada. As of this writing,* the case had not been listed for trial.

Representative Wright Patman, during his 1961–69 probe, turned up numerous instances of questionable foundation activities. The Julius S. Eaton Education Foundation was established to make "interest-free loans to needy students" at the University of Miami, Florida. Patman reported: "The primary purpose of the Eaton Foundation is to recruit prospective players for the Miami University [sic] football team, as it so states in its brochure. Once a year, boosters of the football team who have paid their $100 annual dues get together for a big blowout. Free and tax free, of course. The U.S. government, in effect, picked up the chit."

According to Patman, an unnamed Oregon foundation "occasionally buys beef carcasses and donates them to the city's soup kitchen—however, the steaks, tenderloins, prime ribs, and other choice cuts are missing before the beeves get to the soup kitchen and it is widely believed that these finer pieces wind up in the deep freeze tax free and, for the most part, cost free. The scion of this family is believed to be attending college in a fancy sports car purchased, for the rec-

* June 4, 1970.

ord, 'to investigate the worthiness of applicants for the foundation's bounty.' "

Another Patman finding: "The creator of the St. Genevieve Foundation, Spencer R. Collins, a millionaire in his late sixties, supported twin sisters through several years of parties and gay living, spending an estimated $100,000 on them; part of the expenses being paid by the tax-exempt foundation. One of the twins lived in a posh duplex, spent more than $3,000 on clothes one year. The other twin, ensconced in a five-bedroom mansion on Lake Oswego, was paid $36,000 as a 'caretaker of the house' . . ." Collins' defense was that he needed companionship and knew no other way to obtain it. A jury convicted him of tax evasion.[8]

CHAPTER **7**

Saving Money

JUDGE LEARNED HAND once exclaimed in exasperation that the tax code was a melange of words that "dance before . . . [one's] eyes in a meaningless procession: cross-reference to cross-reference, exception upon exception—couched in abstract terms that offer no handle to seize hold of." [1] The basic code which defines our tax system was not subjected to a complete rewriting by Congress for the two decades 1950–1969. In those years it acquired a heavy and often smelly encrustation of Tax Court decisions; ad hoc rulings by the Internal Revenue Service on specific issues advanced by taxpayers; administrative guidelines composed in the regulationese in which the Treasury Department, but no one else, is so fluent; and special interest legislation

181

which an influential citizen or organization can cajole a Congressman into introducing and which other members accept at announced face value.

Foundation law, a part of this teeming witches' brew, is further complicated by the fact that it is a bastard offspring of estate and charity law. Until the Tax Reform Act of 1969, little specific legislation existed stating what foundations may or may not do. The courts, reluctant to thrust themselves into an area of legislative vacuum, seldom addressed themselves directly to foundation issues. In determining legitimate business activities for a foundation, for instance, lawyers had to hark back to, among other decisions, a 1925 Supreme Court ruling involving an order of monks in the Philippines which got into trouble with the tax collector for selling wine, chocolate, and religious artifacts while at the same time claiming tax exemption. The monks won, the courts holding that their 7,239 peso income from the sales was an insignificant portion of their total revenue of 254,702 pesos and that the "destination, not the source," of the funds was most important in evaluating business activity.[2]

What use did foundations make of this freedom? Representative Wright Patman told the House Ways and Means Committee in 1969: "Philanthropy—one of mankind's more noble instincts—has been perverted into a vehicle for institutionalized, deliberate evasion of fiscal and moral responsibility to the nation."[3]

Foundation fiscal abuses fell into these broad areas:

— Gamesmanship with the tax laws that result in donors, not charity, reaping the chief benefits from "gifts."

— Ultraconservative investment policies which brought minimal returns on foundation assets, and a proclivity of foundation controllers to hoard their wealth, not spend it on charity. The chief utility of the foundation was to maintain control of a business.

— A commingling of business and foundation interests, with pseudophilanthropists using the privilege of tax exemption to the disadvantage of commercial competitors. The popularity of foundations as tax-avoidance vehicles became widespread beginning in 1950 when Congress said, in effect, that foundation philanthropy could regulate itself. In a laborious "reform" of tax laws that year, Congress's sole attention to foundations was the imposition of a mild, easily-avoided ban on the use of foundation funds to purchase businesses. Tax planners seized upon this implicit invitation to bring their profession to a new level of sophistication. If foundations were so useful to the dead rich in avoiding inheritance taxes, why could not the same techniques that had helped Henry Ford and Buck Duke be put to use for the living rich—and the lesser rich?

A major product of the 1950 law was a dramatic proliferation of pocket-sized foundations. According to one Treasury Department estimate, in 1950 there were some five thousand foundations, of which 2,261 had assets of *at least* $100,000. During the next two decades, the number of foundations of all sizes increased either by 17,000 or 25,000, depending upon the different definitions and computations used by the Foundation Center and the Internal Revenue Service. The vast majority of these new foundations, according to IRS, had assets of *less than* $100,000.

Control of a foundation is a privilege advantageous chiefly to the rich or near-rich, for simple mathematical reasons: because of the graduated income tax, it "costs" a person in the upper brackets less out-of-pocket money to make a gift than it does a salaried clerk or middle-echelon executive. In 1969 a person in the lowest bracket who gave a dollar to charity was entitled to a tax deduction of 14 cents; hence his cost was 86 cents. Conversely, in the top bracket, a dollar gift entitled the donor to a deduction of 73.5 cents; hence his cost was 26.5 cents. In such circumstances the Prentice-Hall tax advisory service cheerily calls the income tax surcharge "a further incentive to giving."

TAXABLE INCOME BEFORE CHARITABLE CONTRIBUTION	NET COST	TAX SAVED
$ 10,000	$769	$231
20,000	706	294
30,000	591	409
50,000	475	525
100,000	370	630
500,000	265	735

The preceding table shows the cost of making a $1,000 gift for persons in various income levels, including the surcharge and assuming a joint return.

TAX LAWYERS ARE THE TECHNICIANS who brought foundations within the reach of middle-class business and professional persons. The tax lawyer can make a philanthropist of the meanest of men. He is disturbingly pragmatic, more interested in tax savings for his client than in benefits for charity, and his professional literature and trade meeting oratory reflect the preference.

Attorney Norman Sugarman of Cleveland, who conducts a thriving foundation practice, and who is a regular speaker at tax-philanthropy conferences, quotes approvingly the observation of a fellow tax specialist: "When a client retains me, he is paying me for my services as a tax lawyer, not for my wisdom as a tax philosopher. A lawyer who fails to distinguish between the two when he is representing a client has no business representing him." [4] And attorney Harry Yohlin of Philadelphia, writing about "The Tax Blessings of Charitable Giving," declared he was content to leave to the "social philosophers" the determination of psychic rewards received by the giver: "Our concern will be solely with the material rewards to the donors that the tax laws make possible." [5]

The words "charity" and "philanthropy" do occasionally slip from the lips and pens of tax lawyers—but as a part of such titles as "How to Get Maximum Tax Benefits from Charitable Contributions," in the *Tax Ideas* series of Prentice-Hall; "How to Make Money by Giving It Away: Tax Consequences of Creating a Charitable Trust," in *The Practical Lawyer,* monthly publication of the Joint Committee on Continuing Legal Education of the American Law Institute and the American Bar Association; and "Possible Tax Bonanza in Giving Property Instead of Cash," from Commerce Clearing House, Inc., a reporting service on tax and business law. Prentice-Hall's monthly *Report Bulletin* on wills, estates, and trusts features the "Money Savings Idea of the Month"—almost invariably a tip on how to avoid taxes through manipulation of the laws on charitable giving and bequests.

In theory, a citizen could start a foundation by following instructions in an Internal Revenue Service pamphlet, "How to Apply for Exemption for an Organization," available for fifteen cents at the Government Printing Office. In practice, however, anyone who walks through the Internal Revenue Code without legal guidance risks an expensive stumble. A tax avoidance attorney will form the foundation for him, conduct its affairs so that IRS will remain happy, and reap the maximum possible—or conscionable—tax benefits.

If the attorney has no expertise in foundation law, *The Practical Lawyer,* with fill-in-the-blank simplicity, tells readers "How to Draft the Charter or Indenture of a Charity so as to Qualify for the Federal Tax Exemption." [6] What are the main points? Avoid using "grandiose language [in the title] that may suggest purposes extending beyond the limitation of the charitable exemption. Thus, the simplest names are usually best, such as 'X Foundation,' or 'X Charitable Fund.' " Stay close to home, where tax collectors "are likely to be best acquainted with the integrity and responsibility" of the foundation creator, his lawyer, and his accountant. "Track the statute"—that is, quote section 501c3 of the Internal Revenue Code verbatim—in stating the purpose of the foundation, even if its giving program is no more involved than contributing to the United Fund. (*TPL* admits that statute-tracking "may be somewhat offensive to the lawyer who takes pride in his draftmanship and is not steeped in tax law.")

For the attorney too busy to compose an original charter for his client's foundation, *The Practical Lawyer* provides draft models which the authors feel "satisfy the current requirements" of IRS. Finally, stationery houses specializing in legal supplies can furnish all the "physical property" needed to operate a foundation. The Excelsior-Legal Stationery Company of New York, for example, advertises a "Black Beauty" kit, described as "an all-in-one corporate outfit . . . for non-profit corporations." The Black Beauty includes a book for minutes and bylaws, a pocket-sized seal, fifty membership roll sheets and membership certificates (ornate affairs resembling Latin American military commissions), and a black vinyl "corporate record book" on which can be imprinted, in gold, the foundation's name. The price is $15 to $27, depending on how complete a kit the lawyer feels is required for the foundation.

An organization known as "Americans Building Constitutionally," based in the Chicago suburb of Barrington, carried the do-it-yourself technique a step further in 1966–67. For a fee of $10,500, ABC taught physicians, dentists, and other professional people how to convert their practices into what ABC called "tax-exempt" organizations. Under the ABC format, a physician would turn his practice into a foundation devoted to research and development in the fields of "health, education and welfare," and become its "medical director." The foundation would collect fees from the "subjects"—former patients—and from them pay the physician a salary and his living expenses. At least one physician made his wife (who was also his nurse) the foundation "assistant medical administrator" and gave his four children "educational grants" to attend college. ABC stayed in business long enough to train some eight hundred persons— then attracted the fatal attention of the Internal Revenue Service, which warned participants that the scheme violated tax laws. ABC promptly sank into a legal quagmire, and nothing more has been heard from it.

Once the foundation is operative, no special expertise is required to use it for tax savings. Two afternoons of browsing in the tax-avoidance literature in any law library or in the business reading room of a good public library can give the tax lawyer enough ideas to keep his client happy, and the foundation busy, for weeks. Through this literature the techniques refined in confrontations between the IRS and taxpayers is made available on a mass basis. An IRS lawyer once explained this to me:

> The cycle is predictable. A tax lawyer tries something fancy in Detroit, we challenge him, go to Tax Court, and he wins. The

tax journals and the advisory services report the mechanics of what he did. Within two or three months the gimmick shows up in our offices all over the country. I'm not saying it's bad, because the tax lawyers are just following what the court says is legal and trying to save a buck for their client. What I *don't* like is the constant pushing at the tax laws, the probing for loopholes, the willingness to stretch language to lengths unintended by Congress.

During the years 1950–69—a period lawyers are already referring to wistfully as the "golden era" of foundation tax avoidance—there was no outright ban on transactions between an individual and a foundation he created or controlled—"self dealing," in tax jargon. And here arose the most flagrant foundation abuses. Anglo-American law pertaining to conventional trusts has long recognized the impossibility of insuring that a trustee who is permitted to deal with himself will treat the trust fairly. Therefore the courts barred self-dealing outright. Such was not the case with foundations, and this created a multitude of opportunities for tax avoidance.

— A person could borrow funds from "his" foundation or direct it to lend money to a business that he controlled, or to his friends or associates, at terms he dictated.

For example, Donald G. Griswold, a businessman and church leader in Newport Beach, California, created the Sherry Griswold Foundation honoring a son killed in the Second World War. During a three-year period, according to Tax Court testimony, the Foundation made twelve loans totaling $284,300 for what IRS charged were "clearly non-charitable purposes." Griswold and three corporations he controlled received $197,300; his nephew, $37,500; a

brother, $25,000; a real estate trust in which he was in-
volved, $23,000; a sometime Foundation employee, $1,500.
But the Tax Court would not disturb his Foundation's tax
exemption.[7]

A business with such control over a foundation possessed
valuable competitive advantage over other persons. Mr.
Jones, who had no foundation, had to rely upon after-tax
dollars when investing in his business; when he donated to
a charity such as the Community Chest, he lost control of
the money. But Smith, with a controlled foundation, could
"donate" cash or appreciated property back to it and have
the funds immediately lent back to him. If Smith was in the
fifty-percent tax bracket, he could place twice as much cash
at the disposal of his business as could Jones. The amount
borrowed must, of course, be repaid to the foundation, but
as the Treasury Department has commented, "the present
value to Smith of being able to put twice as much capital
into his business than would otherwise be possible may often
exceed the value of the right to collect the debt at some time
in the future."

— He could use his foundation as a conduit for stock
transactions to avoid capital gains taxes and maximize
deductions for "charitable contributions."

Under the pre-1969 law,* a person who donated appreciated stock to a foundation received a deduction for the
amount of the market value, rather than his actual out-of-
pocket cost. (That is, if a person purchased stock for $1,000,
and it rose to $2,000 before he gave it away, his deduction
was $2,000, and he paid no capital gains on the increase.)

For persons in high tax brackets, such gifts enabled

---

* Congress's attempt to plug this and other loopholes through the Tax Reform Act
of 1969 is discussed in Chapter Nine.

them to "make" money. In a hypothetical case drawn from tax-avoidance literature, Bill Donor, president and founder of the Donor Family Foundation (his wife and attorney are the other directors) three months ago purchased stock for $5,000 that has appreciated in value to $11,000. Donor doesn't think the price will hold, and he wants to dispose of the stock. Yet he hadn't owned it for the six-month period required to treat the profit as a capital gain, and his sixty-four-percent tax bracket means he must pay a $3,840 tax (sixty-four percent of the $6,000 gain). Donor's net thus would be only $7,160 ($11,000 minus the $3,840 tax). What does he do?

Donor and his lawyer hold a "directors' meeting" of the Donor Family Foundation and purchase Donor's stock at the cost price of $5,000. Donor pockets this amount. He also takes a charitable deduction of $6,000—the difference between proceeds from the sale and the fair market value of the stock. In the sixty-four-percent bracket, the deduction is worth $3,840, meaning a total gain by Donor of $8,840 ($5,000 for the stock plus $3,840). Thus the sale through the friendly, controlled foundation has increased his net after-tax yield by $1,680 ($8,840 rather than the $7,160 he would have received through an outright, taxable sale for $11,000). Donor would have been hard-pressed to find a conventional charity to buy the stock at the market price. A community chest will accept donations; rarely will one deal in stocks. Hence, the value of his controlled foundation.

The appreciated stock gambit has endless variations. Near the end of the year, Tom Avoider's tax adviser computes that he "has room" for an additional $5,000 contribution to charity.* Avoider has $5,000 in shares of Consol-

---

* Prior to 1969, an individual could claim deductions for contributions to charity of not more than thirty percent of their adjusted gross income. The 1969 act raised the limit to fifty percent.

idated Gravel Company for which he paid $1,000; in his fifty-percent bracket, the contribution of this stock would save him $2,000 in taxes (one-half the $4,000 difference between his cost and the market value at the time of giving). However, Avoider considers Consolidated Gravel a good investment, and he wants to keep the stock.

Tom Avoider convenes a directors' meeting of the Tom Avoider Charitable Foundation (Tom Avoider, president; his lawyer, vice president; his office manager, secretary). They buy the Consolidated Gravel stock for $1,000, his cost price, and sell it back to Avoider a day later for the fair market value of $5,000. (The foundation gives the $4,000 gain to Avoider's college, enhancing his reputation as a philanthropist.)

Tom Avoider now has his Consolidated Gravel again, but, because of the peculiar mathematics of the tax world, the $5,000 he paid for it was really only $3,000 ($5,000 cash plus the original $1,000 cost, minus the $1,000 he received from the foundation for the first transfer, and the $2,000 tax deduction to which the gift entitled him). But insofar as IRS is concerned, Avoider's "cost basis" for the stock is now the new $5,000 purchase price, and computations on taxes on the future sale of the stock start from that basis. Avoider holds the stock another year; as expected, it rises to $10,000. He sells. His capital-gains tax is $1,250 (twenty-five percent of the increase from $5,000 to $10,000). Had Avoider not "processed" the stock through his foundation, the capital gains levy would have been $2,250 (twenty-five percent of the increase from the original cost of $1,000 to $10,000). So Tom Avoider pockets $1,000, courtesy of the Tom Avoider Charitable Foundation.

— A person can surrender future control of property to a foundation in return for an immediate deduction and continuing use of the property until his death, or another specified date, through a trust arrangement.

An example: In 1963 Mrs. Giles Whiting, a widow in her nineties, began donating a remainder interest in her estate in Westchester County, New York, to the Mrs. Giles Whiting Foundation. The gift each year amounted to twenty percent of the value of the home, and ultimately came to more than half a million dollars. There was no immediate gain for charity. In 1966, for instance, the Foundation listed assets of $456,499 ($66,083 in stocks in addition to the interest in the Whiting home). Yet its income was only $1,434. Mrs. Whiting, meanwhile, enjoyed a tax deduction for the donation of the remainder interest in the home.

The flaw in such an arrangement, as the Treasury Department has commented critically, is that the "donor obtains a current tax advantage for a transfer which confers no concomitant benefit upon charity." [8] Beginning in the 1960s Treasury argued—without convincing either the courts or Congress—that deductions should not be permitted for such gifts until the asset is (1) made productive; (2) disposed of; or (3) applied to charitable uses.

But tax attorneys defend the practice with vigor. Chauncy Belknap, Wall Street attorney who represents the Mrs. Giles Whiting Foundation (the Rockefeller Foundation is also his client), notes that before she gave away the property she had an owner's usual rights—to sell or dispose of it as she chose. "Now she has no rights in the property which can be left by will, and her remaining rights to sell or lease an interest terminating at her death are for all practical purposes without value." [9] Eventually, Belknap stated, the estate will be used as a "center for some charitable use or be sold and the proceeds devoted to charitable purposes."

And he asked: "In any event, is it not clear that the public benefit from having this valuable property permanently dedicated to charitable purposes, even though its active employment for such purposes is subject to a necessarily brief deferment, outweighs in value the tax deductions which the law allowed to the donor?"

A variation of this gimmick is to give charity, in trust, a stock which has little current value, but which can be transformed into a substantial tax deduction. The Institute for Business Planning, of New York, one of the more astute tax-avoidance services, described the mechanics in an article entitled "How to Make Money by Giving It Away," in its semimonthly *Tax Planning Ideas*.[10] The Institute admitted the title resulted from "an Alice in Wonderland provision" of the tax laws. But the only relevant question tax planners ask is "Does it work?" And it does:

Harry Hypothetical is in the fifty-percent tax bracket. He owns a $20,000 block of stock he'd like to retain for his estate because of its long-range growth potential, yet the income is only 1.5 percent a year ($300). On the advice of his tax planner, Harry creates the Hypothetical Memorial Trust Foundation with a life of ten years and one day (by law, trusts must be for more than ten years for this technique to work) and transfers the stock to it with instructions to pay the proceeds to a designated charity. When the trust period expires, the stock is to revert to Hypothetical's wife and/or children.

Although the yield from the stock is only 1.5 percent, for the purpose of computing the value of charitable contributions the Internal Revenue Service "assumes" a minimum yield of 3.5 percent. The Institute for Business Planning says: "The result is that your charitable contribution is worth, under IRS tables, $5,822. This is true even though the income from the stock continues to be only $300 per year and the charity will have realized only $3,000 for the ten-year period!" (The exclamation point belongs to the Institute for Business Planning.) For a fifty-percenter, the $5,822 deduction is worth a tax savings of $2,911.

— A person could donate stock in his business to his foundation and receive a deduction even if the stock paid no dividends and the gain by charity was nil.

Tax planners found this technique particularly useful for owners of small businesses whose salaries absorb the bulk of the profits. Foundation tax returns* reveal instance after instance where foundations were "given" nonproductive stock.

The M. S. Grumbacker Foundation, of York, Pennsylvania, during the fiscal year ending August 31, 1966, listed as its major holding stock in S. Grumbacker & Sons valued at $141,755. Yet the Foundation's total gross income for the year was $85.49, in interest, with none whatsoever from dividends.

The Wheelan Foundation, of New York, owns one-third to one-fifth the stock in seventeen separate Wheelan photographic studios around the country, plus substantial shares of Polyfoto Corporation. Collectively, these assets were valued at $331,081 at the end of 1966. The income was $7,036 in interest, $2,000 from royalties, and none from dividends. The interest was on notes receivable, paid by companies not identified in the Wheelan Foundation's tax returns.

Lex Marsh, a real estate developer in Charlotte, North Carolina, is president, treasurer, and director of the Marsh Foundation, which at the end of 1967 had assets of $225,543

* Examined at the Foundation Center library and at the Washington office of IRS.

($25,395 in cash; $20,544 in notes; $109,580 in corporate notes; and $70,022 in land). Marsh's return from the total investment wouldn't excite an investment portfolio manager—$1,161 for the year, or far less than one percent. The corporate stock—which paid no dividends whatsoever—was in something called Realty Syndicate, Inc., a Marsh company. In routine correspondence with IRS in 1963, Marsh used stationery which listed Realty Syndicate, Inc., among six realty and land companies he controlled. The IRS 990-A forms filed by the Marsh Foundation give no information, of course, on Marsh's personal tax situation. Under the tax code, however, donation of the Realty Syndicate, Inc., stock entitled him to a deduction of $109,580 and produced funds he was able to use elsewhere. As of the end of 1967, the last year for which Marsh Foundation tax returns were available, charity had not yet benefited from the donation of the land.

IN 1950 FOUNDATION ASSETS WERE ESTIMATED at $2,570,000,000; in 1968, at $20,500,000,000.[11] At first blush these figures would seem to support Congressman Patman's charge that the nation is undergoing a "disastrous erosion of our tax base" and an "inebriated orgy of tax avoidance." [12] That tax planners are teaching business and professional persons to use foundations as tax shelters is indisputable. Yet several qualifications are necessary to bring these raw statistics into perspective. Foundation wealth *has* swelled over the years; so, too, has total American wealth. According to Treasury Department computations, since 1930 foundations have increased their share of the total wealth from 0.25 percent to about 0.8 percent, or something more than three-fold.[13] And the Securities and Exchange Commission states that foundations own about 2.6 percent of the stocks registered on the New York Stock Exchange—the same percentage as they did in 1949.

Appreciation of stock values accounts for much of the increase in total foundation wealth. The W. K. Kellogg Foundation (and a related trust whose income goes to the Foundation) since 1930 has received gifts of Kellogg and other stocks valued at $67,076,512. By 1968 the value had swelled to $435,066,494, due to the growth and dividend record of the Kellogg Company. Kellogg stock sold for $1.625 per share in 1931; the 1968 mean price was $41.50. The assets of the Emily and Ernest Woodruff Foundation are almost entirely Coca-Cola stock, which in ten years has appreciated in value from slightly more than $21,573,173 to more than $140,000,000. In 1960 the Pew Memorial Trust's Sun Oil stock was valued at $132,525,801; at the end of 1967, $347,714,414.

There is also evidence that no new mastadon foundations are likely to appear, that America's big fortunes are either safely in foundations already or that their owners are not interested in institutionalized philanthropy. According to Treasury Department figures, eighty-six percent of the 175 foundations with assets of $10,000,000 or more were established before 1949, only fourteen percent thereafter.[14] The youngest foundation among the twenty-five largest is the Pew Memorial Trust, created in 1957; next, the Moody Foundation, in 1942; third, the Rockefeller Brothers Fund, in 1940.

Yet, large sums of money do continue to pass to foundations. Archibald G. Bush, former chairman of the executive committee of the Minnesota Mining & Manufacturing

Company, died in 1966; his estate of $118,000,000, chiefly 3-M stock, went to the Bush Foundation of St. Paul, Minnesota. Publisher Henry Luce left Time Inc. stocks and other securities, with a total value of $74,500,000, to the Henry Luce Foundation. Arthur Vining Davis, former chairman of the Mellons' Aluminum Company of America, left assets valued at an estimated $45,000,000 to separate foundations in Pittsburgh and Miami. George Gund, former board chairman of Cleveland Trust Company, willed $20,000,000 to the George Gund Foundation. The bulk of Alfred P. Sloan's $90,000,000 estate, chiefly General Motors stock, went to the foundation he had generously endowed during his lifetime. Showman Billy Rose gave $10,000,000 to the Billy Rose Foundation. New York investment banker Stephen R. Currier and his wife, the daughter of Mrs. Ailsa Mellon Bruce, died in a plane crash in 1967; they left $20,000,000 to their Taconic Foundation.[15]

The omnipresent Rockefellers begat still another foundation in 1968, this one as the "personal giving vehicle" of twenty-three persons, all fourth-generation members of the clan. The Rockefeller Family Fund, for the moment, is to operate with no endowment, relying upon annual contributions from the children and their spouses. Such was also the genesis of the third-generation foundation, the Rockefeller Brothers Fund, which began modestly, but is now well within the twenty-five largest, with assets of $222,000,000. As the younger Rockefellers gradually acquire control of the family fortune, the new foundation can be expected to take its place in the ranks of the nation's larger philanthropic institutions.

To summarize briefly, although foundation wealth is increasing in gross terms, its share of the total U.S. economy is remaining relatively stable.

Why, then, do foundations have a public image as concentrations of great wealth? The record supports several conclusions. The largest foundations are conspicuously identified with businesses in which they have (or had) a major or controlling interest. According to the Peterson Commission, fifty-seven percent of the foundations with assets of more than $100,000,000 have held, at one time or another, twenty percent or more of the stock in a single company.[16] Ford, Duke, Mott, Lilly, Kellogg, and Danforth are names common to both the world of business and the world of philanthropy. Conversely, only seven percent of the foundations with less than $1,000,000 in assets have ever held twenty percent of the stock in a single company. Foundation wealth is not spread evenly over the entire economy; it tends to collect in lumps.

This is not to dismiss lightly the fact that, collectively, foundations own a lot of money. Of the 596 foundations covered by the 1966 installment of Representative Wright Patman's continuing survey, 136 held stock in 288 corporations, in amounts ranging from five to one hundred percent, with a book value of $2,500,000,000 and an estimated market value of $4,900,000,000. Patman noted: "Even the latter figure is most likely an understatement, however, because in many instances the securities are in closely-held companies that are not traded." [17]

The Ford Foundation—which is, of course, in a class unto itself—as of September 30, 1969, owned Ford Motor Company stock with a market value of $1,166,500,000. It also held almost a billion dollars of common and preferred stock in other companies, $350,656,969 in government and other bonds, and $350,824,168 in various securities. Simply listing Ford's common stocks requires five closely-printed pages in the Foundation's financial statements; the bonds and securities, another twelve. Only eleven of the 171 holdings are valued at less than a million dollars. Ford's holdings of $118,369,438 in oil stocks alone are greater than the assets of all but twenty-four of the nation's 30,262 foundations. Ford has $122,701,600 in utilities stocks, of which $10,830,625 is in AT&T; $88,567,263 in business and electrical equipment, topped by $30,209,375 in IBM; $70,524,675 in banks and finance, from American Express Company ($15,484,250) to Whitney Holding Corporation ($2,736,000); $49,019,876 in chemicals (the big blocks being Minnesota Mining & Manufacturing Company [$5,418,750] and Dow Chemical [$5,380,000]); $81,387,621 in consumer products, from American Machine & Foundry Company ($1,600,000) to Unilever, N. V. ($3,524,125). Ford owns a share of the *New York Times* ($8,994,375), Time Inc. ($2,917,688) and the Columbia Broadcasting System ($2,200,000). Ford owns shares of seven major airlines: American, Eastern, Northwest, Pan American, Trans World, United, and World. Ford owns a minute portion of the military complex, with $6,254,750 in the Boeing Company, $6,714,583 in Litton Industries, Inc., and $1,496,000 in Lockheed Aircraft Corporation.

Ford's bigness is staggering: its total portfolio, at September 30, 1969, market values, was a rounded $2,922,800,000. Anyone frightened by wealth measured in box-car lots can find what solace he may in the fact that it has been even bigger, at its peak of $4,073,000,000 in 1964. Stock market fluctuations can cleave as much as four-fifths of a billion dollars off the portfolio in a single year (from $3,846,000,000 in 1965 to $3,051,400,000 in 1966); market declines in 1969 hit Ford for $678,000,000.* And, from a

* Ford's 1969 financial statement notes this decline of 7.98 percent compared with a 13.04 percent decrease in the Dow Jones Industrial Average and a decrease of 9.30 percent in the Standard and Poor's 500 Composite Index.

strict accounting sense, Ford is $1,300,800,000 in the red: its grants and other expenses since 1936 are that far ahead of income, a sum that has come out of principal.[18]

Ford's major holding is stock in the motor company, a gift, as we have seen, between 1936 and 1950 from Henry Ford and his son Edsel. As of September 30, 1955, the Foundation's entire assets were Ford stock, with an estimated value of $2,500,000,000, or 83.4 percent of all the company stock outstanding. The Foundation trustees decided that year that "it was not wise to have such a concentrated investment in the non-voting shares of a single company." [19] Thus, in 1956 they began selling the Ford stock publicly, and they have gradually reduced the Foundation's share of Ford's outstanding stock from the peak of 83.4 percent to twenty-five percent as of September 30, 1969. These sales have brought the Foundation more than $2,000,000,000; another $100,000,000 has been donated to various universities, symphony orchestras, and charities as capital grants.

Save for the overlapping directorships of Henry Ford II and Benson Ford, the Foundation plays no role in the management of Ford Motor Company. And, based upon the available evidence, the motor company seems to ignore the Foundation. In 1970 a group of conservatives based in Orange County, California, known as "Families Opposing Revolutionary Doctrine"—an awkward title, but one which produced the desired acronym—began a "nationwide boycott" of Ford, and claimed dealer support. Ford's national director, Hurst B. Amyx, of Inglewood, California, asserted: "There is increasing evidence that a sharp division is developing between the Ford dealers and Henry Ford II. Many dealers recognize that our Ford campaign is the only hope they have of getting the Foundation's policies corrected and getting its public off their backs."

Ford recruited a retired air force major general as its president and received serious attention in right-wing periodicals; yet the Foundation claims to have felt no backlash from it. One Ford officer told me:

> Oh, we'll occasionally receive a nasty letter from some Ford dealer who doesn't like the publicity "Ford" is getting from a project. Detroit forwards us a handful of nasty dealer mail each year. But we're pretty well immune to it, and the public doesn't think much of the business connection. I mean, good sense dictates that the staff and the trustees don't go out of their ways to offend Henry the Second. But in the years I've been here I've never heard any mention of avoiding a project because it might make some dealer mad." *

The wealth of the Rockefeller Foundation and its lesser siblings can be summed in three letters: "o-i-l." Standard Oil of New Jersey, the keystone company of John D. Rockefeller's old oil monopoly, accounts for more than $400,000,000 of the assets of the Rockefeller Foundation, the Rockefeller Brothers Fund, and seven smaller organizations.** In addition to $291,000,000 in Jersey Standard stock, the Rockefeller Foundation owns enough shares in other petroleum companies, chiefly Continental, Marathon, and Mobil, to bring its total oil portfolio to $508,582,856 (of total assets of slightly less than $1,000,000,000).

Each of these companies was a member of the Rockefel-

---

* This man had been at the Ford Foundation for slightly more than a decade. Conversely, Ford dealer anger was a factor in the Foundation's decision to discontinue support of the Fund for the Republic during the 1950s.
** The Sealantic Fund, Inc.; Sleepy Hollow Restoration; Colonial Williamsburg, Inc.; the China Medical Board of New York; Standard Oil (Indiana) Foundation; the Agricultural Development Council; and the Rockefeller Institute. Another Rockefeller-related foundation, the Esso Education Foundation, owns slightly more than $1,000,000 in Jersey Standard shares, but relies chiefly upon sustaining annual contributions from Jersey Standard.

ler oil monopoly which the U.S. Supreme Court ordered dissolved in a 1912 antitrust decree; yet, this does not deter Rockefeller portfolio managers from buying their stock. Representative Wright Patman views this with considerable suspicion. He notes that J. Starr Murphy, one-time counsel for the Rockefeller interests, promised, before the Foundation was created, that it would not serve "as a repository for Standard Oil stock." Patman charges: "Despite Mr. Murphy's solemn promise, the Rockefeller foundations are operating in the very fashion that the trustbusters of Theodore Roosevelt's day meant to forbid. . . . Through the supposedly benevolent foundations, the Rockefellers are today still violating the spirit if not the letter of the federal antitrust statutes." [20]

The Justice Department did not respond to Patman's demand that it "do something" about the Foundation's holdings for two reasons. First, though the Rockefeller Foundation holding of Jersey Standard is massive, it represents only slightly more than three percent of the outstanding stock of that company. Furthermore, each of the foundations does attempt to maintain a separate identity. "We do not work together in any way," states Rockefeller Foundation president J. George Harrar. John D. Rockefeller III, chairman of the Rockefeller Foundation, is a board member of the Rockefeller Brothers Fund, the second largest family foundation; but Harrar says, "we have no interaction with the fund." [21] Harrar also asserts that the foundation has— and desires—no role in management or policy of Jersey Standard: "Our trustees . . . many years ago decided that large blocks of stock we had originally held should over a period of years be diversified in order to avoid any suggestion that we might own enough of any stock to be considered influential in the affairs of the company." [22]

The Rockefeller Foundation, because of its deep involvement in Latin-American agricultural programs, studiously attempts to avoid identification with the Rockefeller oil empire. It occasionally slips. In early 1969 the Nixon Administration appointed New York attorney John N. Irwin II as its special emissary to negotiate compensation for the International Petroleum Company, a Jersey Standard subsidiary which was nationalized by the Peruvian government. Irwin is also associate counsel for the Rockefeller Foundation, a fact the State Department claimed it overlooked when clearing Irwin's appointment. The Peruvians chose not to make an issue of a situation in which they could, with justification, have asked, "Does Irwin represent the government of the United States or the Rockefeller oil interests?" Oil is inherently political with Latin-Americans, and the Rockefeller Foundation takes quiet pride in the fact that it has never been evicted from a host country during a time of governmental upheaval.*

The Foundation's hesitancy in political affairs extends even to Governor Nelson Rockefeller, the most prominent of several politicians in the family. Rockefeller asked Harrar, the Foundation's president, to accompany him on the Latin-American tour he made for President Nixon in 1969. Harrar, as a Rockefeller agent, has a long background in Latin-American agriculture, and the Governor said he would be "most useful" as an adviser. Harrar politely refused, and Rockefeller did not pressure him. A collective sigh of relief was heard from the Foundation several weeks later when the Governor's trip turned into one of the worst

---

* A sister organization, the China Medical Board, is not so fortunate. Its chief activity, the Peking Union Medical College, was seized by the Chinese Communists in 1951. As compensation, the Board received $1,283,877 under the War Claims Act.

American disasters in Latin America since the Bay of Pigs. "If Harrar had been on that junket," a Rockefeller officer told me, "we'd have been raising corn in Missouri instead of in Mexico."

EVERY INSTITUTION DESERVES TO BE JUDGED on how well it achieves its basic purpose. The Peterson Commission states: "Thus, a business corporation is measured by its growth in sales and profits; a foundation, by what it contributes to charity." [23] And, since foundation philanthropy is funded by society at large through tax exemptions, the public "has every reason to be interested in a satisfactory return on this capital investment."

If one accepts the Peterson Commission's thesis, the public has grounds for acute displeasure with foundation philanthropy. Put most simply, foundations have not been overly vigorous in earning or in spending money.

The universal measuring stick for investment-, mutual-, and endowment-fund performance is the total rate of return: interest, dividends, and realized and unrealized capital gains. According to an investments study conducted for the Ford Foundation,[24] during the decade 1959–69 ten large general growth mutual funds had an average return of 14.6 percent annually; twenty-one so-called balanced funds, with more bonds than the general growth funds had a return of 9.2 percent annually. In 1968 the average performance was 15.3 percent for general funds, 14.9 percent for balanced funds.

Foundations did considerably worse. Here are median returns computed by the Peterson Commission for a selected group of larger foundations, based on information contained in their 990-A forms.

ASSET SIZE (in Millions)	RETURN (in Percentages)
$1 to 10	6.1
10 to 100	7.7
100 and over	8.0

On the basis of these figures alone, the Peterson Commission concluded that the "investment performance of foundations is sub-par, perhaps significantly, and the cost of this to society could easily amount to hundreds of millions and perhaps over a billion dollars annually." [25] If the assets of foundations are $20,000,000,000, as conservatively estimated by the Foundation Center, every percentage point improvement in return represents $200,000,000 more annually to charity.

The median foundation figures cited by the Peterson Commission are misleading (as the Commission itself stated) because they are based, in part, on book value of assets, rather than the true market value. And there are a host of major foundations—ones among the twenty-five largest—whose annual income is far below five percent.

The Lilly Endowment, of Indiana, with assets of more than $400,000,000, earned a return of 3.5 percent from 1945 to 1965. Since 1966, however, stock values have risen and, despite an increase in the dividend rate, "the yield has averaged only approximately 1.5 percent of market value," according to Byron P. Hollett, attorney-director of the Endowment.[26]

Even more conspicuous is the Moody Foundation, of Galveston, Texas, whose performance is an acute illustration of what went wrong with American foundations during the 1950s and 1960s.

The Moody Foundation's problem is that its holdings are in businesses either founded or controlled by the Moody family, which is not visibly enthusiastic about spending any substantial amount of the Foundation money for charity. In addition, the Moodys have a history of family feuds. The family scion, William L. Moody, Jr., built a $400,000,000 fortune in banking, insurance, hotels, and publishing, all based in the island city of Galveston. He left one dollar to son William L. III (who went to court and won a settlement of $3,640,898). And in 1969 rival factions of the family fought bitterly in the Texas Legislature over proposals to modify administration of the old man's estate. The issues were so obscure and so tangled that they apparently were comprehensible only to lawyers for the opposing Moody factions; but the clan's brawling in a public forum tells much of the intensity of the intrafamilial relationships.

From its founding in 1942 through 1959 the Moody Foundation's assets and income were relatively small. It paid grants of $350,000, or about $20,000 a year, to Galveston churches and orphanages, and to a school for children with cerebral palsy. On December 31, 1959, however, the Foundation received its share of the estate of Moody *père*: more than $100,000,000 in shares of the American National Insurance Company, formed by Moody in 1905, the largest life insurance company—in terms of volume of business— west of the Mississippi; most of W. L. Moody & Company, Bankers,* the largest private bank in Texas; and varied ranch, cotton, and other properties.

For a family supposedly rich in financial acumen as well as in dollars (each of the four family members on the Foundation board carries the accolade "financier" in annual re-

* Now the Moody National Bank.

ports, in addition to other titles), the Moodys' performance with foundation holdings is strikingly dismal, as demonstrated by this table showing a breakdown of the yield of major parts of its investments portfolio in 1962[27]:

STOCKHOLDING	APPROXIMATE VALUE	1962 CASH DIVIDEND	PERCENTAGE YIELD[a]
50% Gal-Tex Hotel Corp.	$ 1,400,000	0	0
50% Silver Lake Ranches Co.	700,000	0	0
100% Texas National Hotel Corp.	1,300,000	0	0
35% American National Insurance Co.	167,300,000	2,420,000	1.4
44% Hotel Wade Hampton, Inc.	300,000	0	0
40% Moody National Bank	800,000	10,000	1.3
35% National Hotel Co.	2,500,000	0	0

[a] Dividend return on book value of stock

Moody family members held key executive jobs in each of the companies and maintained themselves comfortably on salaries. Thus they were willing to plow profits back into the companies, rather than pay them out in dividends. Furthermore, through a maze of trusts, each received a share of the elder Moody's fortune.

The records of Moody and other Texas foundations prompted unhappy stirrings by Texas attorney general Will Wilson, who in 1961 created a division in his office to study charitable trusts. His first report, in December, 1962, decried a rapid increase in "the flight of capital into charita-

ble trusts and foundations." He continued: "This is a
prolific field for conflict-of-interest situations and miscon-
duct, and I feel that a great deal more basic supervision of
actions of trustees is in the public interest." [28]

According to Treasury Department sources, the Moody
Foundation was one of the organizations Wilson warned to
start spending some of the funds set aside for charity. If the
warning indeed was aimed at Moody, it wasn't heeded. Five
years after Wilson's criticism, returns of Moody family businesses remained abysmally low. American National Insurance Company was up to 3.08 percent ($4,175,412 divi-
dends on stock with a market value of $135,555,903). The
Gal-Tex Hotel Corporation paid $2,500 in dividends on
stock listed at $1,576,886; the National Hotel Company,
$7,075 on $2,500,000. Four lesser businesses, including Silver Lake Ranches Co., Inc., alone valued at $697,071, re-
turned no dividends whatsoever. The sole Moody holding
with a tolerably respectable dividend was the Moody National Bank, which paid $74,371 on stock with a book value
of $1,513,500 (and a market value several times higher).

The record of smaller Moody foundations—formed
since the early 1960s by various heirs of William L. Moody,
Jr.—is equally unspectacular. As is the case with their
larger foundations, the Moodys' chief gifts to these smaller
"charities" are stock in family enterprises. The Shearn
Moody Foundation is headed by grandson Shearn Moody,
Jr., thirty-five years old in 1970, and identified in Moody
Foundation annual reports as "financier and chairman,
president, Empire Life Insurance Company of America,
Birmingham, Alabama." At the end of 1964, to cite a typical year, the Shearn Moody Foundation's chief holding was
2,800 shares in American National Insurance Company,
valued at $46,025, which returned a dividend income of

$805. The Foundation made no contributions and listed "legal expenses" of $425. During the year Shearn Moody, Jr., donated $5,793 of American National Insurance stock to his foundation, for which he was able to take a tax deduction.

Shearn Moody's uncle, Robert L. Moody, also has a foundation, which at the end of 1966 had assets of $206,157, chiefly in American National Insurance Company stock. Its contributions that year were $808.50. In 1964 the Robert L. Moody Foundation had an even worse record: assets of $199,690 produced a gross income of $4,285, of which $2,485 went for "legal fees" and $1,825 for charity. In this same year Robert L. Moody received a tax deduction for a contribution of $48,343 in American National Insurance stock.[29]

John T. Jones, Jr., president of the Houston Endowment, among the twenty-five largest with $193,000,000 in assets, has offered a unique defense of poor foundation earnings records. Southwestern foundations created from first-generation wealth are peculiarly diverse, he said. Jones once told a foundation conference:

> Our founders were the opportunists, the wheelers and dealers of the frontier. They were hard rock individualists who started from scratch and made their money whenever, wherever, and however they could. Southwest foundations have precious little AT&T stock, for these were mostly men deeply suspicious of New York with its top-hatted bankers and smooth talking brokers. Instead of the stock, there may be three or four short grass ranches where oil might or might not be found some day, and that are always well stocked with hungry cows. It is likely that the corpus may include not only ranches but also office buildings, pine lands, oil royalties, theaters, maybe a

fleet of leaky shrimp boats, real estate in places no one ever heard of, a string of hotels or motels, and God only knows what all else.[30]

After Jones's despondent description one would wonder why a Southwest millionaire would even bother giving such worthless odds-and-ends to charity and why charity would keep them on the books if he did. But Jones sees no reason to convert these assets into more conventional holdings: "I firmly believe that the corpus of a trust or foundation should be preserved at its maximum earnings power for purposes of the trust. I do not believe this idea would be served by holding an immediate fire sale of assets or by conversion of a high income business lease into limited fixed income securities."

Jones's jocular denigration of the wealth of Southwest foundations does not exactly describe his own Houston Endowment, which owns a hefty chunk of the Houston economy. But as a foundation, the Houston Endowment earns less than would be possible were its overseers to sell all assets and deposit the proceeds in a savings and loan association.

The Houston Endowment was created by Jesse H. Jones (1874–1956), a Houston banker, politician, and publisher who was chairman of the Reconstruction Finance Corporation and secretary of commerce under President Roosevelt. As of December 31, 1967, the Houston Endowment had assets with a market value of $193,126,963, on which it earned $3,015,989 during the year. Its wealth is only partially revealed by the listing of corporate names on its tax returns. There are six separate real estate and "properties" companies which represent, in turn, the Rice Hotel, leading hostelry in the city; two smaller hotels; a downtown department store; a medical building; seven office buildings; and various tracts of land both in Houston and in New York (including one valued at $6,800,000). The Houston Endowment owns outright the Bankers Mortgage Company, valued at $12,451,500, with a 1967 income of $133,464; and it has a twenty-eight percent interest in the Texas National Bank of Commerce, valued at $29,951,292, with a 1967 income of $1,226,390. It owns Jones Lumber Company ($400,000 market value, $15,000 in dividends) and the Houston Terminal Warehouse and Cold Storage Company ($558,450 market value, $9,307 in dividends). And, finally, the Endowment owns the Houston Chronicle Publishing Company, on the books at $35,000,000, with a dividend return of $150,000—a minute fraction of one percent.

Why would the Houston Endowment be content with such low returns on its business holdings? Its officers would not respond to numerous written requests for information. Its record, nonetheless, supports a plethora of conclusions. The most obvious is its use of profits to gain an edge over competitive businesses whose shareholders demand a distribution of profits, rather than an incessant accumulation of capital. Charity, which is the Endowment's sole "shareholder," is powerless to make similar demands. The Houston Endowment's operation of the *Houston Chronicle,* Houston's afternoon newspaper, which boasts the largest daily circulation in Texas, is illustrative.

According to a 1965 report by the Treasury Department,* the Endowment's willingness to defer indefinitely the realization of profits from the *Chronicle* made it possible for funds to be invested in modernization and expansion to

---

* The Treasury Department did not identify the Houston Endowment or other foundations discussed in this report by name. Mitchell Rogovin, formerly IRS general counsel, publicly identified the Houston Endowment in a speech to a philanthropic conference in 1967.

improve its "competitive posture." According to the Treasury Department, the *Chronicle* made competitive efforts which neither the *Houston Post,* the city's morning paper, nor other newspapers of comparable size elsewhere in the country could duplicate. The *Chronicle* had seven wire services: "Other newspapers of similar size have from one to three"; The *Chronicle* "publishes seven separate editions each day," the *Post* but five, and "no comparable evening newspaper in the country publishes seven." The *Chronicle's* subscription rate was $2.00 per month; the *Post's* had been "forced down to $2.25; those of newspapers in comparable cities range from $2.20 to $3.00." During the period of the Treasury study the *Chronicle* purchased—and then killed—its only afternoon competitor, the *Houston Press.* And the Treasury Department concluded that the *Chronicle's* advertising rates "appear to remain substantially lower than those of any similar newspaper in the country." [31]

FOUNDATIONS ACQUIRED MOST of their commercial holdings simply because a man who owned a business gave it to charity, for altruistic or tax purposes. In such instances foundations were a mere by-product of estate or tax planning. Conversely, there are foundations created for the sole purpose of acquiring businesses and other properties, for the benefit of their creators or an institution. A Tax Court judge, commenting in 1969 on the techniques which made such acquisitions possible, declared: "Let there be no mistake about this case; it involves a tax avoidance scheme of massive proportions whereby large amounts of business income are accorded favored tax treatment merely because a comparatively minor portion thereof finds its way into the hands of a charitable institution." [32]

The scheme to which the judge referred—"bootstrapping," in tax lawyers' parlance—was first put to broad use by a rather remarkable Jesuit priest named Lorenzo M. Malone. A banker before he entered the priesthood, Father Malone in 1935 became development officer of Loyola University of Los Angeles. Loyola's fiscal prospects were bleak. In the 1920s a real estate promoter, Harry Culver, had persuaded several major Hollywood film producers to move their studios to his new community of Culver City. To add cultural frosting Culver donated a hundred acres of land to Loyola for a new campus, and told the ruling Jesuits that the movie people would provide funds to develop the property. On the strength of these pledges, Loyola borrowed $500,000 and began building. This was in 1929. The stock market broke, the pledges were not fulfilled, and Loyola crept into the next decade almost completely broke.

For seven years, by dint of industry, personal charm, and persuasiveness, Father Malone managed to raise enough money to keep Loyola alive. As a priest, he was subject to the vows of chastity, poverty, and obedience; he received no salary and lived in a dormitory room cluttered with old clothes collected for students and other needy persons. Father Charles S. Casassa, a colleague, recalls: "You could find a lady's old fur coat there that somebody gave to him. You could find old sports clothes that some student was going to get. You could find a lampshade that somebody no longer wanted at home, and he was going to give away. . . . In a sense, he was a junk collector, but he always had a purpose in it. He was going to give it to somebody."

However, Father Malone realized the futility of attempting to build Loyola into a viable school through sporadic personal contributions. Another associate recalled his frustration at staging bridge parties and bazaars with students and parents and getting "a $25, or a $35, or a $40 contribution."

In 1942 he met Joseph W. Drown, a businessman who had made substantial gifts to Loyola. Drown proposed a solution to Loyola's problems. He owned the U.S. Grant Hotel in San Diego, the city's largest. Drown suggested that Loyola buy the hotel, making a minimal cash down payment, lease the property back to a management company which he would form, and pay the balance of the cost of the hotel from rental receipts from the lessee.

As a tax-exempt institution, Loyola would not owe any taxes on the rental receipts. And from Drown's point of view, the rent would be deductible as a business expense. Drown's profit on the sale would be taxed at capital gains rates. Thus he would make a greater profit than if he held the hotel and continued to take out profits taxable at ordinary income and corporate rates. The rental was set at eighty percent of the hotel's operating profit; ninety percent of these proceeds, in turn, would be paid back to Drown toward the purchase price. The economic effect of the scheme was to divide the net profits of the hotel, twenty percent to the operating company (controlled by Drown); eight percent to Loyola; and seventy-two percent to Drown, the seller.

Loyola officials liked the idea, but suggested the use of an intermediary to make the purchase, since the Society of Jesus does not encourage its institutions to acquire properties and each sale would have to be approved by the order's headquarters in Rome. So in 1945 Father Malone, together with Drown and Paul Cote, a Los Angeles attorney and promiment Catholic layman, established the University

Hill Foundation, for the sole purpose of raising funds for Loyola.

University Hill Foundation's first purchase was the U.S. Grant Hotel. During the next nine years it bought no less than twenty-three other businesses: lumber companies, a printing firm, a foundry, three dairies, factories which made plastics, locks, foam rubber, oil burners and metal windows, a recording company, a scrap metal dealership, and a sand and gravel company.

"The Cote Formula," as IRS later termed the Foundation's technique, was used in each purchase. Drown, Cote, and Father Malone actively sought out closely-held businesses with proven managements, low, fixed assets, and a quick turnover of merchandise. The Foundation obligated itself to pay the purchase only from business receipts; if not enough revenue was produced to fulfill the contract, the deal was nullified with no recourse, the seller regaining his business. The firms kept their old letterheads and phone numbers; frequently, nothing was said to customers (nor even to creditors, in some instances) about the change of ownership. The new "operating corporation"—the former owners, now the managers—many times took the same name as the previous firm.

Justice Arthur J. Goldberg wrote later in a dissenting opinion in a parallel case: "At first glance it might appear odd that the sellers would enter into this transaction, for prior to the sale they had a right to 100 percent of the corporation's income, but after the sale they had a right to only 72 percent of that income and would lose the business . . . to boot." [33] But tax and other advantages more than compensated for any drawbacks. Because the Foundation was tax-exempt, neither it nor the operating company had to pay income taxes on business earnings. Therefore the sellers

received, free of corporate taxation (at a fifty-two percent
rate) and subject to taxation only at capital gains rates, seventy-two percent of the business earnings. By juggling the
purchase price the amount of the "capital gain" to be taxed
could be kept low, thereby allowing the businessman to
keep virtually all the price paid for the company. Without
the sale the businessman would have received only forty-
eight percent of the business earnings, and this would have
been subject to personal taxation at ordinary income rates.

In terms of benefits to Loyola, the plan was strikingly
successful. Between 1948 and 1956 the Foundation gave the
college contributions of $2,194,166. The Foundation also
accumulated another $4,224,310 but withheld distribution
of it after 1956 when the IRS revoked its tax-exempt status,
charging, "It is apparent that your primary activities and
principal expenditures are concerned with your business
ventures and that your exempt activities are incidental."
University Hill challenged IRS in Tax Court—and won,
finally, in 1969, when the court stated that Congress had
had ample opportunity to prevent such foundation transactions, if it thought they violated public policy. The court
noted that laws concerning foundations "have been enacted
gingerly, and have been most carefully drawn against a
background of historical bias in favor of the charitable exemption which still survives with the luster of its public
service emblem untarnished." [34] *

Congress was well aware of the bootstrapping and of the
warning, voiced in 1967 by Stanley S. Surrey, assistant secretary of the treasury for tax affairs, that it was resulting in
a "substantial unplanned shift of productive property to the

* The Tax Court decision was issued January 8, 1969, before Congress began work
on the Tax Reform Act of 1969. Congress's answer to "bootstrapping" is discussed
in Chapter Nine, along with other actions against foundation fiscal abuses.

[tax] exempt sector of our economy," and "broad economic and social changes stemming from the ownership of a large number of businesses by organizations with different motives and different objectives than the entrepreneurs who have thus far constituted our business community." [35]

The tax-avoidance attorneys were also well aware of bootstrapping—and of its value to their rich clients. They predicted, accurately, that the University Hill Foundation technique would be upheld by the courts, and they devised ingenious variations to help clients siphon low-tax funds out of businesses and other enterprises. For example, Prentice-Hall's *Executive Tax Report* headlined in 1963:

BOOSTING PROFITS: HAVE YOU PUT A PRICE
ON YOUR BUSINESS?
YOU MAY BE ABLE TO DOUBLE IT—BY SELLING TO A CHARITY.

This particular hypothetical case said that since a tax-exempt buyer "keeps a hundred cents on the dollar" on business earnings, he should be willing to pay "twice what you figured" when buying a business. As "frosting on the cake," Prentice-Hall added, the seller could remain active in management and draw a "good salary." [36]

A spate of similar advertisements in the *Wall Street Journal* revealed an eagerness of foundations to help businessmen take advantage of the bootstrapping loophole.

TAX EXEMPT INSTITUTION SEEKS CLOSELY-HELD COMPANIES
(BROKERS PROTECTED)

Negotiations conducted on generous pre-tax earnings basis. Include phone number, please, Box D-173, *The Wall Street Journal.*

. . . .

HIGHLY RESPECTED CHARITABLE FUND (NON-PROFIT) WILL PURCHASE

Private or closely-held companies with minimum pre-tax profit of $250,000. Financial and other benefits very rewarding. For private and confidential appointment call or write L. H. [followed by an address and phone number in a New Jersey suburb of New York].

Real estate. Dairies. Lumber mills. Even a bank. And Southwestern oilmen devised their own variation of bootstrapping to siphon petroleum dollars out of the earth at favorable tax rates through the use of organizations that are foundations in name only. This frightfully involved scheme enables the oilmen to stretch benefits of the oil-depletion allowance beyond limits set by Congress and to reduce or eliminate entirely federal income-tax liabilities, sometimes by incurring deliberate paper losses.

The basic ingredient is what the oil industry calls a "production payment," defined, for federal tax purposes, as the right to oil and gas that is still in the ground. A major headache to oilmen is the fact that it takes years to get all the oil out of a well; some wells in the famed east Texas fields have been producing for more than four decades, and the oilmen don't like to wait that long for their money. Through a production payment, an oilman "carves out" a percentage of a field's known reserves and sells them for cash.

But it is difficult for him to use conventional financing in production payment transactions. The courts have defined production payments as a form of "interest in land," and national banks' land dealings are severely restricted, so much so, in fact, that banks seldom will dare to make a direct purchase of a production payment.

It is here that the oil foundations are valuable. Typical of these tax-avoidance organizations is the Bright Star

Foundation, created for a purpose candidly stated (even if inadvertently so) by its secretary-treasurer, attorney Robert B. Payne: "to purchase production payments." [37]

The function of Bright Star and similar oil foundations is to borrow money from banks and lend it to companies which wish to buy production payments. The foundations charge a fraction more interest than they pay to the banks. The production payments serve as collateral, and the foundations repay the banks with continuing income from the production payments. The foundations' "profit" is the minute difference between the interest they are charged by the banks and the interest they collect from companies which purchase the production payments.

The result is an increasingly vast turnover of money. One Treasury Department estimate put the amount at $217,000,000 in 1965, $750,000,000 in 1967, $703,000,000 in 1968, and $814,000,000 in 1969.

Yet the arrangement is such that only a slim trickle of the money handled by the oil foundations goes to charity. The Bright Star Foundation, according to its income tax returns, earned a gross profit from oil production payments of $9,933,119 during the fiscal year ending March 31, 1967. But $9,915,808 was paid out immediately to meet the bank loans and other expenses: After churning this money through its accounts, Bright Star Foundation had a token $100 for charity, paid to the Children's Medical Center of Dallas. Bright Star also listed "miscellaneous expenses" of $1,060, accounting fees of $1,050, and a reporting fee to the State of Texas of $100. Thus its administrative expenses ran twenty-two times its payments to charity. Secretary-Treasurer Payne, however, protests that the reason more contributions were not made is that "I just did not get around to writing any checks." [38]

In truth, Bright Star Foundation did have a slightly better contributions record in several preceding years. During the year ending March 31, 1964, for instance, from gross profits of $3,347,333, it paid $19,000 to Life Line Foundation, Inc., the rightist political propaganda group run by billionaire H. L. Hunt, which lost its tax-exempt status a year later for engaging in partisan political activities forbidden to foundations under the tax laws. Companies controlled by Hunt had a hand in some of the production payments handled through Bright Star.

Dallas banks are happy about such foundation manipulations because of the interest they make on the loans. The First Texas Charitable Foundation (one of three foundations listing its address as Post Office Box 6031, Dallas), for instance, as of November 30, 1967, owed the First National Bank in Dallas mortgages totaling $2,430,036, all covering production payments purchased on an installment basis. The First Texas Charitable Foundation had an extraordinary record that year. It received a gross income from royalty payments of $1,455,158, and made a single contribution—$100 to the Dallas Zoological Society. The Foree Foundation, created by Dallas oilman R. L. Foree, Sr., and a co-occupant of Box 6031, did somewhat better: its contributions totaled $2,110, from a gross income of $33,790. The Foree Foundation, its tax returns indicate, was in the process of becoming inactive as its production payments ran out.*

The oil-foundation gimmick is also popular in New Orleans, where officials and attorneys of the Whitney National Bank are directors of no less than eight foundations. One of

---

* Neither Foree nor William F. Rose, Jr., listed as president of the First Texas Charitable Foundation, responded to the author's request for their comments on such use of a tax-exempt organization.

these groups, the Thirteen Hundred Foundation, had production payments totaling $2,926,353 in 1967–68. It gave $25 to a local Methodist church.

The use of oil foundations to squeeze extra tax savings out of the depletion allowance is a marriage of loopholes which Treasury tax experts outline as follows:[39]

Oil wells owned by the Big Gusher Company produce a gross profit of $10,000,000 in 1969. The 27.5 percent oil-depletion allowance permits the company a $2,750,000 deduction. Yet Big Gusher has operating expenses of $8,000,000, cutting its net income to $2,000,000. Since the depletion allowance may not exceed fifty percent of net income, Big Gusher faces a diminution of its $2,750,000 deduction to $1,000,000.

So Big Gusher sells a production payment for $8,000,000, boosting its total gross income for the year to $18,000,000. Since business expenses remain the same, its net income is $10,000,000. But its depletion allowance is based upon the full gross income—27.5 percent of $18,000,000, or $4,950,000. The $4,950,000 is deducted from the net income of $10,000,000, leaving Big Gusher liable for taxes on the remaining $5,050,000—$2,666,400, at the 1969 corporate rate of 52.8 percent.

At this point Big Gusher is still in the red, for this is more taxes than it would have had to pay if it had not peddled the production payment. Its savings comes the following year. Big Gusher again has $10,000,000 of gross income, but it must pay $8,000,000 of this to the purchaser of the production payment. Thus its income is cut to $2,000,000. Its business expenses remain at $8,000,000, producing a paper loss for the year of $6,000,000.

The paper loss, according to Treasury experts, eliminates federal tax liability for the second year. It is also enough to offset the $5,050,000 income for the preceding year, entitling Big Gusher to claim a refund of the $2,666,400 taxes it paid, and to provide a carryover of $950,000 to be applied against taxes in future years.

"Charitable" foundations are at the core of this tangle.

The Internal Revenue Service, in court cases begun in the early 1960s, charged that the oil foundations were businesses operated for profit, and therefore ineligible for tax-exemption. IRS lost. In the case of Bright Star Foundation, T. Whitfield Davidson, an octogenarian U.S. District Court judge in Dallas, commented: "The foundation was organized by some wealthy outstanding citizens of Dallas, some of them engaged in the banking business." [40] For no other cited reason, Davidson ruled against IRS. Another federal judge disposed of four more oil-foundation cases in a bloc without substantial comment, denying IRS claims for more than $125,000 in allegedly avoided taxes.

The judiciary's attitude towards oil foundations was pragmatically stated by the Fifth U.S. Circuit Court of Appeals in disposing of an IRS challenge to a deal wherein oil-man D. K. Caldwell of Tyler, Texas, "sold" five producing oil properties to the D. K. Caldwell Foundation for $1,005,000, payable from proceeds, and at a tax saving of $327,087.45. The court said: "A taxpayer is entitled to take any legal course with his property or business which lightens or lessens his tax load . . . and . . . the fact that an arrangment reduces his taxes is of no moment in determining its validity . . ." [41] But a dissenting judge warned of the use the tax-wary oil industry would make of the approved loophole: "It seems to me that, if by this process the taxpayer could convert his ordinary income from these properties to capital gain, then hereafter there will be no necessity for an owner of oil royalty interests to receive therefrom ordinary income."

CONDUIT SALES OF STOCKS. BOOTSTRAPPING. Oil foundations. The tax avoidance stratagems demonstrate a peculiar capacity of Americans to demean noble ideas for money. This kind of modern philanthropist, when he sits down with his lawyer and accountant to draft a "giving" program, thinks not of what worthy cause will benefit—but of what he will save. That he is credited with giving a crippled children's hospital $5,822 during a ten-year period when it actually receives only $3,000 is but a quirk of the law over which the tax specialists jest at their annual meetings. But that these games are played at the expense of citizens too poor to run "charitable foundations," or to hire tax attorneys, is another matter. Each boast of sharp-dealing, even if uttered in the private pages of tax-avoidance literature, diminishes confidence in the tax system—and in the entire philanthropic establishment.

Serious foundation executives resent the tax lawyers' cynicism. But they seldom say anything critical of it. The reason they remain silent—or, at the minimum, speak off-the-record—is obvious: alienate a contributor by impugning his motives, and the money stops.

The president of a medium-sized New York foundation (assets of $100,000,000 to $150,000,000), which has wide support from other foundations, told me in the spring of 1969, when Congress was preparing to give all foundations the thrashing only some of them deserved:

Week after week these so-called estate planners invite me down to their nice offices on Wall Street, and tell me what

great things they are going to do for us. I'm not particularly
stupid, and I've been around long enough so that most of the
tax lawyers realize it. But I sit there and see the same old
schemes unfold: a remainder interest in a dog of an old mansion out on Long Island (we won't get involved with such
things; it's rough enough dealing with the trust department of
a bank); a block of stock in a family firm that hasn't paid a
dividend since 1931, and has the market value of a roll of . . .
well, a roll of wall paper; stock in an oil company that has a
suspiciously high over-the-counter value, or so they claim
anyway, compared to the price our benefactor paid for it.

I'm lucky because I have trustees who won't let our name
be used for more obvious schemes. But it's easy to get hooked.
What do you say to a rich man who gives you forty shares of
AT&T one year and next time around wants to unload 3,000
shares of Unamalgamated Old Sludge Petroleum Company
on you at a value so unrealistic it isn't even laughable? You
take the junk and don't make any promises, and let him fight
it out with IRS if they question its value when he claims a deduction.

Burton Raffel, just before he resigned from the Foundation Center, the closest thing to an "official" collective voice
of the foundations, criticized the tax specialists in a *Foundation News* article. Commenting on the plethora of "how-to"
articles in tax journals, Raffel concluded: ". . . while the
authors' scholarship is exemplary, the philanthropic foundation should require something more, even of its legal advisers. . . . This is not to advocate human-wave assaults on
the federal tax bastions, nor to suggest that lawyers counsel
fiscal masochism. But I do strongly advocate that we sur-
round philanthropy with more rather than less far-seeing,
humanistic thought—and with less rather than more
money-motivated utilitarianism." [42]

Mortimer Caplin, while Commissioner of Internal Revenue during the Kennedy-Johnson administrations, criti-

cized tax specialists who strain against the limits of the law: "Foundations should not simply obey the law—or rather, they should not confine themselves to avoiding its penalties. Borderline transactions, strictly legal perhaps, but in spirit running distinctly against the statutory grain, should be as carefully shunned as are the clearly-proscribed transactions. In other words, foundations should strive to understand and cooperate with the law, rather than to outwit or to take advantage of it." [43] And Caplin's successor, Sheldon Cohen, once declared: "While I respect those lawyers who are willing to join issue with the IRS on legitimate questions of tax law, I have no respect for the attorney who sees in tax planning a game of catch-as-catch-can. Whether the taxpayer is caught or not, the net effect is . . . a reduced respect for the integrity of the tax bar and the law itself." And Cohen warned, prophetically, that "those who want to play the game for their own selfish motives invite a reaction which will not benefit foundations generally." [44]

F. Emerson Andrews, who spent four decades in foundation work, beginning as a consultant to the Russell Sage Foundation and ending as president of the Foundation Center, questions the propriety of a lawyer representing both the donor and the donor's foundation. "Sometimes the law has forgotten who its client is," Andrews says. "When the lawyer is paid with a foundation check, is not the client the foundation, devoted wholly to tax-exempt purposes? If there should be a conflict of interest between the public purposes of the foundation and the financial advantage of the donor, should not the lawyer decide that conflict of interest in favor of the public purpose of the foundation from which he receives his pay? I just raise this question. Sometimes it has been decided the other way." [45]

How can conflicts of interest arise from dual representation? Though there are numerous actual cases, the libel laws here dictate retreat to a hypothetical one. John Avoider owns stock in the Good Grief Oil Company. During the weekend the Justice Department announces an antitrust action that is sure to tumble the value of Good Grief when the market opens on Monday. John Avoider hastily convenes a directors' meeting of the John Avoider Charitable Foundation, which votes to buy his Good Grief stock at the Friday closing price. On Monday the stock drops by fifty points, and the John Avoider Charitable Foundation suffers a loss of $50,000.

Why would the foundation accommodate Avoider by relieving him of the Good Grief stock? Because Charles Z. Barrister, attorney, was hired to reduce John Avoider's tax bill, and he is a director of the John Avoider Charitable Foundation. To Barrister, the foundation is a legal convenience, and it was Barrister who recommended the stock transaction. Serving as an unsalaried director of the foundation is an ex officio adjunct to Barrister's role as well-paid tax counsel to John Avoider.

Because of their ability to guide philanthropic activities of their clients, should not lawyers demand that the foundations they help create give more than an occasional courteous bow and handful of silver to the public interest?

Norman Sugarman, the foundation-law specialist we met earlier, has argued in several forums that he and other lawyers have no extraordinary obligation to police philanthropy. "It would be very easy to assert that lawyers and accountants should, in the public interest, take on the responsibility to set high standards for the operation of charitable organizations, and to see that they are conducted without possible criticism by anyone," Sugarman told a foundation conference in 1967. But he calls this view "unduly narrow":

> . . . the responsibility for foundation conduct—good and bad—is broadly based. No one connected with the field can avoid his own responsibility by shifting it to the legal or accounting profession.
>   . . . a lawyer performs a very particular function: to serve the best interests of a specific client. His professional responsibility is to advise the client—the foundation—what it can and cannot do under the law.[46]

Sugarman argues that everyone involved in philanthropy—donors, trustees, foundation executives, government officials, and Congress—share the responsibility for setting standards. And he does not like the accusation that foundation abuses result from "clever little schemes on the part of lawyers."

> There is no more reason to generalize, from a few cases, about the lawyer's overall responsibility than there is to generalize about the businessman's, or the doctor's, or the dentist's, to the public in the charitable field. Further, there is at least the question whether so-called abuses have been based on professional advice—or have occurred without regard to or in spite of advice from lawyers and accountants to stay off those shoals. . . .
>   The lawyer who is engaged to represent the donor of a charitable gift must have as his single-minded purpose the matters for which he is engaged. . . . If his client can avoid a capital gains tax by a contribution of appreciated securities to a foundation, it is the lawyer's obligation to so inform his client. The lawyer's obligation is that he so advise his client that, to the extent reasonably possible, the client pays the amount of tax the law requires, and not more. . . . [His recommendations] are not compelled by a vague duty to the public. They are "good business" for the client.

To attorney Milton Young, another able and respected foundation specialist, the tax practitioner's first responsibility is "to be proficient in his skills and ethical in his application. He has a duty to appraise a suggested course of action, to see that it is neither technically unsound nor morally repugnant." But at the same time he has a duty "to help evolve a workable system of taxation." For instance, "gifts of appreciated property to charity are proper, and serve a social as well as a tax purpose. Yet, when a false appraisal is used, it precipitates Congressional inquiry, which may result in a change in the rules of the game affecting all taxpayers, including the ones acting in good faith."

To Young, "the guide for ethical behavior is, in a large measure, subjective. The tax practitioner has met the test if he goes to sleep each night without shame for what he has done that day, and without dread of what he has to do tomorrow." [47]

Nevertheless, different things keep different people awake at night, and the tax avoidance literature speaks for itself.

THAT FOUNDATION FINANCES received any adverse public attention at all can be credited to Representative Wright Patman, an ideological descendant (but not a formal student) of the nineteenth century Southern Populists who fought against economic domination of their region by railroad monopolies, absentee farm owners, and "Wall Street bankers."

Patman is a cherubic little fellow in rimless glasses whose forte is the ability to look absolutely harmless while plotting great mischief against bankers, Treasury Department officials, and other persons he considers malefactors.

Patman came to Washington in 1928, at age thirty-two, as a representative from northeast Texas's First Congressional District, and brought with him fundamentalist views of wealth: capitalism is splendid when the system permits every citizen and businessman equal economic rights. But banks which use interlocking directorates with industrial firms to thwart competition are evil and deserve a clubbing, and rich men who evade taxes while exuding piety are scoundrels and should be made to play by the same rules as the rest of us.

For Patman, foundations are a natural target: they are big, they are wealthy, they are mysterious institutions run by the same stuffed shirts and "pious phonies" who dominate the Wall Street banking community which he has fought for decades. Put an unmarked list of foundation trustees alongside an unmarked list of bank directors, Patman once mused, "and you can't tell Brand X from Brand Y, they're the same people."

Patman began his crusade against the foundations with a series of floor speeches from May through August, 1961:

> I am . . . concerned with, first, foundation-controlled businesses competing with small businessmen; second, the economic effect of great amounts of wealth accumulating in privately-controlled, tax-exempt foundations; third, the problem of control of that capital for an undetermined period—in some instances perpetuity—by a few individuals or their self-appointed successors; and fourth, the foundation's power to interlock and knot together through investments, a network of commercial alliances, which assures harmonious action whenever they have a common interest . . .[48]

The House Small Business Committee, of which Patman was chairman, authorized him to investigate "the impact upon small business of the activities and conduct of tax-exempt foundations and charitable trusts." [49] He created a special foundation study subcommittee and asked more than five hundred foundations for information on their holdings, trustees, and program. He published the findings over the next seven years, in a series of "reports to the subcommittee" that ultimately totaled more than 5,000 pages. The laborious compilation of statistics was done, for the most part, by Patman's sole subcommittee staff member, Harry A. Olsher, with the occasional assistance of an accountant, J. J. Seidman, and the General Accounting Office of Congress. But the tone of the reports, and the interpretation of the data, were vintage Patman populism. They deserve a mixed report card.

On the positive side, Patman detailed for the first time the extent of foundation holdings. Through use of subpoena powers, he forced such secretive foundations as the Pew Memorial Trust of Philadelphia to release data on their holdings and grants. His criticisms of secrecy pressured the Internal Revenue Service into opening for public inspection most of the information contained on the foundations' 990-A forms, their annual tax returns. (Representative John Moss of California had tried unsuccessfully to open these records in 1958, through his freedom-of-information subcommittee.) Also through subpoena, Patman obtained and published details of stock manipulations of foundations controlled by New York financier David Baird, who was under IRS investigation and whose organizations later lost their tax-exemption.

Patman found scores of foundations that had not reported their business holdings, as required by law, and forced IRS to tighten its enforcement procedures.

Fearing exposure by Patman, foundations corrected some of their sloppy, questionable grants procedures. "When it comes to the proper policing of tax-exempt foundations, the IRS appears to be totally impaled in the quicksands of absolute inertia," Patman once stated, in wondrously scrambled metaphors.[50] Even the Foundation Center's F. Emerson Andrews, most vociferous of the Patman critics, admitted: "It is probable that . . . the foundation world stirred to more self-appraisal and more cooperation [because of the probe]. Foundation conferences were never better attended than when the Patman investigation was a program item." And Andrews credits Patman for "presenting detailed financial data usually reliable for the individual foundations, however distorted in interpretation . . ." [51]

Yet the Patman investigation was sorely flawed. No foundation ever received a chance to submit, through testimony or other communication, a rebuttal to Patman's many and often off-the-mark charges of wrongdoing. Major errors were pointed out to Patman and Olsher, but they went uncorrected in the formal record. In one installment Patman accused a New York foundation of giving $1,654,765 to its donor's estate to pay a tax deficiency. If this in fact had happened, the foundation and its trustees would have been in grave violation of the law. Actually, it turned out, the foundation *received* this amount from the estate after a court trial.

Patman's work was as devoid of achievable goal as are many foundation research projects. The Small Business Committee had no authority to write legislation affecting foundations; that must come from Ways and Means, and Chairman Wilbur Mills of Arkansas, although Patman's friend, was frequently miffed at the invasion of his territory.

At various times, Patman proposed (1) a moratorium on the creation of new foundations; (2) a twenty-five-year limit on their life; (3) a ban on business holdings of any type; (4) the treatment of contributions and capital gains as current income which must be spent in the year of receipt; and (5) taxes of varying percentages on foundation income. The strangest proposal of all, made in 1968, was that foundations, "for the duration of the Vietnam War . . . donate their gross receipts . . . to the Federal government in support of our defense of democracy in Southeast Asia and other uses vital to our national interest . . ." [52]

Patman's investigation was restricted to a varying group of foundations which he said represented "about one percent in each state sampled." [53] A careless reader might conclude that if the one percent "sampling" had $7,000,000,000 in income during the ten year period 1952–62, the total income for all foundations was a hundred times as much, or $700,000,000,000. On closer examination Patman's "sampling" proved to have come off the tip of the iceberg; the group on his list represented ninety percent of the assets of all foundations. His 1968 report stated: "The value of the 596 foundations at the close of 1966 was 50 percent greater than it had been six years earlier, at the end of 1960. Those assets totaled $15.1 billion at the close of 1966 compared with $10.2 billion at the end of 1960 (with market values of stocks being used wherever available)." [54]

There are curious omissions from this statement. First, the 1960 asset figure, taken from his first report, is for 534 foundations; the 1966 figure, for 596 foundations. (At other points the "sample" contained 522 and 575 foundations.) Some of the original 534 had been culled from the "sample" over the years without notice. One of them, the James Foundation, of New York, had dropped from assets of

$85,000,000 to zero upon dissolution. Nine of the additions to the list had assets of $20,000,000 or more. Other additions were not even foundations: the System Development Corporation, with receipts of $102,000,000 in 1966, and the Rand Corporation, with $45,000,000, are both think-tanks which are financed by government and other contracts. Emerson Andrews correctly notes: "No percentage increase for a particular group of foundations is valid when radical and arbitrary changes are made in the group within the time span examined." [55]

Patman's selection of target foundations revealed a regional bias. His reports did not take up the "bootstrap" sale technique which oilmen used to avoid taxes (and which the IRS considered to be a major foundation abuse). His reports studiously avoided criticism of the two largest Texas foundations, the Houston Endowment and the Moody Foundation, although they own more active businesses than any other foundation among the twenty-five largest and have the worst return/asset ratio. (Olsher resigned from the foundation subcommittee in the spring of 1969 to become president of the Fund for Public Policy Research, created that year in Washington. The fund is described as a "non-profit organization devoted to impartial research, analyses and studies in the areas of taxation, fiscal policy, monetary policy, and related fields including comprehensive study of the Internal Revenue Code. The Fund is financed by a $1 million grant from the Houston Endowment . . ." [56])

In terms of bulk, the Irvine Foundation of California received more attention from Patman than any other organization. Patman's fifth installment, issued April 28, 1967, is best described by a paragraph of his covering statement: "The contents consist entirely of exhibits relating to the James Irvine Foundation–Irvine Company, of California, and its impact on the economy of Orange County, California." The document contains 1,131 pages, measures a foot at the spine, and weighs slightly more than four pounds; it is, quite probably, the largest single publication ever issued with the Congressional imprimatur. And this report, published under auspices of a Congressional subcommittee, has a history that points strongly to misuse of Congressional authority for the direct benefit of a private party to a law suit.

The Irvine Foundation owns fifty-three percent of the shares of the Irvine Company, which in turn owns 88,000 acres of land—the Irvine Ranch, in common parlance—south of Los Angeles, comprising nearly twenty percent of the area of Orange County, with a value estimated at from $250,000,000 to $1,000,000,000.

Patman's probe of the Irvine Foundation coincided with a challenge to Irvine foundation and company management by Mrs. Joan Irvine Smith, a dissident minority stockholder and a granddaughter of James Irvine, who assembled the ranch from old Spanish land grants. A petite, tough-minded blonde in her thirties, Mrs. Smith charged her adversaries with mismanagement and nonfeasance: for not developing the Irvine land at a faster rate; for accumulating supposedly excessive reserves, instead of paying dividends to her and other minority shareholders; for carving out sections of the ranch for industrial development and putting them under the control of separate management companies; for an interlock (five of seven persons) of the Foundation and company boards. Mrs. Smith pursued these charges through state and federal courts in California beginning in the 1950s, but without success.

In 1963–64, Mrs. Smith took a new direction, charging

that her grandfather's stock in the Irvine Company (fifty-three percent of the outstanding shares) was not legally transferred to the Foundation during his lifetime, and belonged to the surviving heirs. Had Mrs. Smith been able to substantiate this claim in court, she, her mother, who is the wife of U.S. District Judge Thurmond Clarke of Los Angeles, and other heirs would have gained control of the Irvine fortune. Thus her tenacity, despite a nearly unbroken string of defeats in the board room and in court.

Mrs. Smith found an ally in the Patman subcommittee. From 1963 through 1967 the Patman subcommittee—actually, Olsher, writing in the Congressman's name, with his permission—sent more than twenty requests to the Irvine Foundation for documents, including minutes of board meetings, data on its business dealings, and copies of internal reports on its plan for development of the Irvine Ranch. For three years the Foundation gave Patman the requested data—not always as quickly as he asked, and in one instance only after he rustled a subpoena. All these documents, of course, would be extremely valuable to Mrs. Smith in her attempt to prove her grandfather had never transferred his stock to the Foundation. And, in April 1966, the Foundation suddenly realized that was exactly where many of the documents were going.

The Irvine Foundation president, N. Loyall McLaren, wrote Patman on April 15: ". . . information has come to our attention that minutes of meetings of the directors of the James Irvine Foundation, which had been submitted to you, were turned over to Mrs. Smith and her press agent, Mr. Chip Cleary. Neither of them is connected with the foundation, nor, so far as I am aware, with your committee. I am appalled that your committee would serve as the intermediary through which the foundation's minutes and rec-

ords were made available to them or to anyone else."
McLaren said the Foundation would not send any further
material to the subcommittee until he was assured they
"will not be made available to unauthorized third parties."

McLaren's letter began an acrimonious exchange of correspondence. Patman wrote on April 18: "From the very
beginning of our studies, the information we have gathered
has been made available to the public so that the people
could evaluate the operations of tax exempt foundations.
. . . All of our endeavors are designed to benefit the public,
and their deep interest has been indicated by thousands of
letters from all parts of the country, including Orange
County and other areas of California." Patman accused
McLaren of "demanding secrecy" and threatened him with
a subpoena.

McLaren replied that although Patman's letter "bears
your signature or a facsimile thereof, it is difficult for me to
believe that you could have authored or authorized such a
letter. . . . There is no principle of law or government
which says that corporate records may be demanded by a
Congressional committee and turned over to private persons
simply because the corporation enjoys a Federal tax exemption." McLaren complained in another letter that Foundation officers had seen Olsher in Newport Beach, California,
"in conference with Mr. Lyndol Young," Mrs. Smith's attorney. He called this meeting "confirmatory of our earlier
concern that the resources of your subcommittee were being
utilized to assist Mrs. Smith in her controversy with the
foundation and its directors."

Just as the Irvine officials feared, the documents obtained through the Patman subcommittee were incorporated into a suit which Mrs. Smith filed on August 10, 1966.
The Irvine officials reiterated their protests, retaining the

prestigious Washington law firm of Covington & Burlington
to present their case directly to Patman and urge him not to
"take sides in private litigation."

Patman deftly cut the ground from under them by or-
dering publication of all the Irvine material as a Congressional document, thereby putting it into the public domain,
and protecting Olsher from charges that he had spirited papers obtained under Congressional authority to private
parties.[57]

Despite Patman's help, Mrs. Smith lost her case.

Unperturbed by this quiet controversy, which was outside the sight of the public, Patman plodded on with his investigation, publicizing foundation wealth, publishing detailed descriptions of the "abuses" he found around the
country (many of them, actually, in Tax Court cases
brought by IRS), goading IRS into an intensive audit program.

Inevitably, Patman began to attract the attention of a
tax-conscious public—and of a Congress which heard citizen demands for an end to tax avoidance by loophole.

CHAPTER 8

Activism and Acrimony

IN A CYNICAL MOMENT of self-denigration a philanthropoid once lamented to me: "A foundation would answer a drowning man's cries for help by studying the physical properties of salt water." Foundation-sponsored empirical research follows a dreary cycle: a famed educator is commissioned to study urban schools, collects data for two years, spends another year writing, and another two years reporting to learned meetings and possibly a "White House conference." Everyone exclaims over the problems he has documented and agrees that Something Must Be Done. An "action" commission is recruited by the President, the governor, or the mayor. At its first meeting it discovers the figures with which it is dealing are six years old. So a famed educator is commissioned to study urban schools. He collects data for two years, spends another year writing . . .

In 1966 the Ford Foundation boldly moved from empiricism to activism. No longer would it merely study America's problems; it would try to solve them, by getting down into the street and siding with the people most affected. Activism was not new among foundations, but the few who had been bold in the past had also been relatively poor: the Stern Family Fund, the Field Foundation, the New World Foundation, among others, had bankrolled community action groups.

Ford, however, had something more than $3,000,-000,000 to dedicate to the elimination of what its president, McGeorge Bundy, called "the corrosiveness of prejudice" in American life. When so much wealth moves, even on tiptoes, it can cause a tremor in the United States.

McGeorge Bundy was Ford's point man, the term the infantry uses for the soldier who walks ahead of the platoon, unafraid to venture down dark paths towards unseen dangers, drawing fire if the enemy is there, deciding whether to shoot back or to withdraw. As point man, Bundy was in the field of fire of an awesome collection of American institutions: conservative segregationist politicians in the South; machine politicians in the North; the university establishment; the public school bureaucracy—in total, enough power to overwhelm almost any man or organization, regardless of how wealthy.

Not so with Bundy, who is blessed (or cursed, as some would prefer) with the special strength of self-assurance; the very smart, like the very rich, are different from you and me. And the very smart, when they have the means, also have the irritating tendency to do what is best for us, whether or not we agree.

Bundy's presence at Ford resulted from several coincidences of timing. By the end of 1965, with the Johnson administration securely through the transition from the Kennedy years, Bundy was weary of trying to adapt himself to a President with whom he was never temperamentally at ease. Johnson's closeness to Secretary of State Dean Rusk diminished considerably Bundy's power as White House national security adviser.

The Ford Foundation, concurrently, was looking for a new president. From 1951 to 1953 an activist president, Paul Hoffman, who had been Truman's Marshall Plan administrator, had run the Foundation, and times were tumultuous. Ford's support of the Fund for the Republic attracted red-hunting Congressmen. Hoffman later recollected: "Every time we got a dozen letters objecting to something we'd done—a radio show or an overseas program or what not—I'd have to spend hours reassuring the board." [1] H. Rowan Gaither, Hoffman's immediate successor, was safe; so was Henry Heald, whom Bundy was to replace. A Ford officer told me: "Heald's background was in education, and he made his name as president of New York University. The Foundation directors were ready to change their emphasis from passing out money to universities to more significant matters, and they needed a man with a broader background."

The "change in emphasis" of which this officer spoke was the realization—in the American business community as in the board rooms of alert foundations—that the civil rights revolution was inexorably spreading from challenges to the blatant, but admitted, segregation of the South to the more subtle racial rigidities of the big cities of the North and East. In Detroit the simmering racial tensions among workers at his own motor company warned Henry Ford II of the crisis rapidly sweeping down upon urban America. Race, pollution, decay, poor schools—the American mess was suddenly very visible.

The Establishment knew it must regroup, not only to assure its own preservation but also to guarantee that it had a voice in the imminent rebuilding of urban government. One instrument through which this was to be done was the Ford Foundation. Hence, in late 1965, the third coincidence of timing: McGeorge Bundy was tired of Lyndon Johnson, and vice versa; the Ford Foundation was looking for a new president; and the Ford Foundation was ready for an abrupt change of course.

No man can train for a position such as the Ford Foundation presidency, especially when the job description is still evolving, as it was in late 1965. What Ford wanted, simply, was a strong-minded man with intellectual depth, administrative skill, and leadership ability, at high enough a level to direct a $3,000,000,000 organization. Ford director John J. McCloy, one-time U.S. high commissioner in Germany, had known Bundy in the foreign-policy community—first as the son of a high War Department official in the Roosevelt administration; next as the biographer of Henry L. Stimson; last as the Kennedy-Johnson national security adviser. Another director, Julius K. Stratton, former president of the Massachusetts Institute of Technology, had known Bundy in the Cambridge academic community, as a Harvard dean.

"Julius Stratton came to me that winter [of 1965–66] and asked if I'd like to come to Ford. That was it," Bundy says. With a minimum of negotiations the marriage was consummated, and Bundy left the national security office in the basement of the White House for a job that provided him more than twice the money ($75,000 annually, instead of $30,000); roughly the same type of chauffeured limousine (his foundation-owned Lincoln is slightly larger than sedans in the White House motor pool); and considerably more direct responsibility (in Washington, Bundy answered to Lyndon Johnson, which meant he had an all-consuming boss; at Ford, he answered to directors who hired him because they believed in him and were willing to permit him to do what he wished within broad policy lines).

At the staff level, Ford learned within a week it had an entirely new breed of president on the premises. Heald had believed in the channel system of command: he relayed his orders and received his information through staff officers. Now the phone would ring, and a program officer nine echelons from the top would pick it up and hear a measured voice, "This is McGeorge Bundy. I was reading your paper on ——, and I want you to tell me more on several of these points." (Bundy laughed when told several years later that the calls had jolted his staff: "JFK operated that way, too. He'd go right to desk officers at State when he wanted a point of information. You aren't jumping channels if you want information or guidance before talking to someone, or simply to ask, 'Are we doing something about this subject?' There's a difference between doing this and going directly to program officers on actual operations; that I would never do.")

Bundy also tightened Ford's internal bureaucracy, squeezing half a dozen formerly separate domestic programs into two offices; releasing senior officers from administrative duties and making them direct advisers to the president; bringing in new program officers to replace some older men who chose to leave when he became president.

And Bundy took direct charge of the Division of National Affairs, the major work of which was "enlarging the opportunities of minorities."

Foundation supplicants also learned that Bundy's presidency meant a jarring, jaw-dropping surprise. During the fifteen-year period 1950–65 Ford had given grants totaling slightly more than $1,500,000,000, of which around $1,000,000,000 went for educational affairs, the largest amounts in the form of capital grants to colleges and universities. Chiefly because of these grants, Ford spending was running almost double its annual income of $150,000,000 per year. Bundy put the colleges on notice that this could not continue, that Ford did not intend to dismantle itself simply for the convenience of higher education.

"There is no solution to the problems of the private colleges and universities in simply giving away the Ford Foundation," he wrote in his 1966 annual report. "It is quite understandable that any given dean or president should feel sure that he needs our capital more than we do—when I was a dean, I felt that way myself. The trouble is in the arithmetic: the present needs of deans and presidents, strung end to end, would go three times around the endowment of the Ford Foundation, without a pause for breath." (The universities reacted so angrily—to the tone as well as the content of the message—that Bundy offered a mock apology in the next annual report, because "I forgot that the academic world is not in the habit of laughing much at itself.") As compensation, Ford began a study on how universities could improve the performance of their endowment funds. With capital portfolios of $12,000,000,000, Ford noted, an improvement of only one percent per year would increase their return by $120,000,000 per year, more than double what Ford spent for education and research in 1966.

But the universities were not appeased. Previously, more than a score of the nation's largest institutions could rely upon Ford for an annual contribution of several millions of dollars each. Now Bundy had the audacity to suggest that conservative university trustees were not earning the highest prudent return on endowments, and that the sons of the rich should pay the actual cost of their education, not a fraction.

Thus, in his first year Bundy—or, more accurately, the reoriented Ford board—grossly irritated the Foundation's single largest constituency. In past years the universities did not complain if Ford channeled funds into specified areas, for there was always enough left over for general purposes to make almost any grant profitable. Too, the Ford money provided extra income for professors astute enough to attract research grants, lessening demands upon administrations for salary increases. Could this cut in income be tolerated? The universities were sorely aggrieved, and so told Ford—and were ignored.

"Ford shouldn't be stirring up trouble for the sake of doing so," McGeorge Bundy told me one quiet afternoon in 1969. Nor was he pleased that some persons described Ford as "liberal" or "activist." To Bundy, the question of what a foundation should do "ultimately becomes whether we'd be able to live with ourselves without facing urban and equal-opportunities problems. . . . They're the necessary Number One problems for anyone concerned with the welfare of the citizen. It's because these problems are so edgy that we've been controversial. We're unwilling to go hunting for trouble; but we're not so unbecoming as to avoid it." [2]

Ford found the trouble close to home, in the miserable

New York public school system, whose utter failure in educating its increasingly black student population would have been a national disgrace, had anyone really cared.

Here are some random statistics: eighty-five percent of Harlem children were more than two years behind the accepted norm in reading; in a single year, one Harlem high school produced only thirteen youngsters with academic degrees.[3] Although half New York's schoolchildren were black or Puerto Rican, there were only four Negroes and no Puerto Ricans among the system's approximately 900 principals at the end of the 1966–67 school year.

There are a number of reasons for this. During its heyday years of the 1930s New York schools were a lighthouse system. Through vigorous citizen struggle the schools got rid of the suffocating hold of city and state politicians, but, in doing so, they fell victim to an administrative bureaucracy that was even more deadly, because it was *within* the system itself. The professional staff members of the Board of Education controlled, in most minute detail, the operations of the 900 schools and one million students in the system. The system permitted no true neighborhood voice in school rule. As the city's problems of race and poverty intensified during the 1950s and 1960s, the system could not meet the new conditions. Teachers lost faith in their city and what it could accomplish; why should they frustrate themselves trying to teach "uneducable" slum children? Teachers considered slum schools "penal colonies." Chronic Monday and Friday absenteeism emptied classrooms of teachers and pupils alike. Job security deteriorated into sloth, with teachers inching along for years, building up tenure and civil service status.

Some of the results were that blacks lost faith in achieving an equal educational system; they tired of the refrain from teachers and principals: "It isn't *our* fault your children can't learn; it's the fault of *your* home and *your* community." The blacks responded: "You are paid to teach, to deliver a certain product. When overwhelming numbers of our children fail to learn, you are not delivering. You are not meeting your professional obligation."

With blacks nearly a majority in the system, the goal of "integrated education" became an unattainable myth. Even more cruelly, blacks saw no chance of controlling schools that were destined, by geography or by bureaucratic design, to be almost or entirely black. Integration, when granted, was an act of condescension. Blacks felt that the "dependent status of the Negro in American society is perpetuated by the notion that the only way to help the black child is to seat him alongside white children." [4] The blacks wanted more—an education system that would give them stronger racial identity and pride. Black Power advocates argued that Negroes who achieved quality education under their own aegis would be prepared to be integrated into white society with a background of parity rather than deficiency. The "system" was run from the Board of Education, however, and the Board of Education wasn't interested in listening to lower-class blacks who know nothing of formal pedagogy.

On the first day of the 1966 fall term Harlem parents flung down the gauntlet to the school bureaucracy by declaring a boycott of Intermediate School 201. If IS 201 could not be integrated, either through busing, gerrymandering, or some other device, give control to the community. Harlem was tired of hearing principals and teachers complain they "couldn't teach" local youngsters; if these people couldn't, Harlem would find teachers who could. Parent boycotts spread across the city, with demands for "commu-

nity control" crashing down upon a surprised school administration like thunder, interjecting a somber new element
into New York's racial crisis and sending city politicians in
search of a solution.

"What got us involved, I suppose, is when Lloyd
Garrison, the president of the New York Board of Education, called out to Bundy, 'Help!' " This comment, by a
Ford officer intimately connected with what came to be
known as "the school decentralization fight," points up an
often-blurred fact about the Ford Foundation's role in it.
Ford participated by invitation of the school board. Ford
did not, as charged by the Left and the Right, provoke a
confrontation with the New York school bureaucracy simply as an exercise in power—showing a city and a teachers'
union what $3,000,000,000 and single-minded men can ac-
complish when they set their minds to it. The American
Conservative Union, in a polemical broadside entitled "The
Financiers of a Revolution" (which perhaps by accident,
but perhaps not, bore a bright red cover), called Ford the
"catalyst of New York school disorders." [5]

David Halberstam made the process sound equally simple through the voice of an anonymous informant he quoted
in an unfriendly 1969 *Harper's Magazine* piece on Bundy:
"He arrives in New York. What's the worst problem? Answer, race. What's the head of the dragon? Answer, the
schools. What's the worst problem with education? Answer,
the bureaucracy. How do you break up the bureaucracy?
Click, click, click . . ." [6] Joseph Alsop commented that the
launching of the demonstration school projects "opened the
whole Pandora's box of race hatred in New York." [7]

These statements are oversimplifications; the confrontation would have occurred regardless of Ford. Community

militants were on a collision course with the teachers' union and the school bureaucracy. That Ford was caught in the crunch is relevant for several reasons. First, for one of the few times in history, a foundation was doing more than just talk about "reform of the big city schools": it was actually promoting reform. Second, when Ford got into trouble—the inevitable fate of anyone who tampers with New York's entrenched and inter-supporting, if diverse, power structures —the liberals and academicians who talk so fulsomely about foundations constituting a "powerful instrument for evolution, growth and improvement" [8] said not a word in its defense. ("Our good liberal friends never felt comfortable with blacks who said 'shit' at public meetings," says a Ford officer.) By the time the controversy stilled, Ford was either bent upon destroying society with tax-free funds, in the opinion of the Right, or of fostering a "let-them-eat-cake" scheme of institutionalized segregation upon blacks and Puerto Ricans, the theory of socialist Michael Harrington.[9] Ford was also "anti-Semitic," "anti-union," "anti-teacher" and "anti-community."

Bundy was conspicuous throughout the school decentralization fight because he had a dual role: he was president of Ford and chairman of an ad hoc committee appointed by Mayor John V. Lindsay to draft a policy on citizen participation in school affairs. Ford's involvement began soon after the IS 201 boycott, when the New York school board asked that it supply officers to meet with community leaders and representatives of the United Federation of Teachers and the Council of Supervisory Associations (CSA) to devise a blueprint for giving parents a role in school policy-making. For Bundy and Ford, the request was a chance to expand their urban education programs beyond mundane remedial-reading and team-teaching projects to do something more important: "more direct and effective parent and community participation in school affairs." [10]

Bundy had signaled Ford's readiness for an activist role in an Urban League speech earlier that summer: ". . . the city is as good a proof as any that those who wish to be judged neither stupid nor wicked have a lot to do. For the city is like the Negro in this: it is past the point when all it needs is equal treatment; what it needs now is what the farmer needed, and got, a generation ago—it needs *help*. A lot of the people who own our cities don't seem to know it yet. It is time to get moving." [11]

Bundy's chief adviser was an earnest young man named Mario D. Fantini, who worked in slum schools in Syracuse before joining Ford as a program officer. Fantini felt that "*real* public control of public education could provide more effective education" and that it could "foster the revitalization of one of the most fundamental goals of education: to make better citizens, all along the age spectrum." Fantini argued that "the public has a right to determine educational policy and to hold professionals accountable for implementing policy. Thus, when 70 percent of ghetto children are not reading at grade-level, their parents have a right to question professional performance since the schools are supposed to educate everyone." Furthermore, "public education is a universal right," available not only to the "normal" but also to the physically and otherwise handicapped, and to "those who are unresponsive or hostile to the prevailing process." [12]

Fantini doubted the lasting value of such "compensatory education" programs as Head Start, calling them "strengthened doses of prescriptions that have been ineffective before—more trips, more remedial reading, etc.—without real difference in kind." Similarly, the "model school" experiments in Washington, Philadelphia, and elsewhere were imprisoned by the "bureaucratic rigidity" of the systems of which they were a part; "the mother system is frequently unwilling to give her precocious, adventurous children much latitude."

What, then, was the solution? Total system reform, and one led not solely by "professionals . . . who have shifted their struggle from the front lines to universities or the authors' desks" but also by parents and the community at large. Only this mass group would give reform the "powerful energy source" essential to success.

In sum, Fantini proposed doing for the schools what Eugene McCarthy and other practitioners of the New Politics proposed doing for the political system—giving the people a share of the action.

And here the Ford Foundation came into direct conflict with the system. Structurally, New York schools, and schools elsewhere, are designed to keep parents and the community at a respectful distance. A parent who wants to know more about what happens in Johnny's school is deterred by what Fantini calls "the inertial mass of the system or by the aura of professional exclusivity." Schools limit parent visiting days to two or three times annually; PTA meetings are polite teas at which probing questions seem rudely inappropriate. Teacher selection, curricula, and performance data are all inside matters and no concern of the parents.

The Council of Supervisory Associations, which Bundy and Fantini tried to interest in decentralization, is composed of school officials of the rank of assistant principal or higher; it runs New York schools on a day-to-day basis, and its power, in the realistic sense, is greater than that of the elected board.

After some initial staff-level contacts Bundy began meeting CSA officers and rank-and-file. One Ford officer describes Bundy's experiences:

> Mac had the notion that, as a former educator and administrator, he could talk man-to-man with the supervisors. We thought they would have the best interests of the system at heart and come up with some constructive suggestions. At one of the first meetings he made some opening remarks, and then asked for ideas he could recommend to the school board to improve community relations. These supervisors thought a long time, and finally one of them said, "more vocational training."
>
> This jolted Mac, but he kept trying. "O.K.," he said, "we're not getting anywhere at this level of the bureaucracy, so let's go to a deeper layer." At the next meeting the talk got around to specifics of community control, and after considerable give-and-take one of the women administrators declared she wouldn't accept community control under any circumstances.
>
> Bundy turned white when he heard this. I think he finally realized the supervisors weren't serious, that the system would not reform itself, and that some outside impetus was needed. Bundy crossed a personal Rubicon that night.

In the spring of 1967, at Ford's urging, the Board of Education announced a "policy on decentralization" in which it proposed to set up "demonstration projects" in certain districts "for increasing parental and community involvement . . . [to] strengthen our educational program." Ford had a role in choosing the three pilot projects at which decentralization would be tested: IS 201; the Ocean Hill-Brownsville school district, where the vast Brooklyn slums of Bedford-Stuyvesant and Brownsville merge; and Two Bridges, on the Lower East Side of Manhattan. Finally, Ford furnished the money with which community groups planned the experiments: $51,000 to the Community Association of the East Harlem Triangle, for the IS 201 area; $44,000 to Our Lady of the Presentation Church, for Ocean Hill-Brownsville; and $40,000 to the Two Bridges Neighborhood Council.

Using the Ford money, and following procedures approved by the Board, Ocean Hill residents in the summer of 1967 elected a local governing board for their schools. In turn, the local board elected Rhody McCoy, a veteran black teacher, to the position of district superintendent, rejecting the candidacy of a white principal who had the tacit support of the Board of Education. In selecting principals for Ocean Hill's eight schools, the local board ignored civil service lists and the established "seniority principles" so dear to the school bureaucracy. During the ensuing year, the following happened, roughly in this order: (1) the United Federation of Teachers called a city-wide strike, ostensibly to protest pupil-teacher ratios, actually to object to supposed threats to "job security" posed by community control; (2) Ocean Hill community representatives charged the school board and UFT with undermining the decentralization experiment; (3) faced with court challenges to legality of the Ocean Hill board, Ford temporarily stopped payments, converting it into little more than a debating society; (4) McCoy ordered nineteen teachers and supervisors transferred from Ocean Hill, charging them with "sabotage" of the demonstration project; (5) the UFT began the 1968 school year with another systemwide strike, focused on the job security of the nineteen ousted persons. During the resultant acrimony, as Michael Harrington said, "no decent person on either side could be happy." [13]

The dispute quickly took on serious racial connotations: black militants infused student programs not only with

black nationalism and African history, but with more so-
bering stuff. A play written by the poet LeRoi Jones had a
student chanting these lines;

> Who murdered the black man?
> Whitey! Whitey!
> Who should we lynch?
> Whitey! Whitey!

A mimeographed flyer distributed in Ocean Hill-
Brownsville schools read, in part:

> One thing we learned and we learned it from you
> And it's screw the next man before he can screw
> you.
> So here Judas pimps we'll give you a clue
> Shape up or ship out before this "fall"
> Or all you mothers against the wall.[14]

Jewish and other white teachers who defied the UFT
strike and continued working at the demonstration schools
suffered abuse of another sort. One of them has written: "I
have been called everything from 'scab' to 'Commie bastard' to 'nigger-lover lout.' " [15] The UFT president, Albert
Shanker, ironically, was a major circulator of the anti-
Semitic trash produced by the black extremists, declaring at
one community meeting: "If community control, as we see
it at Ocean Hill-Brownsville, wins, there will be 'Jew Bastard' signs and swastikas in all the schools." The president
of the Jewish Teachers Association demanded that the Ford
Foundation withdraw support from Ocean Hill-Brownsville: "I, and those to whom I have spoken, are beginning to
have doubts about the anti-Semitic influence in the Ford
Foundation and/or some of its officers and/or directors in
their persistence in allocating funds to the Ocean Hill-

Brownsville demonstration project which we have charged with anti-Semitic prejudices in its dealings with the educational personnel."

After all the turmoil, there was only partial success.

The New York legislature, bowing to a peculiar alliance of conservatives who opposed community rule for ill-disguised racial reasons and of teacher unionists who opposed it because they feared loss of job security, ordered disbanding of the three experimental community-run school districts. The legislature did write a decentralization program, but one which was tailored by the UFT. Although the city was split into thirty-three supposedly "autonomous" districts, the central Board of Education retained the right to hire, assign, and negotiate contracts with teachers and other personnel—the key issue of the confrontation. The Board also kept the power to control district budgets and to overrule, suspend, or oust any local board or member. The only powers given the local boards were hiring the local superintendent and setting his salary, contracting for repairs and maintenance for up to $250,000 a year, and picking textbooks from an approved list.

What did Ford accomplish by participating in the decentralization controversy? Did the experience gained outweigh the many political black eyes suffered by the Foundation (and by Bundy personally)? Did Ford overstep itself as an extragovernmental force in what was in essence a public-policy decision over who was to control New York public schools?

Ford officers, although they may differ over the wisdom of details of the way the decentralization experiment was conducted, are of a single mind on the central issue: the time is past when a serious foundation can nibble around the edge of big city problems; a foundation must confront directly the problems of racism in housing, in schools, in jobs, lest it lose contact with the constituency it is attempting to help. For this reason, one of these men puts it, there was some optimism at Ford:

> Decentralization is the greatest thing that ever happened to Ford. To use a battlefield analogy, we bloodied ourselves by going against the toughest problem in the toughest city in the country. This is not the sort of thing you can expect to win— all you can do is attract the attention of the people who will join your team, and give them something to rally around. We sorted out New York and made people choose sides. If you believe that the mass of people here aren't racists—which is all you can believe, if you want to keep any sort of faith at all— that's a good thing. Sure, the teachers are down on decentralization now. But who would have thought the legislature would have passed as liberal a decentralization plan as it did? After all, permitting the community to select its own superintendent is one heck of a gain.

Bundy has stated strongly that he has no compunctions against using the Foundation as an independent extra-governmental force, as he did during the Ocean Hill-Brownsville dispute. "It makes no sense, in the last third of the twentieth century, to suppose an arbitrary division between what is done publicly and what is done privately," he said in a speech in May, 1967. "One of the obligations of the private organization is, in fact, to concern itself with the relationship between the problem it is attacking and *that part of the problem which, of honest assessment, it believes is a part of the responsibility of political institutions and political forces.*" [16]

Once one sorts out the responsibilities, however, the question remains of how far the private organization should go in correcting what it considers to be defects of "political institutions and political forces." It well may "make no sense" to suppose a division between the private sector and government. But section 501c3 of the Internal Revenue Code, in defining organizations eligible for tax-exemption, lists groups "no substantial part of the activities of which is carrying on propaganda, or otherwise attempting to influence legislation, and which does not participate in, or intervene in (including the publishing or distributing of statements), any political campaign on behalf of any candidate for public office." And the Supreme Court has ruled: ". . . Since purchased publicity can influence the fate of legislation which will affect, directly or indirectly, all in the community, everyone in the community should stand on the same footing as regards its purchase so far as the Treasury of the United States is concerned." [17]

DURING THE WINTER AND SPRING OF 1967, urban America feared the coming "long hot summer," that overworked euphemism for black rioting. One predicted flash spot was Cleveland, a city which in 1966 had suffered bloody strife which killed four persons, injured more than fifty others, and damaged millions of dollars of property.

The Cleveland tension was racial. While Cleveland's population had declined by more than 100,000 persons between 1960 and 1965, the proportion of blacks had increased from 16.1 to 34.4 percent. The Justice Department's Community Relations Service and the U.S. Civil Rights Commission, in their soundings of community attitudes, reported that blacks felt increasingly helpless in a city where urban renewal had failed and where unemployment was high; that they were further disillusioned because the city had lost access to federal funds because of fiscal incompetence at city hall. The Cleveland branch of the National Association of Social Workers, whose members worked daily in the Hough ghetto, warned as summer approached: "Unless and until the problems of racial discrimination and poverty are effectively dealt with, none of us is safe."

That was the situation in early July, 1967, when Ford directors met to consider, among other items of business, a grant to the Cleveland chapter of the Congress of Racial Equality (CORE). Ford's National Affairs Division sketched a brief picture of the tension in Cleveland and also gave some background on CORE, much of it disturbing. For a year national CORE officer Floyd McKissick had been prominent in the Black Power movement. McKissick considered civil rights "dead." He advocated black nationalism and separatism; he scorned cooperation with whites and with long-established black groups like the Urban League and the NAACP. He had termed CORE "an effective revolutionary movement." CORE had no effective central organization and, with McKissick outspokenly hostile to whites, big portions of CORE's financial support was melting away.

However, several large chapters operated more or less independently of McKissick. In Baltimore, CORE claimed success with a broad project supported by moderate blacks and white businessmen: it sponsored college scholarships, a nonprofit low-cost housing project, a voter registration and education campaign, a school dropout and job training program. In Cleveland CORE boasted a leadership nucleus of a dozen or so young black males described as having "a sense of balance, more interested in effective programs than in radical posturing." These Cleveland blacks wanted Ford

Foundation help in starting a program similar to those in Baltimore.

Ford's directors talked about CORE for more than two hours, and their chief concern, according to men who were present, was whether Ford should risk public identification with a group whose national leaders advocated a reverse racism, anathema to the equality programs the Foundation had supported, by word and dollar, for years. Would the Cleveland blacks dissociate themselves from McKissick? one director asked. Couldn't the National Affairs Division find another competent group to run the program? asked another. Is this really the sort of thing a foundation should do? said yet another. Look at what happened to Sargent Shriver and the poverty program, and all the money that· was wasted in the ghettos. There are long-established lines of communication to the black community and leaders of national stature. Shouldn't we stick with our friends and not support upstarts who want to wreck half a century of work toward racial harmony?

After an hour the board seemed far from any consensus. Seldom do Ford directors overturn a staff recommendation; yet CORE clearly was a potentially dangerous partner. Cleveland CORE's independence notwithstanding, the directors had to decide whether this was the sort of organization with which the Establishment members of the Ford board wished to form a partnership. In the board room that day were such men as Julius A. Stratton; Eugene R. Black, the banker, financier, and presidential confidant; John H. Loudon, board chairman of Royal Dutch Petroleum Company; and Bethuel M. Webster, partner in a Wall Street law firm. These were not men inclined to spend Ford money on any organization which intended to destroy society.

Then came the commanding opinion of Henry Ford II,
the man who frequently remained silent during such de-
bates until a consensus was struck—the man who listened,
and learned, and weighed arguments until some balance
tipped inside his head. Henry Ford II, to be true, was but
one director of fifteen, and, in the strictest sense, his voice in
the Ford board room was no more authoritative than any
other. In fact, he and his brother Benson are at times almost
embarrassingly gracious in avoiding any semblance of
"bossing" the Foundation. But Henry Ford II does speak for
several hundred millions of dollars of personal wealth, and
the Foundation was formed with his father's money, and the
Foundation does carry his family name. And regardless of
the legal distinction between the Ford family, Foundation,
and motor company, in the public mind they are almost
synonymous.

So all it took, really, was one sentence from Henry Ford
II: "If you're going to work in civil rights, you can't stop at
Roy Wilkins and Whitney Young."

That was it. The directors—some of them with
"fingers crossed," as they said later—approved granting
$175,000 to CORE for a scaled-down version of the Balti-
more program: training of youth and community workers,
voter registration, and planning for economic development.
The voter registration plan, peculiarly, received little attention from the directors, since the professional staff said it
paralleled similar, noncontroversial work done in the South
for almost a decade by the Ford-supported Southern Regional Council. The staff said voter registration was "within
the legitimate scope of foundation interest" because it enabled ethnic groups to accelerate their own development
through participation in the political process.

During the next several weeks Ford and CORE staff members worked together on contract details, saying nothing publicly of the pending grant. Then word began seeping around Cleveland and reached a regional correspondent of the *New York Times,* who asked the Ford office for confirmation. He was persuaded to delay his story until July 14, when a formal announcement was made:

> Three grants aimed at improving race relations and opportunities for minority groups in the city of Cleveland were announced today by the Ford Foundation.
> The grants were:
> — $127,500 to the Greater Cleveland Associated Foundation for the Businessmen's Interracial Committee on Community Affairs for job-training assistance, fact-gathering and analysis, and small grants to neighborhood groups;
> — $175,000 to the Special Purposes Fund of the Congress of Racial Equality (CORE) for training of Cleveland youth and adult community workers, voter registration efforts, exploration of economic-development programs, and attempts to improve program planning among civil rights groups;
> — $200,000 to the National Conference for Interracial Justice and the American Council for Nationalities for joint education efforts to improve understanding between Negroes and white ethnic groups.

The four-page press release went into unusual detail on the purposes of the grants, and the *Cleveland Press* and *Cleveland Plain Dealer* reporters assigned to the story came all the way to New York to discuss them with Bundy and John R. Coleman, the program officer. Bundy took great pains to stress in his statement that the grants did not imply Foundation endorsement of Black Power and other controversial CORE ideas:

> In this case, as in many others, we are supporting one part of the work of an organization that has other activities on

which we as a foundation make no judgment. We believe that Cleveland members of CORE will do good work in a cause which we seek to support. Our trustees have reviewed this proposed action with particular care, and they have instructed us to make our decision on the merits, and not on the question whether other actions or statements from other members of CORE are "too controversial." This policy is one which we have followed over the years with other bodies— universities, state governments, cities, and voluntary associations of all sorts. The national officers of CORE have dealt with us on this matter in a businesslike way, and neither Mr. Floyd McKissick nor I supposes that this grant requires the two of us—or our organizations—to agree on all public questions.

The CORE grant was at once the bravest and the most naïve action ever taken by a major foundation.

Ford was brave, in that it put the Ford Foundation's $3,000,000,000 ringingly behind Bundy's declaration that "full equality for all American Negroes is now the most urgent domestic concern of this country." It also fulfilled his pledge to act outside the "familiar listing of jobs and education and housing." [18]

No foundation was obligated in any way to follow Ford's example and spend its money on community-action programs. But the example had been set, and by men with impeccable financial, social, and academic credentials. There has long been an adage in foundation philanthropy: "When Ford takes a project, that's the Good Housekeeping Seal of Approval, and we know we're safe if we spend our money there."

Ford was naïve, because in its haste to do the right thing, it made several rather fundamental errors that could have been predicted. Indeed, the most lasting result of the CORE grant is that similar projects will never again be conducted by tax-exempt foundations. Ford's major error was that its voter-registration project was approved exactly one month after Ohio state representative Carl Stokes, a black, had announced his candidacy for the mayoralty. Two years earlier, Stokes had come within 2,143 votes of being elected mayor. Using the Ford funds, CORE registrars concentrated their efforts in the Hough and Glenville ghettos, almost solidly black, working alongside volunteers from the Southern Christian Leadership Conference, the Urban League, and other civil-rights groups. The *Cleveland Plain Dealer* reported on August 23, the last day for registrations, that both the civil-rights people and Democratic registrars "insist they are conducting citywide voter drives." But, the paper added, the efforts "are certain to benefit Stokes."

And they did. Some 25,000 new voters were added to Cleveland rolls. Although registration forms are not counted by race, some sixty-five to seventy percent of 17,000 new voters registered at one downtown office were said to have been black.[19] On October 3, Stokes defeated incumbent Mayor Ralph Lochner, a fifty-one-year-old, Rumanian-born lawyer, in the Democratic primary by an 8.7 percent margin; 96.7 percent of the vote in predominantly black wards went to Stokes. In the general election on November 7, Stokes edged past Republican Seth C. Taft, grandson of President William Howard Taft, by 2,350 votes of 257,207.

Bundy now argues, fervently and sincerely, that Ford was doing nothing more than giving Cleveland blacks an opportunity to avail themselves of the Civil Rights Act of 1965, and that political activity via the ballot box is vital "because of the alternatives that may otherwise develop in time of trouble"—that is, rioting.[20] According to Bundy,

Ford officers asked themselves whether the fact a black man was running should keep the Foundation "from doing something we would otherwise have done." Voter registration is a revered American institution, Bundy notes: "Motherhood, boy scouts, voter registration, everyone's for it, as an alternative to rocks and fire bombs. And it turned out that way in Cleveland." [21]

That is the emotional Bundy speaking. The legalistic Bundy also had an answer:

> We operate on the premise that the Internal Revenue Service has the responsibility for determining whether a grant-receiving organization is exempt under section 501c3 of the tax code. But this doesn't absolve us from responsibility: we monitor, and we evaluate, what the recipient organization is doing. But the policing function for obedience to the law does not belong to us, it belongs to the Internal Revenue Service. We can't possibly make a judgment on each of the hundreds of organizations with which we deal as to whether they are engaging in prohibited political activity—talk about having a bureaucracy now, why we'd have a bureaucracy here like no one could imagine. If we went around the country investigating all those organizations, we would *really* be a hidden government, and more powerful than a foundation has a right to be. Anyway, CORE kept out of the 1967 Cleveland election; our monitors saw to that. In one respect you could even call the grant a handicap for Stokes, because CORE had worked hard for him in 1965.[22]

Bundy's statement is incomplete. CORE was not simply one of the "hundreds of organizations" with which Ford deals; it was something special, and it was so recognized by the extraordinary attention the staff gave the grant application. And there is yet another flaw in Bundy's rationale, one which one of his own staff members now says was "so obvious that there should be a mass examining of heads around here, including my own, for missing it": Restriction of a voter registration drive to a black area during a campaign in which a black candidate depends on black votes is inescapably "political," regardless of what the sponsors call it. "What we should have done," this staff member says, "is to have covered the entire map, to have found groups to run registration campaigns all over Cleveland and not just in Hough/Glenville. I'd have done it by the map—block out the areas of underregistration, and go after the whole thing, regardless of who lives there, blacks or Slovaks or Wasps. This way, we couldn't be accused of running a 'black' voter registration drive, but an 'unregistered' voter drive." [23]

By Bundy's account, Ford is absolved of the charge that it "supported" Stokes because Stokes' candidacy was not declared (although it had been rumored) when talks on the CORE grant began in February, 1967. Furthermore, Bundy states, the possibility of Stokes' candidacy was not a factor in Ford's decision: "We have never examined the question of the relations between any voter registration campaign and the election of any candidate, and I think it would be improper for us to do so." [24]

Yet the political implications were recognized by Ford staff members, to the extent that they originally saw the grants as a means whereby Cleveland's anti-Lochner forces, as well as CORE, could "confront" the incumbent administration. (This premise was later discarded.) During the planning the project officer, John Coleman, met a reluctant Lochner to discuss the grant (Lochner wouldn't see Coleman in his office; he insisted on neutral territory, and brought along an aide as a witness). Lochner welcomed the "constructive" features of the grant—that is, the ethnic group projects—but was cool toward voter registration, an attitude which Coleman attributed to "political expediency," in a report to the Foundation.

Another Ford error lies in the manner with which it unveiled the grants. The simultaneous grants to the other Cleveland organizations (the Businessmen's Interracial Committee and the nationalities group) were public-relations afterthoughts, added "to create padding around the CORE grant," as a Ford officer has stated. The businessmen's grant was simply an expansion and continuation of an existing Ford program. The nationalities project had been submitted earlier by another group and rejected by Ford at a low staff level. When Ford decided to proceed with CORE, an officer recollects, "we suddenly realized that this was about to backfire on both the Foundation and on CORE, that the tightly-organized, highly-political European ethnic groups in Cleveland would dump all sorts of abuse on us for giving the blacks preferential treatment."

The nationalities group application was hastily pulled from the files, reworked, and approved—to the surprise of the Cleveland organization, which first learned from reporters that Ford had $200,000 if someone would come for it.

Ford officers now say there were "legitimate grounds" for the non-CORE grants; but they concede they would *not* have been made in July, 1967, if at all, had not the Foundation wanted attractive wrapping for the CORE money. It is no overstatement to say that Ford gave $200,000 to the nationalities group and $127,500 to the businessmen's group in the hope—and the realized expectation—that they and the persons they represented would remain silent and not protest the $175,000 that CORE received.

The backlash from the CORE grant was predictable, and it did not come solely from racists and archconservatives angered by the election of the first big-city Negro mayor in United States history. The *Boston Globe* asked: "If one foundation can help elect a good mayor, why cannot another elect a bad one?" The real question, to the *Globe,* was "how and by whom the foundations, now virtually independent governments within a government, are to be controlled." Or, as Daniel Patrick Moynihan has asked, "How much public money would American liberals be willing to see President [George C.] Wallace expend for the purpose of increasing the participation in public affairs of those elements in the population he regards as simultaneously deprived and underorganized? . . . [this] is an obvious point and need not be pressed, save to note that what is involved, in a word, is integrity. And common sense." [25]

Representative Wright Patman asked: "Are the giant foundations on the road to becoming political machines? . . . Does the Ford Foundation have a grandiose design to bring vast political, economic and social changes to the nation in the 1970's?" Pointing an alarmed finger at the assets of Ford and the Rockefeller Foundation, Patman told the House Ways and Means Committee: "I need not tell you gentlemen what can happen in a local, state or national election where this kind of money is turned loose, directly or indirectly, in behalf of their favorite candidates." [26]

A PECULIAR CAMPAIGN soon after Ford's Cleveland experience showed the dangers of putting foundation projects into juxtaposition with politics. Frederick W. Richmond, a wealthy Manhattan businessman and industrialist, also controls a foundation which bears his name, and which was formed in 1962. In November, 1967 the Frederick W. Richmond Foundation suddenly discovered the Williams-

burg area of Brooklyn—an ethnic melting pot with many
Jewish, Italian, Puerto Rican, Polish, Irish, and Negro families. Williamsburg is also the Fourteenth Congressional
District. The start of the spending coincided with the start
of Richmond's campaign against Representative John
Rooney in the Democratic primary. Here are some of the
things philanthropist Richmond did, through his foundation, while candidate Richmond was campaigning.

— It announced a $20,000 "scholarship grant" to the
Yeshiva of Satimar-United Talmudical Academy, payable in monthly stipends of $1,000 or $500, each of which
was publicized by the academy. A flier distributed by
Richmond's campaign staff showed him talking with the
rabbi and stated that he "once considered becoming a
rabbi himself."

— It gave $5,000 to the Sacred Heart Day Care Child
Center, popular among Italian-American mothers in
Williamsburg. A publicity handout showed him with
the pastor.

— It set up a series of "neighborhood study clubs" and
spent $43,000 on them. (Other Democratic politicians
in Williamsburg called them "nothing more than Richmond's version of the old neighborhood ward clubs." [27])

— It contributed $500 to the Puerto Rican Trade Com-
mittee, $50 to the Hispanic Society of the Fire Depart-
ment, $50 to the Zion Baptist Church, and $2,700 to the
Urban League.

According to the Foundation's tax returns, some of
the funds it received during this period were gifts from companies controlled by or friendly to Richmond. For example,
during the fiscal years 1967 and 1968 the Foundation received $113,500 from the Walco American Corporation, a
holding company controlled by Richmond. On May 3,

1968—six weeks before the primary election—the Foundation received $1,000 from the National Valve and Manufacturing Company of Pittsburgh, of which Richmond is a director. And Thomas G. Wyman, identified as a Richmond fund-raiser, gave $3,500 to the Foundation in February, 1968, during the political campaign.

Congressman Rooney angrily called these contributions "a bonanza of the type that one seldom encounters in business. The corporation is not only allowed to take a deduction on its tax return for a 'charitable contribution' but it is also permitted to undercut one of the most sensitive laws in campaign politics—the Corrupt Practices Act which prohibits political contributions by corporations."

Called before the Ways and Means Committee in 1969, Richmond denied any wrongdoing. He said the gifts began because "as I walked the district I saw poverty all around me and the Foundation made a number of gifts to try and help out." [28] He added: "I feel strongly that the law should not require me to give up a tax deduction for charitable contributions simply because I want to run for Congress. The law should not require that the beneficiaries of my charitable activities and those of the Foundation should suffer because of my personal and entirely separate political ambitions."

Richmond did admit, under questioning: "There is no question that my political organization did get as much public relations benefit out of those grants as they possibly could, but the grants were made solely and separately from any political activities I happen to have had."

FOR FORD, 1967 AND 1968 WERE TRAUMATIC YEARS. "For years the academicians and the liberals and the so-called good people had stood off in the corner and sniped at Ford for being a do-nothing organization," one of its officers told me. "We were .the fat cats, the aloof ones, the lazy money bags, the ivory tower philanthropists. Oh, I could argue against a lot of that crap, but why bother? What *does* bother me is that when we did start doing things, and were criticized for getting into controversial areas, these so-called activists had found something else to carp about. Now we weren't lazy, we were arrogant sons-of-bitches who were tearing up the world. We were responsible to no one, we were too powerful for our own good, or that of anyone else. After two years of this sort of bitching—and from the so-called best people—I think our directors would have been justified in shucking the whole damned thing and turning our income over to the New York Public Library or the Bronx Zoo. Oh, they would have howled again, but so what? I don't think they have a voice any more—they forfeited it, through cowardice, during the decentralization thing particularly."

But Ford didn't "shuck the whole damned thing." Instead it reached deeper into the hungry underbelly of America for new clients who had not shared the affluence of the 1960s. Each time it did so, Ford only found troubles— and more territorial barriers which were impolitic for foundations (or any other "outside interest") to cross.

One such venture was with the 4,500,000 Mexican-Americans of the Southwest. Poor, jobless, and uneducated, and, like the blacks, increasingly urbanized, their *barrios* were the Latin equivalent of the Negro ghetto. But the *chicanos* are politically weak; their communities are divided, argumentative, and lacking any overall sense of purpose. Although 1,500,000 Mexican-Americans live in California, for example, not one is in the legislature. A UCLA study project which Ford funded before deciding to enter *chicano* affairs concluded:

> New generations demand new solutions. The leadership is now aging and there is acute need for persons who understand and can work within the Anglo governmental structure. Because of their cultural isolation, the Mexican-American leaders have only elementary notions of the techniques of national pressure. There are no full-time lobbyists or public relations experts, no newspapers or magazines of any consequence and of potential influence as opinion molders. Little communication exists between the major centers of Mexican-American population. . . . The Negro protest movement is enormously sophisticated by comparison.

Soon after Bundy took office, three Mexican-American consultants recommended starting a national Latin organization modeled after the NAACP or Urban League, to coordinate regional groups and to work toward national goals. This led to the creation of the Southwest Council of La Raza (literally, "the race," but in a broad nationalistic sense). La Raza, in turn, was commissioned to fund and direct local boards, drawn heavily from existing organizations, in Los Angeles, San Antonio, and the San Francisco bay area. The aims were the full panoply of community action projects: leadership development, voter education and registration, guidance on obtaining federal funds for model cities, and neighborhood-improvement programs. In 1968 Ford granted $290,000 to La Raza and $340,000 to three local boards.

Inevitably, more problems arose for Ford. The San Antonio board, while broad-based (with three Anglos), included a county commissioner, Albert Pena, and a Texas state senator, Joe Bernal, both political foes of U.S. Representative Henry B. Gonzalez, the idol of Texas liberals early in his career, when he was the outsider, flailing at reactionary dragons. Once inside the system, Gonzalez seemed to enjoy it. To Gonzalez, the advanced New Dealism of his good friend Lyndon Johnson was more comfortable and practical, politically and personally, than militancy. Texans came to admire Gonzalez more for what he had been than for what he was. "Henry went to the [LBJ] ranch too often," an observer said of him. Gonzalez underestimated how much his constituency was stirring, and with what unprecedented urgency, at the same time that he was opting for Johnsonian gradualism.

"The old ways of boss rule, discrimination, disrespect and apathy are out now for an influential minority among Texas *chicanos*," wrote the radical Texas editor Greg Olds. "There is a war of sorts on now, a war of liberation being fought against whoever stands in the way, be they school board member, city councilman, county commissioner, school principal, or employer. Those enlisted in the fight are determined and not easily discouraged; they are ready for protracted struggle." [29]

In the vanguard of the struggle was the Mexican-American Youth Organization, or MAYO, created with Ford money. MAYO went to the dusty Texas border country, where *chicanos* work under peonage conditions, and supported striking farm workers and boycotts of discriminatory schools. When right-wing Texas officials ordered VISTA volunteers out of border towns, MAYO arranged rallies at which youths shouted "brown power" and *"viva la raza"* and waved clenched-fist salutes at photographers. In San Antonio, MAYO organized a Universidad de los Barrios—a university of the slums—with Ford money. Calling this institution a "university" was hyperbolic; it offered classes but served chiefly as a youth center—and was popular.

Not so with MAYO itself. Mexican-American politicians, businessmen, lawyers, physicians, and merchants who had "made it" under the system saw the militants as firebrands who would jeopardize the gradualistic progress being made in Texas. But County Commissioner Albert Pena sympathized with MAYO, and he protested to state officials when its leaders were harassed while attempting a protest march in Del Rio. Albert Pena was also one of the anti-Gonzalez politicians on the board of the Ford-funded San Antonio adjunct of La Raza.

Another Ford-funded group, the Mexican-American Legal Defense Fund (MALD), usurped many of the protective functions Gonzalez had served as *patrón* of San Antonio's Mexican community. MALD, created in May, 1968, with an eight-year, $2,200,000 grant, gave *chicanos* the access to lawyers blacks had learned to expect from OEO and Community Legal Services. Old-line Mexican-American politicians had not discovered that federal courts are a more effective route to civil rights than appeals to the dubious good natures of local racist politicians. Now, in one suit, MALD challenged state school fund distribution that saw San Antonio slums receive $246 per pupil per year and wealthy Houston suburbs $1,149. In another case, MALD challenged the exclusion of Mexican-Americans from grand juries and draft boards. Swimming pool segregation, police brutality, job discrimination at air bases, even segregation at the Dallas County jail and in west Texas barbershops—all came under MALD attack.

Gonzalez waited, and finally found a target for counterattack in a young brown-power advocate, Jose Angel Gutierrez, a salaried employee of MALD at the Universidad de los Barrios. At a San Antonio press conference in April, 1969, Gutierrez charged that the "vicious cultural genocide being inflicted upon La Raza [the Mexican race, not the organization] by gringos and their institutions not only severely damage our human dignity but also make it impossible for La Raza to develop its right of self-determination." He denounced assimilation and said MAYO wanted only to survive "as a free and complete family of *Mexicanos*." Then he declared:

> We realize that the effects of cultural genocide takes many forms—some *Mexicanos* will become psychologically castrated, others will become demagogues and gringos as well, and others will come together, resist and eliminate the gringo. We will be with the latter.

Gutierrez defined a gringo as a "person or an institution that has a certain policy or program or attitude that reflects bigotry, racism, discord and prejudice and violence." Asked if he considered Gonzalez a gringo, Gutierrez replied: "He has demonstrated some tendencies that fit in that category."

Gonzalez, in turn, denounced Gutierrez for "race hatred" and the Ford Foundation for supporting groups with leadership "that is clearly irresponsible." Gonzalez declared:

> . . . rather than fostering brotherhood, the foundation has supported the spewings of hate, and rather than creating a new political unity, it has destroyed what little there was; and rather than creating new leadership, it is simply financing the ambitions of some men who are greedy and some who are ruthless and a few who are plainly irresponsible. . . . It saddens me that a foundation dedicated to constructive action has let its resources be used for action that is destructive and counterproductive. I hope that racists are not the new leaders that the foundation hopes to see created; I hope that little men are not permitted the luxury of using money intended for very large purposes . . .

Gonzalez also charged (inaccurately, as it turned out) that two murders were committed at the Universidad de los Barrios, and in one speech he even insinuated there was a link between the Ford project and Cuba: "Some of them [brown-power advocates] openly say that their symbol is Che Guevara and Castro . . . they blame the establishment for everything that is wrong. However, there is method in their madness. *None of this was done in this fashion until the Ford Foundation money came into their hands. Some money even indirectly came from Castro himself . . .*" * Conservative border Congressmen Abraham Kazen and Eligio de la Garza echoed Gonzalez, Kazen saying, "He has been a true leader of his people and I commend him for the position which he has taken against violence and for law and order." [30]

Gonzalez's demagogic tone caused more disgust than alarm at Ford. Staff officers had concluded—as had Sargent Shriver of the Office of Economic Opportunity earlier—that sometimes slum youths are not as level-headed and rational as Eagle Scouts. One officer said: "If these people didn't have a slight burn on in the first place, they wouldn't be neighborhood chiefs. You've got to have the patience, and the skill, to channel this rage, and you've got to be able to take a deep breath and ignore the bluster. Hell, you hear more inflammatory remarks on the floor of Congress on any given day that you do among militants—it's a matter of definition. I get madder listening to Mendel Rivers yap about some bomber than Rivers does listening to Rap Brown talk about Strom Thurmond."

But Gonzalez had Ford at a tactical disadvantage. He was on the House Banking and Currency Committee,

---

* A State Department intelligence expert in Cuban affairs, queried about this charge, said he had seen no evidence Castro supplied funds to the south Texas brown-power movement.

whose chairman was Representative Wright Patman, ever
ready to embarrass Ford. In addition, three persons prominent in MAYO ran for the San Antonio city council, and
there was circumstantial evidence that, although they lost
the election, a MAYO voter registration drive, financed by
Ford, was of benefit to their campaigns. Mitchell Svirdoff,
head of Ford's Division of National Affairs, tried to placate
Gonzalez, promising to tighten controls over MAYO spending. But Gonzalez was adamant: he wanted Ford to drop
MAYO, and he threatened to seek revocation of Ford's tax-
exempt status if it did not do so. Ford yielded in June, 1969,
refusing further funding to MAYO on the stated grounds of
"political involvement." But it stood firm on funding of the
Southwest Council of La Raza and the Mexican-American
Unity Council, the major grant recipient in San Antonio.

Not all persons at Ford were happy with the decision.
"Gonzalez had just enough facts on his side to make his case
palatable," stated one officer. "The temper of the times
being what they were, it wasn't politic to brawl with him or
Internal Revenue Service. The important thing is that he
damned well didn't run us out of San Antonio and south
Texas as he wanted to do." Svirdoff says simply: "Gonzalez
had some legitimate complaints, and some that weren't so
valid. But MAYO was sufficiently involved in politics that
we didn't think it wise that it receive further Ford Foundation funds." [31]

To Congress, however, the Mexican-American grants
were further violations of Congress's territorial rights.
"Brown power" and "black power" are perjorative fright-
words, and, in the shorthand mentality of American politics, Congress never attempted to go behind the slogans and
understand Ford's goals in Ocean Hill-Brownsville, south
Texas, or elsewhere. That these projects existed was reason

enough for Congress to consider itself in an undeclared state of war with the Ford Foundation, and Congress is an institution peculiarly equipped to fight a war of attrition. From its privileged position, Congress must but sit and wait, confident that any opponent as large and active as Ford eventually will stumble and be vulnerable to a swift rabbit punch.

FORD'S STUMBLE WAS AN ADMITTED ERROR of judgment by Bundy in making travel-study grants totaling $131,069 to eight aides of the slain Senator Robert F. Kennedy. Ford had made some two thousand previous such awards, the criteria being, according to Bundy, "whether the professional interest and concerns of individuals are interests and concerns which we are trying to advance under the guidelines and programs approved by our trustees." He also referred to the aides as men "who had been uniquely stricken in a moment of terrible tragedy." The aides, their subjects, and the amounts of their grants were as follows[32]:

— Jerry Bruno, $19,450 for a seven-month study "of the methods and styles of national political campaigning in the United States."

— Joseph Dolan, $18,556 for a six-month study "of the teaching methods, text materials and other writings used in university and law school courses which deal with the lawyer's role in the legislative process."

— Peter Edelman, $19,090 for a five-month study of "community development and social programs in various countries, with special emphasis on the degree to which the participation of individual citizens is encouraged in planning and policy making and to which the processes of government have been successfully decentralized." His itinerary included travel to Scandinavia, Eastern Europe, the Middle East and Africa, India, Singapore, and Japan.

— Dall Forsythe, $6,390 for a four-month study "of the changes that have occurred in participation by citizens in political processes, especially in the nominating processes of the Democratic Party."

— Earl Graves, $19,500 for a six-month study of "opportunities for black citizens to engage in small private enterprise business in the United States."

— Thomas Johnston, $10,190 for a three-month study "of the feasibility of a national and/or international newspaper transmitted through the medium of television," with travel in Europe and Asia.

— Adam Walinsky, $22,200 for a six-month study of "community self-determination, self-control, and self-improvement" based on the studies of community action programs in Watts, Ohio, and the Mississippi Delta.

— Frank Mankiewicz, $15,692.50 for a five-month study of the changes effected by Peace Corps projects in Latin America and the Caribbean.

Congress interpreted the grants as either "severance pay" or sub rosa financing for a shadow Kennedy political machine (a mystifying scheme in view of the fact that a majority of the Ford trustees are Republicans). Senator John J. Williams, the Delaware Republican, introduced a bill prohibiting any foundation payments to persons within two years of the time they left government—aimed squarely at the Kennedy grants.

Senator Albert Gore said petulantly during hearings on the Williams bill:

Mr. McGeorge Bundy directed an award to employees of a former Senator because they were heartbroken at his demise, and I certainly sympathize with their sorrow. But did you consider giving an award, a trip around the world, to any of Senator [Eugene] McCarthy's supporters? They were not only broken-hearted but broken-nosed. They were disappointed and beaten up . . . [there] has been a big anti-Democratic tide sweeping the border states area. Should I seek re-election next year, I will certainly have to swim against the stream, and the current's rather swift. Were I to be defeated, my employees would be very broken-hearted . . ."

In January, 1969, when Dean Rusk left the office of secretary of state, the Rockefeller Foundation gave him a one-year appointment as a "consultant" with undefined duties and responsibilities. Not a whisper of criticism was heard, from Congress or elsewhere.

AT THE BEGINNING OF 1969, other foundations, tentatively, hesitantly, began to follow Ford's example and fund community action projects. Even the ultracautious Rockefeller Foundation, which had restricted its major grants to foreign work—first in public health, next in agriculture—shifted its "equal opportunities program" from an emphasis on experimental projects in higher education to "more direct involvement with the problems of the urban ghetto." [33] Rockefeller funds went to ghetto schools in Los Angeles, Minneapolis, Cleveland, Gary, and Philadelphia; veteran social radical Saul Alinsky received grants for his community-organizer training program in Chicago.

Rockefeller, however, moved cautiously: its school grants were only slightly more than $1,500,000, a fraction of what it spends on population control and agriculture. Its preoccupation with research, rather than direct action, was reflected in $625,000 of grants to the Metropolitan Applied

Research Center in New York so that Dr. Kenneth Clark could study urban ghettos—"their characteristics and causes, and the possible remedies for their ills." One philanthropoid told me: "The last thing that anyone should do is criticize Rockefeller, for they seem to be moving. But they are at the stage Ford was ten years ago—research rather than action."

At Ford's request the Carnegie Corporation in 1967 granted $15,000 "to secure legal and other technical assistance needed" for New York school decentralization. The Rockefeller Brothers Fund, usually bolder than the main Rockefeller Foundation, joined Carnegie to form the New York Urban Coalition in 1968; its goal was involving the private sector in solving urban problems. Smaller foundations followed suit. According to a Foundation Center survey of 1968 grants, one dollar of every five was spent on problems of the cities and the poor.[34] A trend was clearly developing.

But a countertrend was even stronger. The American public, long satisfied with do-nothing Congresses and do-less public officials, could not reconcile itself to activist foundations. The conservative "we've-done-enough-for-the-blacks" sentiment so pronounced in the nation during the 1968 Presidential election was at cross-purposes with Ford and other foundations. The foundations' new visibility propelled them into public consciousness—and under circumstances that aroused their enemies without winning new friends. Bundy's identification with Vietnam made his name anathema on the Left. His identification with Ford's aggressiveness in the cities, the schools and elsewhere, made his name anathema on the Right. Scientists and scholars who no longer received large grants from the foundations decided, in petty selfishness, that it was fashionable to snipe at their erstwhile friends.

The disclosure by *Ramparts Magazine* in 1967 that the Central Intelligence Agency has used foundations as conduits for covert payments to student, labor, and other groups for more than a decade soured American liberals to whom under-the-table financing is an untouchable practice. To the CIA, this method was necessary because the rightist Congresses of the early 1950s would not approve payments to left-wing foreign and domestic groups whose favor the government wished to court. That the CIA had financed what liberals would normally have considered to be the "right people" was irrelevant—to the liberals. That the foundations were willing to act as partners of the CIA meant they were unworthy of trust.

Another enemy of foundation activism was a goodly number of the foundations themselves. Foundation executives who have made careers of faintheartedness saw Ford's troubles as proof of their premise that he who sits silently by the roadside of life might collect dust, but not criticism. During interviews with dozens of foundation officers during the spring and summer of 1969 I heard a recurring question: "What does Ford think of McGeorge Bundy now that he's got them into all that mess? Has Ford changed its mind about getting involved in things that foundations have no business doing?" In most of these men I sensed an ill-concealed gloating: they had found security through stodginess, and they were glad to see Bundy in trouble.*

Bundy's discomfort meant assured continuance of their own good lives: a check to a hospital here, to a college there,

---

* Deliberately malicious, I told one of these comfortable toads that Ford was so pleased with Bundy that his salary was being raised to $150,000. This misinformation ruined his day.

an occasional speech to a foundation conference on the good job that foundation executives are doing; the studied courtesy to the foundation's founding family at the quarterly directors' meeting; the fawning praise they could expect from university presidents and development officers on their annual tours of client campuses.

Thus the storm gathered. Congressman Patman, meanwhile, drummed away at foundation finances, attempting to convince the public that foundation philanthropy was nothing more than sophisticated tax-dodging. In the public mind "foundation" became the connotation for power-mad, leftist agitators who were not only cheating the government of taxes but also supporting the Sinister Forces of Change.

And then Justice Abe Fortas of the United States Supreme Court was revealed to have accepted a check from Louis Wolfson's foundation.

CHAPTER **9**

The Retaliation

IN 1910 INDUSTRIALIST ANDREW CARNEGIE gave $75,000,000 in United States Steel bonds to the Carnegie Corporation, his foundation, with the stipulation that the income be used to pay $25,000 annual pensions to former United States Presidents and their widows. Carnegie wanted to spare future Presidents from dying in lonely penury, as did U. S. Grant. But an angry public accused Carnegie of trying to "curry favor," and he was forced to withdraw his offer. The $75,000,000 remained with the Carnegie Corporation, but the income went to colleges and other noncontroversial institutions.

Two generations later a foundation endowed in honor of and bearing the name of J. Edgar Hoover, director of the

Federal Bureau of Investigation, unhesitatingly accepted
stocks with a book value of more than $800,000—and a
market value twice that amount—from liquor baron Lewis
S. Rosentiel, whose career was marked by conflicts with the
Securities and Exchange Commission, the Federal Trade
Commission, and various state liquor control bodies. One of
Rosentiel's lawyers, Roy M. Cohn, was under constant federal investigation during the period; at the time of the largest single Rosentiel gift, he was awaiting trial on federal
criminal indictments. The J. Edgar Hoover Foundation
spent little of the contributions; what it did disburse went
chiefly to the J. Edgar Hoover Library at Freedoms Foundation, the rightist anti-Communist outfit at Valley Forge,
Pennsylvania.*

But Hoover's effective superior in government was in no
position to complain of any conflict-of-interest: Lyndon B.
Johnson, several times during his Presidency, accepted
foundation support for projects with political overtones.

No less an authority than Eric F. Goldman, a White
House staff member from December, 1963, to September,
1966, states that at the peak of the 1964 campaign Johnson
seized upon an offer by John Gardner, then president of the
Carnegie Corporation, to finance a "national service plan"
whereby young people would be brought into government
for fifteen months of training and service.

Goldman liked the idea, he recollects, because he
thought it "might possibly build greater understanding between President Johnson and the younger age group during
the election and for future years of his Administration." [1]
Youth's reaction to the Johnson campaign previously had
been lukewarm. So Goldman says he persuaded Gardner to

* See Chapter Six.

put a $225,000 initial appropriation before the Carnegie Corporation board at a special meeting. Johnson approved of the plan, and he announced the "White House Fellow" program from Washington on October 3, 1964, a month before Election Day. (Gardner later joined the Johnson Cabinet as Secretary of Health, Education, and Welfare.)

Again, in 1966, the Albert and Mary Lasker Foundation gave the White House press office $3,000 to defray expenses of reporters who accompanied the First Lady on a trip to Big Bend National Park. The grant, listed on the Foundation's tax return under "civic and miscellaneous contributions," paid for press buses and hospitality parties. It helped "maximize" coverage of the trip just prior to the 1966 Congressional elections. The Foundation also helped Mrs. Johnson organize the Society for a More Beautiful Capital and gave it an initial grant of $47,917 in 1966. The society's activities, of course, enhanced Mrs. Johnson's reputation as First Lady.

The foundation dealings with Hoover and the Johnsons were possible because there was no outright ban on a public official accepting money or indirect favors from a tax-exempt organization. The interplay between foundations and government is intense and continuing, on both a policy and a personal basis. National administrations for decades have drawn upon foundations for high-level appointees, including cabinet rank. John Foster Dulles was chairman of the trustees of the Carnegie Endowment for International Peace when President Eisenhower tapped him for the post of secretary of state. Dean Rusk went from the post of Assistant Secretary of State in 1953 to the presidency of the Rockefeller, and he remained there until President Kennedy brought him back into government as Secretary of State. In 1969 Rockefeller gave the retiring Rusk a one-year "transitional grant" which afforded him time to rest and compile his papers. W. Willard Wirtz served simultaneously as Secretary of Labor for Kennedy-Johnson and as a trustee of the Stern Family Fund. Clifford Hardin, a Rockefeller trustee, became President Nixon's Secretary of Agriculture. Arthur F. Burns, counselor to Nixon and then chairman of the Federal Reserve Board, remained a trustee of the 20th Century Fund. C. Douglas Dillon, Kennedy's Secretary of the Treasury, and Robert V. Roosa, a former Treasury Undersecretary, are on the Rockefeller board.

Few lower level officials sever foundation connections when entering government. Here are two examples from a single foundation: Erwin N. Griswold became a trustee of the Walter E. Meyer Research Institute of Law while dean of the Harvard law school and continued serving when he became Solicitor General of the United States; similarly, Eugene Rostow was an institute trustee while a professor at the Yale law school and so remained while Undersecretary of State for Political Affairs.

In the judiciary, Chief Judge Charles E. Wyzanski, Jr., of the U.S. District Court in Boston, has been a Ford Foundation trustee for more than a decade. Warren E. Burger was a trustee of the Mayo Foundation while a judge of the U.S. Circuit Court of Appeals in Washington; he resigned several months after becoming Chief Justice of the United States. Judge Dudley B. Bonsal of the U.S. District Court in New York has been a director of the American Bar Foundation.

Elsewhere on the federal level, Adlai Stevenson served as a director of the Field Foundation while U.S. permanent representative to the United Nations; a colleague on the Field board was Ralph J. Bunche, UN Undersecretary.

In Congress, Senator Edward W. Brooke of Massachusetts is a trustee of the Council on Religion and International Affairs. Mrs. Frances P. Bolton, while a U.S. Representative from Ohio, was president and prime mover of the Accokeek Foundation, which worked vigorously to persuade Congress to acquire and preserve the Maryland shoreline across the Potomac River from Mount Vernon. John P. Saylor, a Democratic representative from Pennsylvania, served Accokeek as trustee and secretary. Representative Jonathan B. Bingham of New York is a trustee of the 20th Century Fund. Senator Edward Kennedy has put material into the *Congressional Record* praising the Pan American Development Foundation, of which he is a director. On December 12, 1969, for instance, he spoke in favor of putting $15,000,000 into the aid program to guarantee loans made by PADF and similar foundations. Kennedy did not mention his connection with PADF in this speech.[2] Representative Bradford Morse of Massachusetts is also a PADF director.

Examples could be listed indefinitely, from every level of government: from John B. Connally, who served the Sid W. Richardson Foundation while Governor of Texas; to New York Mayor John V. Lindsay, a trustee of the Carnegie Endowment for International Peace; to John C. Danforth, Attorney General of Missouri, and trustee of his family's Danforth Foundation, one of the twenty-five largest.

Yet none is more curious than J. Edgar Hoover's relationship to the Dorothy H. and Lewis Rosentiel Foundation—both because of the conflict-of-interest questions it poses for the nation's chief policeman and because of the double standards of acceptable conduct which Congress applied to Hoover and to Abe Fortas, the Supreme Court justice driven into resignation because of the exposure of his connection with a foundation. The principal characters in the Hoover situation are as follows.

Lewis Rosentiel, the whiskey distiller, head of Schenley Industries, Inc., during the 1960s began giving away much of the fortune he had amassed during his lifetime. Rosentiel had a tragically unhappy personal life. His first wife, Dorothy, died in 1944, and he had several unpleasant divorces thereafter. Schenley and its distributors had running fights with state liquor boards and law enforcement agencies in Massachusetts, California, and Florida during the 1950s and 1960s because of connections with rackets figures. Rosentiel personally remained untainted by any charges, however.

The J. Edgar Hoover Foundation was incorporated on June 10, 1965, by Louis B. Nichols, who had been top assistant to Hoover at the FBI until he retired in 1957 to become executive vice president of Schenley's. The Internal Revenue Service gave the Hoover Foundation tax-exempt status on October 28 of the same year. This was almost record time; normally tax-exempt organizations must operate for a full year before IRS grants exemption. The charter, granted in the District of Columbia, states that the purpose of the Foundation is "to safeguard the heritage and freedom of the United States of America and to promote good citizenship through and appreciation of its form of government and to perpetuate the ideas and purposes to which the Honorable J. Edgar Hoover has dedicated his life." It proclaims that the Foundation is dedicated to "combat communism or any other ideology or doctrine which shall be opposed to the principles set forth in the Constitution . . . or the rule of law."

Officers and directors of the Hoover Foundation, with a single exception, are with either Schenley or the FBI. Nichols is president. Two former FBI agents are vice presidents and directors: William G. Simon, once agent-in-charge of the FBI's Los Angeles field office, now a Washington attorney; and Donald J. Parsons, who after his retirement from the Bureau became president of Parsons Paper Company of Washington. C. D. (Deke) DeLoach, a top deputy to Hoover, until he retired in July 1970 to join Pepsico, is secretary. Both the treasurer, N. J. L. Pieper, and the assistant treasurer, Patricia Corcoran, worked with Nichols at Schenley's. The only non FBI-Schenley person involved in the Foundation is Robert F. Sagle, a Washington attorney whose office at 910 17th Street, N.W., is also the Foundation's mailing address.

Roy Cohn gained national prominence in the 1950s as chief counsel to the late Senator Joseph McCarthy's investigative committee. He, Hoover and Rosentiel form a sort of three-sided mutual-admiration society, drawn together by a common commitment to anti-Communism. Cohn became friendly with Nichols and Hoover while working in Washington. In the 1960s Rosentiel hired him as counsel in a protracted, acrimonious divorce case brought by his fifth wife, Susan Rosentiel. Cohn's law firm of Saxe, Bacon and Boland also did legal work for Schenley Industries. In 1966 the Rosentiel Foundation paid the Cohn firm $6,500 "for legal services rendered" for its part in helping in the defense of a civil action against the Foundation by one of Rosentiel's daughters, Mrs. Louise R. Frank.[3] Cohn has been credited with helping Nichols obtain his job at Schenley. And the American Jewish League Against Communism, of which Cohn is president and founder, helped get the J. Edgar Hoover Foundation rolling with a $500 contribution.

But Rosentiel is the major benefactor of the Hoover Foundation; indeed, the FBI director's Foundation appears to be little more than a conduit for funds provided by the liquor tycoon. Rosentiel began with a gift of $35,000 of Schenley Industries stock in 1965; in 1966, he gave $6,500; in 1967, another $60,000.

And then, in 1968, he donated stock with a book value of $724,628.99, but with an appreciably higher market value. (For example, on August 30, 1968, the Hoover Foundation sold, to Glen Alden Corporation, a block of Schenley stock which had a market value at the time of receipt of $89,649.40. The sale price was $192,050.00, a gain of $102,400.60. Based upon these figures, the 1968 gift of $724,628 would appear to be worth around $1,500,000 at actual market value.)

Such a large contribution to a foundation created to pay homage to an active public official is unprecedented. That Hoover permitted the Foundation to bear his name is all the more remarkable in view of the fact: at the time it was made Rosentiel was under active, vigorous investigation by the Securities and Exchange Commission arising from the sale of Schenley to the Glen Alden Corporation; and his sometime lawyer and adviser, Cohn, was under federal indictments for bribery, conspiracy, extortion, and blackmail, in cases developed in part by the investigatory work of agents of Hoover's FBI.

Furthermore, Cohn was in continuous trouble with the Justice Department and other federal agencies both prior to and during the period in which he and client Rosentiel were assisting the J. Edgar Hoover Foundation. In 1964 Cohn was acquitted in a perjury and conspiracy case. In

1965, the year Cohn helped start the Hoover Foundation, he complained in court petitions that Internal Revenue Service had him under investigation on the basis of information obtained through a mail cover that had been ordered by U.S. Attorney Robert Morgenthau. In 1966 and 1967 Cohn and associates appeared frequently before federal grand juries looking into the condemnation of Fifth Avenue Coach Lines by New York City. In a 1968 civil decision a U.S. district judge ruled that Cohn and two associates, through self-dealing transactions, used Fifth Avenue Coach for illegal purposes; in a separate action, the SEC charged Cohn with misappropriation of funds from Fifth Avenue Coach. And in November, 1968, Cohn was indicted for allegedly paying a $75,000 bribe to a New York City official to give him confidential papers relating to the bus company condemnation proceedings.

This latter case took a bizarre turn in the spring of 1969 through an action of Hoover that had the net effect of helping Cohn's defense. During pretrial proceedings Cohn charged that U.S. Attorney Morgenthau had used wiretapping and illegal bugging devices during the investigation that resulted in the indictments. Three FBI agents—Donald E. Jones, with twenty-three years' service; Russell F. Sullivan, fifteen years; and Jack D. Knox, six years—specifically denied allegations about the use of electronic equipment to hound Cohn, whereupon Hoover ordered the three agents transferred from the New York field office, denying them the customary thirty days' advance notice.

The transfers were significant because of Cohn's repeated charges that the trial was politically motivated. He claimed that Morgenthau was conducting a "personal vendetta" because of allegations by McCarthy's old investigating committee that Communists had infiltrated the Treasury Department when Morgenthau's father, Henry, was secretary of the treasury. Cohn was counsel of the committee at the time. Morgenthau denied this charge each time Cohn raised it, saying there's no law against prosecuting a man just because you don't like him. Of the agents' transfer, the FBI has said only that the men were disciplined because they did not ask permission from FBI headquarters before submitting the affidavits, as is required by Bureau regulations.

The case ultimately resulted in Cohn's acquittal, after an eleven-week trial ending in December, 1969. As of this writing* Cohn still faced trial on charges of defrauding Fifth Avenue Coach of some $75,000, of filing false and misleading reports with the Securities and Exchange Commission, and also of criminal misconduct in a transaction involving an Illinois bank.

In its charter the J. Edgar Hoover Foundation said that it intended to propagate the thoughts of the director through what on face value seemed to be a well-organized program: "conduct education programs; organize study groups; give lectures; establish scholarships and endow chairs . . . [and] circulate magazines and books and pamphlets."

In fact, the J. Edgar Hoover Foundation has done little more than channel token amounts of money to the Freedoms Foundation at Valley Forge. One room of Freedoms Foundation's American Freedoms Center is devoted to the J. Edgar Hoover Library on Communism and Totalitarianism, which is said to contain "one of the largest collections on these subjects available to the public." Freedoms Foun-

* June 4, 1970.

dation states: "Primary sources written by Communists are to be found here, although most of the material is devoted to pointing out the fallacies of the Communist ideology and the necessity for combatting this menace if our American Way of Life is to be preserved." The library supposedly is for the benefit of "graduate students, foreign students, teachers, economists, thought leaders and others studying the American Way of Life." [4]

Two things somewhat diminish the library's value as a research center. It is in an inaccessible rural area on the fringe of the Philadelphia suburbs, a five-dollar cab ride from the nearest commuter train station, a forty-five-minute drive from downtown. The "collection" itself is a mishmash of volumes obtainable from any serious public library, many of them hand-me-downs from the American Legion library in Indianapolis.

Traffic was sparse the day I was there. One man was reading a newspaper, and a single librarian was rustling papers on her desk. The "pro-American section" is padded with seldom-circulated multiple copies of books by Hoover (eighteen copies of *A Study of Communism*, ten of *Masters of Deceit*) and by turncoat Communists (seven copies of *I Led Three Lives*, by Herbert J. Philbrick). The "pro-totalitarian section" reflects a comical lack of intellectual objectivity and common sense by the library staff. Edgar Snow's works on Communist China—one written while he was a staff writer for the *Saturday Evening Post* in the 1940s—are hard by a forty-volume collected works of Lenin. "We bought them from Moscow for a dollar a copy," an earnest young woman librarian confided to me about the Lenin set. "We fooled them. We used home mailing addresses of staff members so that the Communists wouldn't know where they were going.

We do the same thing to get literature from the Chinese Communists."

A scholar could quibble with a library that labels its resources "good" or "bad," rather than simply putting the books on the shelves and permitting researchers to decide for themselves. But few people take the Freedoms Foundation seriously, other than the men who conceived it and the staff people who make their livings there. It is useful only as a specimen of political pathology—a place where an exhibit of buttons seized at a "Communist" rally includes the "I'm a Nervous Nellie" classic worn with pride by the staff of Senator J. W. Fulbright.

An immense color photograph of J. Edgar Hoover stares at visitors, sharing the wall with a display, "Terror at the Hands of the Red Guard," and an equally mammoth photograph of James S. Copley, proprietor of the right-wing Copley newspaper chain, chief patron of the room (he donated a 150-year-old rug). His likeness is accompanied by a plaque engraved with a phrase that won him a $5,000 "Freedoms Award": "Faith in America, as echoed in our simple pledge of allegiance, can and will be the destroyer of atheistic communism."

This is where the J. Edgar Hoover Foundation chooses to spend its money. During the first four years of its existence the Foundation's total expenditures were as follows:

1965	Book for J. Edgar Hoover Library	$	7.20
	Subscriptions for J. Edgar Hoover Library		30.00
	Literature donated for summer institute (at Freedoms Foundation)		227.90
	Contribution to Freedoms Foundation		100.00
	TOTAL	$	365.10

1966   Books for J. Edgar Hoover Library $ 3,000.00
       Compensation for librarian, J. Edgar
           Hoover Library   1,500.00
       Scholarship to attend teaching
           seminars at Freedoms Foundation   400.00
           TOTAL $ 4,900.00

1967   J. Edgar Hoover Library $ 1,000.00
       Contribution for memorial pew at
           Freedoms Foundation Chapel   450.00
           TOTAL $ 1,450.00

1968   American Bar Association Fund for
           Public Education, teacher training
           institute, on crime control and
           prevention $ 5,000.00
       Freedoms Foundation—J. Edgar
           Hoover Library   2,500.00
       Freedoms Foundation—five teacher
           scholarships at same institution   2,125.00
       Southeastern University—assistance
           to three FBI clerical employees
           in continuing education   1,500.00
           TOTAL $11,125.00[5]

For their contribution, Rosentiel and Cohn received the
valuable, if intangible, benefit of being known as the benefactors of a foundation honoring the director of the Federal
Bureau of Investigation. Rosentiel's tax savings were also
considerable, but the Schenley stock which he contributed
returned relatively little cash income to the Foundation. At
the end of 1967, for example, the fair market value of stocks
held by the Hoover Foundation totaled $130,373. Yet dur-

ing the three years these holdings returned only $5,822. The sole stock transaction ever reported by the Foundation was the sale of a block of Schenley stock to Glen Alden Corporation, which in 1968 was in the process of purchasing control of Schenley from a willing Rosentiel. In 1968 the Foundation earned interest of $1,704 and received dividends of $2,242, from assets that had a year-end value of $947,915. Had the foundation sold its Schenley stock at book value ($871,972) and deposited the proceeds in a savings account the earnings would have been twenty-fold greater. And the capital gain reaped on a sale of a portion of the stock, as we have seen, revealed the book value to be far less than the actual market value.

Yet earning the maximum return on its assets is not the chief purpose of the J. Edgar Hoover Foundation. In short, the Foundation is a vehicle through which Rosentiel, Cohn, and their friends can glorify the life and thought of J. Edgar Hoover.*

The existence of the J. Edgar Hoover Foundation and the source of its support were not state secrets in Washington. Each of the Rosentiel grants was reported in *Foundation News*, the semimonthly publication of the Foundation Center, and its tax returns are a matter of public record in room 1317 of the Internal Revenue Service Building in Washington. Yet not a single member of Congress has dared ques-

---

* Conceivably, Hoover's foundation could support interests of the director which are more valuable to society than the Valley Forge library. During 1970 appropriations hearings for the FBI Hoover noted that the Boys Clubs of America, of which he is a director, are doing a "fine job," but "they are very short of funds, and they are not manned in adequate numbers. . . . It takes a great deal of money to finance an organization of that type and size." [6] The nearly million dollars controlled by the Hoover foundation, if invested on behalf of the Boys Clubs of America, would make a better monument to Hoover's memory than a collection of books at Valley Forge.

tion the propriety of the director of the FBI implicitly giving the Justice Department's seal of approval to the controversial Rosentiel and Cohn, and to the rightist Freedoms Foundation.

CONGRESS'S TOLERANCE OF HOOVER is all the more marked when put into juxtaposition to its pained, loud, and more than a little hypocritical, outrage at a case which was in many respects parallel to the Hoover situation—Justice Abe Fortas's agreement to accept a $20,000 annual fee from the family foundation of financier Louis Wolfson.

There are similarities. Hoover, as FBI director, and Fortas, as a Supreme Court justice, both had extraordinary responsibilities in administering justice in America. Both Cohn and Wolfson were involved in activities that were under active investigation by the federal government, and both were ultimately indicted. Although Hoover did not profit materially by the donations to his foundation, he did receive a healthy infusion of the adulation which he has relished throughout his career. Although Fortas's fee from the Wolfson foundation was to be but a fraction of his court salary, $20,000 per year *is* more than the median family income in the United States. There the similarities end: Fortas was driven from the bench in disgrace; the J. Edgar Hoover Foundation and Mr. Hoover remain active.

This is not to imply that Justice Fortas was guilty of anything less than an incredible indiscretion—what the *New York Times* called "the biggest scandal ever to hit the Supreme Court." Even by his own carefully tailored account of the incident, Fortas committed an act which common sense, if nothing else, should have dissuaded him from.

That Abe Fortas and Lou Wolfson came together in the summer of 1965 seems in the natural scheme of things. Both men were born in the South of immigrant Jewish parents: Wolfson in 1912 in Florida; Fortas in 1910 in Memphis. Both men were imbued with a strong appetite for wealth and power, and both men achieved it early. Wolfson made his first million dollars by twenty-eight, through his father's junk business. In the next two decades he became famous as a corporate raider in construction, shipping, and transit—seizing tired companies with dazzling ease and melding them into a multimillion-dollar empire.

Fortas, meanwhile, was a New Deal undercabinet officer at thirty-two; when he went into private practice in 1946, business poured in from the great corporations facing government problems which they thought his insider's connections could help solve. By the 1960s Fortas's income was credibly estimated at $250,000. Fortas was the confidant of Presidents, and he made the most of his privileges. With consummate vanity, he listed himself in a legal directory as "presidential adviser" and gave an address, "Care of the White House, 1600 Pennsylvania Avenue, Washington, D.C."

When Lou Wolfson came to Abe Fortas's law firm in the spring of 1965, he was in deep trouble. For more than a year the Securities and Exchange Commission had been probing his dealings in stock of Merritt-Chapman & Scott, the construction firm that was the linchpin of his pyramided financial empire. New York Shipbuilding Corporation, one of his many firms, was falling to pieces, and Wolfson was besieged with civil suits. Fortas did what he could to help.

The two men had other conversations, completely unrelated to law. Fortas stated later: "[Wolfson] told me about the Wolfson Family Foundation and his hopes and plans for it. He knew that its program—the improvement of community relations and the promotion of racial and religious cooperation—concerned matters to which I had devoted much time and attention. Mr. Wolfson stated that he intended to increase the Foundation's resources, and he hoped that the Foundation might expand its work so as to make unique and basic contributions in its field. As we proceeded in our discussions, Mr. Wolfson suggested that he would like me to participate in and help shape the Foundation's program and activities." [7]

In October, 1965, President Johnson appointed Fortas to the Supreme Court. There are two versions as to how this came about. Johnson has said, both publicly and privately, that Fortas resisted, yielding only when he was told: "I am asking thousands of boys to go to Vietnam; how can you tell me that you won't answer my call to go to the Supreme Court?" Fortas's wife, the tax attorney Carolyn Agger, has been depicted by the Washington newspapers as grievously upset by her husband's acceptance of the appointment. According to this story, Mrs. Fortas didn't want her husband to abandon his legal career at the height of his earning prowess, saying petulantly that Johnson "wasn't doing Abe any favor by forcing this assignment upon him." But a top Johnson adviser of the period gives a story not so replete with sacrifice and financial self-denial: "To use some of Johnson's vernacular, Fortas jumped on this like a dog on a bone. The tacit understanding was that he would move up to Chief Justice if and when Earl Warren retired. The public moaning was to gloss over the fact that Johnson was putting a close personal and political friend onto the Supreme Court."

Lou Wolfson's SEC troubles were undiminished at the time of the Fortas appointment. Yet Fortas's transition from lawyer to Supreme Court justice did not affect their discussions about the Foundation. Fortas went on the Court in October. "Shortly thereafter, Mr. Wolfson was in Washington and again conferred with me about the Foundation's work and my possible association with it," Fortas stated. "I again indicated my interest in the Foundation's program and in expanding its scope, and we discussed the possibility of my participating in the project on a long-term basis. Because of the nature of the work, there was no conflict between it and my judicial duties. It was then my opinion that the work of the court would leave me adequate time for the Foundation assignments."

In this respect Fortas could have relied upon the experience of a colleague, Justice William O. Douglas. In 1961 Douglas became president of the Albert Parvin Foundation, at a salary of $12,000 per year. Parvin, whose main business is a hotel supplies company, has also had his rough moments with the Internal Revenue Service and the SEC, although never to the extent of a criminal proceeding. But Parvin was also a key figure in the Parvin-Dohrmann Company, which owns the Alladin, Fremont, and Stardust hotel-gambling casinos in Las Vegas. Not surprisingly, many of the Las Vegas associates have police dossiers; one was caught up in the Bobby Baker scandal.

Another principal in Parvin-Dohrmann was the FOF Proprietary Fund, Ltd., of Geneva, Switzerland, part of an overseas complex of mutual funds run by Bernard Cornfeld. In addition to intermittent SEC problems, Cornfeld had something else in common with the Parvin Foundation: both were supporters of the Center for the Study of Democratic Institutions, an intellectual lamasery outside Santa Barbara, California. This circle eventually takes on the configuration of a pretzel. Justice Douglas is board chairman of the Center. Harry Ashmore, who won a Pulitzer Prize as a courageous Arkansas newspaper editor during the dark days of Little Rock, is executive vice president of the Center; he is also a director of the Parvin Foundation. Fortas's wife, Carolyn Agger, is the Parvin Foundation's lawyer. Among the public figures who have received honoraria for speaking at Center brain-storming sessions are Senators J. W. Fulbright and John Sherman Cooper and Chief Justice Warren E. Burger, the latter when he was on the U.S. Circuit Court of Appeals in Washington.

That Justice Douglas worked with the Foundation at such a fee, and that its major recipient institution paid U.S. Senators fees of up to $500 per day, disturbed no one except the *Los Angeles Times,* which kept on top of Parvin-Dohrmann with objective but unblinking reportage. Nicholas von Hoffman, the *Washington Post* columnist, caustically commented in May, 1969, that the liberal press ignored a possible scandal because editors "are reluctant to bring out such questions about men they admire and who are in many respects admirable." Von Hoffman stated: "If it were discovered that H. L. Hunt was paying Justice Byron R. White to run a foundation that had Sen. John Tower on the payroll, you can bet your sweet bippy there would be a big noise." [8]

That there wasn't a "big noise" in Santa Barbara well might have led Fortas to conclude that he was free to strike his own arrangement with the Wolfson Family Foundation. This he did, within two months of donning his judicial robes. In December the Wolfson board approved "an agreement under which I was to perform services for the Foundation. It was understood between us that the program in question was a long-range one and that my association would be meaningful only if it were on a long-term basis. The agreement, therefore, contemplated that I would perform continuing service, and instead of fixing variable compensation from time to time for work being done, it provided that I would receive $20,000 per year for my life with arrangements for payments to Mrs. Fortas in the event of my death."

In January, 1966, four months after becoming a member of the nation's highest court, Fortas received a check for $20,000, drawn on the Wolfson Family Foundation and payable to Fortas personally. The justice deposited it in a personal account in a Washington bank.

In June, Fortas flew to Jacksonville, Florida, for a meeting of the Foundation trustees; after it ended, he went to Wolfson's ranch at nearby Ocala and was an overnight guest. Foundation business was discussed.

During this period Wolfson's SEC troubles neared a climax; the financier frantically insisted he was guilty of nothing more than technical violations of new SEC rules in the Merritt-Chapman transactions, while the government pressed for a criminal indictment. Screaming "vendetta," Wolfson scrambled from politician to politician, pleading with persons with whom he had been friendly in the past to intervene and stop the SEC. He showered impassioned letters indiscriminately across Washington and New York. Florida's two Democratic Senators, George Smathers and Spessard Hollings, made inquiries at the SEC and were advised, "Keep away from this one, you might get burned." They did.

At least two, and possibly more, of these letters went to Justice Abe Fortas. One of them was a short "for-your-information" covering note attached to a lengthy brief outlining Wolfson's role in the Merritt-Chapman sales, giving his in-

terpretation of the SEC rule he was alleged to have violated. The other was much more personal: a rambling de-
nunciation of SEC personnel and other persons in the
financial community, whom Wolfson said had been out to
"get" him for more than a decade; bitter disappointment
with "so-called friends" who had sought Wolfson's favors
when he was powerful, only to turn their backs on him now
that he was in trouble; a plea for advice on how to get out of
the situation.

These letters—which the Justice Department obtained
from Wolfson by subpoena in May, 1969—were, by the
most charitable interpretation, an astounding act of impu-
dence. Wolfson was not naïve. He was a highly intelligent
businessman who had dealt with courts and with lawyers,
and he knew the impropriety of attempting to discuss a case
with a judge, even one who was a personal friend and a
former lawyer. By most sinister interpretation—one which
the Justice Department never attempted to prove—the letters were an effort to extract a quid pro quo from Fortas.
The justice had accepted money from Wolfson, and now
Wolfson demanded services. The longer of the two letters
stopped just short of asking Fortas to perform any specific
acts; but it was a general plea for help.

It was at this juncture that Fortas decided he should
have nothing further to do with the Wolfson Family Foundation. According to Fortas' account, there were two reasons for his decision:

> My work for the court was much heavier than I had antic-
> ipated and my idea of the amount of time I would have free
> for non-judicial work had been a substantial overestimate. I
> had also learned shortly before informing the foundation of
> my decision to terminate the arrangement, that the SEC had
> referred Mr. Wolfson's file to the Department of Justice for

consideration as to criminal prosecution. I therefore wrote a letter to the foundation, addressed to its general counsel, dated June 21, 1966, cancelling the agreement we had entered into, subject to completing the projects for the year. I cited as my reason only the burden of court work.

In September and October, grand juries indicted Wolfson in two matters: for conspiring in the sale of $3,500,000 of unregistered stock in a company named Continental Enterprises, allegedly inflicting heavy losses on innocent public investors; and for perjury for his testimony about "insider manipulations" of Merritt-Chapman stock.

Not until two months after the second indictment, in December, 1965, did Fortas return the $20,000. "I concluded that, because of the developments which had taken place, the services which I had performed should be treated as a contribution to the Foundation," Fortas explained.

There the matter rested for more than two years. Because the $20,000 was returned within the year it was paid, the Foundation did not list the transaction on its 1966 tax return. In late 1968 a Justice Department investigator who read some of the Fortas-Wolfson correspondence during the grand jury proceedings tipped *Life* reporter William Lambert. The magazine published the story in May, 1969, a few days after Wolfson entered prison to begin serving a one-year term in the Continental Enterprises case. The revelation that he had accepted money from a man who was now an imprisoned felon drove Fortas from the bench. He left with the following protest: "There has been no wrongdoing on my part. There has been no default in the performance of my judicial duties in accordance with the highest standards of the office I hold." But not even Fortas's friends would deny that he had committed "grave improprieties

. . . which made his resignation from the Supreme Court imperative," as a *Washington Post* editorial commented.

THE FORTAS-WOLFSON EPISODE was an aberration of foundation philanthropy, with as much relationship to Ford and Rockefeller programs as a Supreme Court proceeding has to a kangaroo court. But it was, in the words of a foundation executive, "the grant heard around the world."

To the public, Fortas's indiscretion was further evidence that these mysterious foundations, with their penchant for generous grants and privacy, were out to subvert the nation. Something in the American folk ethic objects to "easy" money. A grant or a consultant's fee means that someone is receiving money for thinking, not for physical labor. During his grant year a professor or scholar doesn't keep office hours; he is apt to work at home, and he may be seen sitting on the porch reading or drinking iced tea suspiciously early in the afternoon or appearing unshaven at midday. Fortas never deigned to submit any physical evidence that he performed any useful work for the Wolfson Foundation, which, with its relatively limited funds and activities, did not even have a salaried staff. What could Fortas conceivably contribute to warrant a $20,000 annual fee?

Shed of the euphemisms, both public and official Washington concluded, rightly or wrongly, that Wolfson had signed on a Supreme Court justice as his personal fixer and that he expected a wave of the Fortas wand to drive away the SEC and the Justice Department.

The Fortas scandal came at the worst possible time for the foundations. In January, 1969, the House Ways and Means Committee had begun hearings on a sweeping reform of the tax laws, with the national mood clearly hostile to rich men who avoided taxes by any means, foundations or otherwise. By widely-publicized Treasury Department computation, 154 individuals with adjusted gross incomes of $200,000 or more (and twenty-one of them over $1,000,000) escaped taxation altogether in 1966 by "piling one [tax] advantage on top of another, an intolerable situation," in the words of the Ways and Means Committee.

The committee had before it Treasury Department proposals first made in 1965 for curbing some of the financial abuses we discussed in Chapter Seven: self-dealing between a foundation and its donor; low payouts from assets for charitable purposes; retention of stock in family businesses that paid no dividends, yet entitled the donor to tax deductions; and the assorted "bootstrapping" techniques through which foundations purchased businesses. The announcement of these hearings contained no reference whatsoever to possible legislation restricting the grant activities of foundations.

Yet the committee almost immediately dived into the subject of political activism and into an examination of whether foundation philanthropy remains relevant in America. McGeorge Bundy spent some three acrimonious hours explaining and defending Ford's grants to Cleveland CORE, the Kennedy aides, and principals in the school decentralization fight. Congressman Rooney told of his experience with philanthropist-politician Frederick Richmond. The Southern Regional Council's voter-registration campaigns took licks.

But some members were more concerned about a somewhat deeper question: Was it proper for foundations to enjoy an extragovernmental freedom not available to the average citizen? Representative John W. Byrnes, the committee's ranking Republican, put it this way:

> Some people, because of their wealth, are able to enjoy the luxury of deciding for themselves that they want to put their money into areas wherein they can control what services are going to be conducted. . . . The vast majority of the American people do not have this choice. They are not only paying for things about which some of them are not very enthusiastic, but they must also pay a higher price to carry on these services simply because some people with wealth have said that they do not want to support any of these services. . . . Should we permit a segment of our society to set up a government of its own to render philanthropic services?[9]

Early in the hearings—which stretched from February through April in the House, and three further months in the Senate—the foundations sensed that Congress would impose grant restrictions. The Fortas disclosures, which came during actual drafting of the tax reform bill in the House, made a crackdown inevitable, with the degree of severity the only question. The foundation provisions that ultimately emerged were in two broad categories, financial and operational, and were a mixture of good and mischief.

FINANCIAL PROVISIONS

The act imposed a four-percent tax on the net annual investment income of foundations—interest, dividends, rents and royalties, and capital gains. The $35,000,000 estimated annual revenue from this tax would finance stricter surveillance of foundations by the Internal Revenue Service. Foundation spokesmen protested during hearings that the tax would deprive charity of needed

funds; Ford alone now must pay in the neighborhood of
$6,000,000 annually, which is equal to one-fifth the budget
of its National Affairs Division. But the tax does *not* diminish the value of foundations to philanthropists who choose
to contribute to them.

The act banned self-dealing. In this category, "disqualified persons" include anyone who has contributed more
than $5,000 to a foundation, or more than two percent of its
assets; the foundation manager; and various business associates of the controlling party. Philanthropists can no longer
use foundations as conduits for stock deals, borrow money
from them, or receive compensation from them. For a first
violation of self-dealing bans, the parties are penalized five
percent of the amount involved in the transaction; for second and subsequent offenses, two hundred percent.

The act requires foundations to spend at least 4.5 percent of the value of their assets beginning in 1972; 5.0 percent in 1973; and 5.5 percent in 1974. This provision struck
directly at foundations such as the Houston Endowment
and the Moody Foundation whose assets consist chiefly of
low-yield stocks in family business. It also should make serious foundations wary of accepting gifts of such nonproductive property as rundown real estate and vacant land.

The act limits business holdings of foundations, but it
gives them ample time to bring them down to the new limits. The foundation, together with all "disqualified persons"
involved in its operation, may continue to hold up to a fifty-
percent interest in any business which it had on May 26,
1969, the date the Ways and Means Committee first announced proposed changes in the law. In this category, if
holdings are not more than seventy-five percent, ten years is
allowed to reduce them to fifty percent; if existing holdings

are between 75 and 95 percent, the reduction must occur within fifteen years; if more than ninety percent, within twenty years. But holdings acquired after May 26, 1969, together with those of all disqualified persons, may not exceed twenty percent. For example, if a disqualified person owns fifteen percent of the stock, any holding greater than five percent must be disposed of either by the foundation or the disqualified person.

The act imposes taxes on bootstrap deals, such as those used by University Hill Foundation and the oil foundations. If the purchase is ninety percent on credit, for example, ninety percent of the net income that flows through the foundation to the original owner is taxed at regular income or corporate rates. (The tax advisory services immediately pronounced bootstrapping a dead gimmick.)

The act cuts into gifts of appreciated stock. Under the new law, if stock is held for less than six months before it is donated, the deduction is the actual cost, not the market value at the time of giving. (Example: Under the old rule, if you gave $10,000 of stock that cost $4,000 three months ago, the deduction was $10,000, with no tax on the $6,000 paper gain. The new rule holds the deduction to $4,000.) But for stocks held for more than six months, the old rules still apply.

Tax advisory services which analyzed the new provisions concluded that large, well-staffed foundations should have no trouble complying with the law, complex though it may be, but that "the Mom-and-Pop foundation will be severely hit. The price of compliance will be high and a slip can be costly to Mom and Pop individually if, as is usually the case, one or both run the foundation. *In fact, many of them would be well advised to close up shop and distribute the fund to a public charity.*" [10] (That language comes from Prentice-Hall.) Other services were equally glum. In sum, they say, the era of the mass-produced but minute foundation that is run from a lawyer's desk drawer could be at an end.

OPERATIONAL PROVISIONS

"I have to laugh about 'significant operational changes' due to the Tax Reform Act," an officer of one of the larger foundations wrote me a few months after Congress finished work. "Some people say the biggest change will be $6,000,000 less with which to do our thing. Others say that $6,000,000 tax will be as peanuts when everyone adds up the price of the red tape in which we are swimming. Try an experiment and ask a hundred liberal, well-educated people what Congress did to the foundations, and weep."

Restrictions imposed on foundation grants derive more from Congress's ,implications than from Congress's specific language. The new law, because it *is* general, gives foundation officers the responsibility for determining whether a grant is permissible and provides for fines both for them and the foundation if they err. McGeorge Bundy of Ford wrote in his 1969 annual report that "my current belief is that the new law will permit and protect the effective continuation of all the basic programs of this foundation." But three pages later he worried that the new law "presents particularly sensitive questions of interpretation." [11]

Outright lobbying remains illegal. To this, Congress added a ban on "expenditures on attempts to influence legislation through attempts to affect the opinion of the general public." House members of the conference committee that wrote the final bill commented that they "desire to make it clear that . . . this language is not intended to prevent the examination of broad social, economic and similar problems of the type the government could be expected to deal with ultimately, even though this would not permit lobbying on matters which have been proposed for legislative action." [12]

Permissible activity thus lies somewhere between those bounds. Foundations with community-action programs decided, in the months immediately after passage of the new law, that discretion henceforth would be their guideline.

One of the twenty-five largest foundations, for example, in mid-1969 received a proposal for a legal services program modeled after Ford's Mexican-American Legal Defense project. The program officer was ordered to hold it until Congress had acted, so that the foundation would know the scope of the new law. The decision: We can't approve the project; it's too risky.

A smaller foundation long noted for gutsiness in tackling public issues declined a proposal for a study of state regulatory commissions. The reason: Any honest work is bound to result in recommendations that the agencies be overhauled, and that puts us into the political process.

Indeed, as *Science,* publication of the American Association of Science, lamented, the curbs threaten foundation interest in "almost everything worth studying, for almost any study worthy of foundation support might, directly or indirectly, influence a decision of some governmental body."

The new law also forbids "attempts to influence legislation through communications with government personnel who may participate in the formulation of legislation except in the case of technical advice or assistance provided to a governmental body in response to a written request by such body or person." The exception is providing "nonpartisan analysis, study or research" or information pertaining to the foundation's tax-exempt status.

This provision marks an end to one of foundation philanthropy's most useful, if intangible, functions—the Senate or White House staff member picking up the phone to ask a foundation expert to write a section of a bill on aid to education or health service, or a foundation executive asking a federal department to take over a program which his organization has developed. Ford's National Affairs Division, for instance, helped write laws creating the Office of Economic Opportunity, a key agency in the Johnson Administration's War on Poverty. Ford and the Carnegie Corporation also developed the highly acclaimed educational TV show *Sesame Street* and persuaded the United States Office of Education to fund it. Bundy thinks that the "hardest task of accommodation" in the new law may come on the question of "influencing legislation."

The new voter-registration rules forbid a repetition of what Ford did with Cleveland CORE, but they left alive such broad registration drives as those conducted by the Southern Regional Council and the League of Women Voters. The new rule is that foundations can support voter drives run by organizations (1) whose principal activities are nonpartisan; (2) which work in five or more states; (3) which derive more than fifty percent of their support from gross investment income; (4) which receive no more than twenty-five percent of their support from one source; and (5) which do not accept contributions subject to the condition that they be used in only one specified election period.

One immediate result was that Ford ordered the Mexican-American Youth Organization to halt voter registration in the *barrios* of San Antonio and elsewhere in Texas.

In the field of individual grants, Congress said that hereafter they must be made on an "objective and non-discriminatory basis" and must be reported fully to the Treasury Department. Bundy, who opened this particular Pandora's box with the Kennedy grants, called the solution "workable."

Peculiarly, few of the twenty-five largest foundations which commented publicly opposed the operational restrictions. Foundations which spend their money in "safe" areas (Duke, on medicine and education; Lilly, on Indiana colleges; Mott, on local charities in Flint, Michigan) had no reason to oppose an end to community-action programs of Ford and other foundations. Indeed, one Ford staff man told me caustically: "For the fat heads, the new law is all the excuse they need to continue sitting on their rumps. They're happy. Congress has forbidden them to do what they had no intention of doing anyway, and they no longer look lazy in comparison to us. They'll use the fuzziness of the language of the new law to keep the hell away from meaningful projects."

But the conservative foundations did succeed in beating back another proposal that struck to the core of their privileged status. The Senate version of the tax-reform bill would have required existing foundations to go out of business by 1995 and would have limited the life of new ones to twenty-five years. Senators had several reasons. Any foundation that really tried could find a worthwhile client to take its money after a quarter of a century. "Immortality" for vast pools of wealth is poor public policy. Too many foundations had used their money in ways the founder never contemplated, and would not condone were he alive.

To the philanthropoids, such a rule was professional genocide. They argued, in rebuttal, that no rich man would leave his fortune to a foundation were he to know it would be broken up in twenty-five years, with the money distributed no one knows where. The foundations won this argument, thus insuring their continuation as the final resting place for many of America's big fortunes.

CHRONOLOGICALLY, my work on this book coincided with Congress's work on the Tax Reform Act of 1969, and I early noted a common attitude among foundation officials I interviewed around the country. Why is Congress picking on us? they asked. Is it because we don't have a constituency to protect us? (as was protested by an officer of the Duke Endowment). Or was it because someone finally noticed that the emperor is an old fraud who isn't wearing any clothes? (the sardonic quip of the manager of a small, activist foundation in New York).

The foundations' formal language was as pained. John J. McCloy, who has been a director of both the Rockefeller Foundation and the Ford Foundation, complained to the Senate of the "atmosphere of hostility" to foundations, and he said: "I am aware that there is a sort of grand skepticism abroad in the land challenging our government, our existing institutions, and, indeed, many of our modes of life. But this, if we are to remain rational, does not mean that we should first destroy everything we have built up and start with a clean slate." [13] McCloy objected to the "abrupt and too far-reaching reversal" of public policy that had encouraged "the creation of charitable foundations through constructive tax incentives." Alan Pifer, president of the Carnegie Corporation, declared that Congress should not "enact politically responsive legislation . . . because of the publicity given to a few egregious cases of bad judgment by foundations in recent months." [14]

Why, then, had not the foundations taken the initiative a decade earlier to persuade Congress to bar self-dealing and other tax schemes which demeaned philanthropy?

Why, then, had not the Council on Foundations and the Foundation Center—the supposed spokesmen for *responsible* foundations—spoken out for reform, rather than denouncing Representative Patman for "rabble rousing . . . gross exaggerations and distortions," as did F. Emerson Andrews in a Foundation Center pamphlet in 1968? [15] A converted enemy makes the best ally. Had the foundations joined Patman in pursuing foundation evils, they could have aimed his blunderbuss at deserving targets, for anyone who has been around foundations a few months certainly learns the villain's identity and location. Any reasonably astute child quickly learns the desirability of being able to select the switch with which he is to be punished. And any reasonably astute person should have sensed that the Patman exposures ultimately were going to result in restrictive legislation.

The foundations did nothing. The Treasury Department's 1965 study contained well-reasoned, inclusive proposals that would have stripped philanthropy of its worst abuses. Had the foundations thrown their considerable weight behind these proposals—after all, the best tax lawyers in the land are at their beck and call, ready to present expert testimony—Patman's campaign would have been defused, and foundations would no longer have been vulnerable as "tax dodges" and "havens for rich men's money."

The foundations did nothing. Thus, they were pitiably hapless targets in 1969 because Congress could attack them both for their financial shortcomings and their questionable grants. A Ford officer told me emphatically: "Ourselves we could defend, and in good conscience. But the average citizen—and the average Congressman, for that matter—couldn't draw a distinction between Cleveland CORE and that nonsense of Frederick Richmond's."

Foundation officers gave me varied excuses when asked about their lack of activity in reform and self-regulation. Manning M. Pattillo, president of the Foundation Center, is a precise man who formerly worked in Christian education at the Lilly Endowment and the Danforth Foundation, two of the less exciting outposts of the foundation world. Pattillo seemed surprised that I had even asked such a question. "We don't think it is our function to tell other foundations how to run their business," he said. "Nor do we think it is our function to become so involved in politics that we suggest legislation to Congress. We're not accustomed to this sort of thing—fighting legislative battles. The attacks of the 1950s [by a McCarthyite House committee, the report of which Bernard DeVoto described as useful if "one wants to grow paranoia from seed"] made foundations cautious of group activity. We don't want cooperation to be mistaken for a conspiracy. The Foundation Center is not a pressure group. If there are abuses of the law, it's up to law enforcement agencies to police them. Too, nobody can pretend to represent 23,000 foundations across the country." [16]

An officer of the Rockefeller Foundation insisted, and with a straight face, that his organization had "no friends in Washington" to whom it could appeal for help. "I doubt if anyone here even knows either of our New York senators," he said. One simply cannot accept this answer: Dean Rusk, a former Rockefeller president, was in the Kennedy-Johnson cabinets for eight years. Clifford Hardin, a Rockefeller trustee, followed as Nixon's secretary of agriculture. And Nelson A. Rockefeller certainly has a phone number or two in Washington. But the Rockefeller Foundation, too, remained silent, adding its own voice to a refrain I heard so often it became tiresome: "We kept our own house in order, so why should we worry about what someone else is doing?"

I heard this sort of nonsense for six months before the truth suddenly came to me: if foundations had been so important to American health, education, and welfare; and if foundations did benefit as many persons as they claimed (the Duke Endowment, for instance, claims to "touch" seventy percent of the residents of the Carolinas annually); and if foundation philanthropy is a vital private sector activity; then their achievements the past half century would h'ave built them a constituency strong enough to give pause even to Congress.

Congress *does* listen to what people back home are saying, and in 1969 Congress heard markedly few grass-roots voices raised in praise of the foundations. Indeed, the only nonfoundation witnesses to defend the foundations before Congressional committees were foundation supplicants, such as the Association of American Medical Colleges, the Association of American Universities, the Council on Library Resources, and the Southern Association of Colleges and Schools. And these groups' chief concern was the proposed levy on foundation income, which would cut the amount of money they get from foundations.

The general public recognized the foundations for what most of them are: institutions which exist to benefit the rich and the near-rich; quiet billions controlled by trustees indistinguishable from the men who run the local bank and administered by philanthropoids who build cuckoo clocks and try to pass them off as cathedrals.

But let us credit the foundations with consistency: they spent half a century politely exploring the defects of society, rather than actively correcting them. Why should they be expected to do more about the defects of philanthropy? There is both irony and a certain justice in their chastisement: Patman conducted the empirical research so dear to philanthropoids and produced the voluminous reports (more than 5,000 pages) cherished by foundations as physical evidence that work is being done.

But, as every philanthropoid learns early in his career, research is something one puts on the shelf and forgets while one moves on to another project. This is, after all, what foundation philanthropy did for half a century.

WHAT FURTHER, IF ANYTHING, should be done about foundations? One's first reaction is to dismiss them as simply another of many flawed institutions in America and to leave them alone to continue building their childish sand castles on their private beaches, as so many of them have done throughout their existence.

But Ford did show that foundations can do more, provided they are willing to risk hostile public opinion and governmental reprisal. What must be done, I suggest, is to give foundations freedom to perform as they please, short of direct intervention in a political campaign, *provided* that the public has a participatory role in their conduct and that there is full disclosure of what is happening and when it is happening.

Foundations should be energized by energizing the men who run them. Congress refused to decree a twenty-five-year life span on foundations, a procedure which would have had the desirable effect of turning the money to fresh hands at the end of that time. As an alternative, it should impose a twenty-five-year limit on the time a donor or his heirs could have any voice in a foundation or in the selection of its directors. If the donor wants his tax-exemption, give him a decent period of time to be an independent philanthropist, and then permit the local government in the foundation's chief place of business to appoint a trustee. Give the local branch of the American Association of University Women or the AFL-CIO council or the American Legion or the Parent-Teacher Association the authority to select another member. For that matter, let the police chief pick a man, or take the second name on page 73 of the phone book. Whatever scheme chosen would not be perfect, but it would result in diversity and would be superior to the present stultifying procedure of self-perpetuating boards which choose their own successors.

Open the foundations' board meetings to the public, and bar the trustees from gathering privately ahead of time to decide what they are going to do. No one would come to most of the meetings, but I'd be curious as to how Ford *decides* to spend that $229,000,000 annually. Require the foundations to give the public access to research reports and itemized expenses of its grantees. The knowledge that an enterprising reporter *could* publish this information would make foundations and their supplicants wary of going down foolish rabbit paths.

In sum, what the rich do with their money in private is their own business. But once they claim the privilege of tax-exemption, each of us acquires an interest in the dollars involved, and we deserve to know how and why they are being spent. Most of us would quickly be bored silly and go away, but the foundations would operate in the constant knowledge that someone could ask at any minute: "What have you done for America recently?"

APPENDIX

The Twenty-Five Largest American Foundations

FOUNDATION	ASSETS, 1969 (Millions of Dollars)
1. Ford Foundation	$2,922
2. Rockefeller Foundation	890
3. Duke Endowment	629
4. Lilly Endowment	580
5. Pew Memorial Trust	541
6. Charles Stewart Mott Foundation	413
7. W. K. Kellogg Foundation	409

* Formed June 30, 1969, from a merger of the Old Dominion Foundation and the Avalon Foundation, both controlled by the Mellon family. Not to be confused with the A. W. Mellon Charitable Trust of Pittsburgh, which deals with local charities.

† Based upon estimated valuation of $500,000,000 for 80,000-acre Irvine Ranch in Orange County, California, in which the Foundation has a fifty-three percent interest. The Foundation carries the ranch interest on books at a token one dollar.

SOURCE NOTE

BECAUSE this is a book about foundations, the primary source of information was the foundations themselves: through interviews with more than 120 of their officers and staff members; through examinations of their 990-A forms, the tax return for foundations, on file at the Foundation Center's Washington office and at the Internal Revenue Service; through the printed annual reports of the 140-odd foundations which issue them; and through correspondence with foundation executives.

Early in my work I discovered that philanthropoids can be uninformative even when they are talkative—some simply because they had never stopped to analyze their job and what they intended to accomplish, or were expected to accomplish; others because they were shy of publicity because of the Patman investigation and the tax reform effort then in progress in Congress; still others because they cling to the notion that what foundations do is no one's business but their own. When speaking on a not-for-attribution basis, however, many of the philanthropoids unburdened themselves with confessional candor, both about their own work and about foundation philanthropy in general. For obvious reasons, these persons are not identified by name or foundation in the text or in notes. In several specified instances, details of incidents were changed to conceal where they happened.

Of the several hundred persons who contributed to this book, I wish especially to thank Mrs. Lois A. Murkland, director, and Mrs. Margot Moore Brinkley, librarian, both of the Foundation Center's Washington office. For two months these gracious ladies cheerfully assisted me in locating 990-A forms for some 3,000 foundations and guided me through the material in their library.

CHAPTER NOTES

CHAPTER 1

1. F. Emerson Andrews, *Philanthropic Foundations,* New York, Russell Sage Foundation, 1956, p. 11.
2. House Select Committee on Small Business, *Tax-Exempt Foundations: Their Impact on Small Business,* Appendix to Hearings, October and November, 1967, Volume II.
3. Wright Patman, "Chairman's Report to the [House] Select Committee on Small Business," *Tax-Exempt Foundations and Charitable Trusts: Their Impact on Our Economy,* December 31, 1962, p.v. (Patman I hereafter.)
4. Wright Patman, "Subcommittee Chairman's Report to Subcommittee No. 1, [House] Select Committee on Small Business," *Tax-Exempt Foundations and Charitable Trusts: Their Impact on Our Economy,* December 21, 1966, p. 4. (Patman IV hereafter.)
5. Louis Lefkowitz, quoted in House Committee on Ways and Means, *Tax Reform 1969,* Hearings, February-April, 1969, Part 1, p. 433. (Ways and Means hereafter.)
6. Manning M. Pattillo, quoted in Senate Finance Committee, *Tax Reform Act of 1969,* Hearings, September-November, 1969, Part 6, p. 5351. (Senate Finance hereafter.)

7. Paul Ylvisaker, quoted in Daniel P. Moynihan, *Maximum Feasible Misunderstanding: Community Action in the War on Poverty,* New York, The Free Press, 1969, p. 190.
8. Dean Rusk, *The Role of Foundations in American Life,* lectures delivered at Claremont University College, 1961.
9. James A. Perkins, "What the New Foundation Executive Should Know," *Foundations: Twenty Viewpoints,* ed. F. Emerson Andrews, New York, Russell Sage Foundation, 1965, p. 71.
10. McGeorge Bundy, quoted in Ways and Means, p. 378.
11. Robert Ardrey, *The Territorial Imperative,* New York, Dell, 1966, p. 3.

CHAPTER 2

1. Raymond B. Fosdick, *The Story of the Rockefeller Foundation,* New York, Harper & Brothers, 1952, p. 5.
2. John T. Jones, speech before the New York University Sixth Biennial Conference on Charitable Foundations; proceedings published: New York, Matthew Bender, 1963. (Sixth Biennial hereafter.)
3. Senate Finance, p. 5724.
4. Amherst H. Wilder Foundation, *Diamond Anniversary Report,* 1959.
5. Charles A. Dana Foundation, *Charles A. Dana Foundation: A Review, 1963–67.*
6. Senate Finance, p. 6138.
7. F. Emerson Andrews, *Philanthropic Giving,* New York, Russell Sage Foundation, 1950, p. 37.
8. Warren Weaver, *U.S. Philanthropic Foundations,* New York, Harper & Row, 1968, p. 24.
9. John D. Rockefeller, quoted in John T. Flynn, *God's Gold,* New York, Harcourt, Brace & World, 1932, p. 114.
10. Frederick T. Gates, quoted in Fosdick, *Rockefeller Foundation,* p. 1.
11. Mark Sullivan, *Our Times,* New York, Scribner's, 1928, p. 327.
12. Allen Nevins, *John D. Rockefeller: A Study in Power,* New York, Scribner's, 1940, Volume II.
13. Frederick T. Gates, quoted in Abraham Flexner (with Esther S. Bailey), *Funds and Foundations,* New York, Harper & Brothers, 1952, pp. 27–29.
14. Ida Tarbell, *History of the Standard Oil Company,* New York, Macmillan, 1904.
15. Starr Murphy, quoted in Senate Committee on the District of Columbia, *Hearings on Senate Bill S. 6888 to Incorporate the Rockefeller Foundation,* March 11, 1910.
16. Material on the Walsh Commission findings and Rockefeller's testimony are from the proceedings of the U.S. Commission on Industrial Relations, 1914–15, and the final report.
17. Samuel S. Marquis, *Henry Ford: An Interpretation,* Boston, Little, Brown, 1923, p. 104.
18. Henry Ford, quoted in Nevins, *John D. Rockefeller.*
19. Nevins, *John D. Rockefeller.*
20. Henry Ford, quoted in House Select Committee to Investigate Tax-Exempt Foundations and Comparable Organizations, Hearings, 1953.
21. Paul Sarnoff, *The Money King,* New York, Ivan Obolensky, 1965.

22. Russell Sage, quoted in John Caldwell Myers, "Russell Sage's Career as a Litigant," *Bench and Bar* (New York), 1906.
23. James Buchanan Duke, quoted in Ben Dixon MacNeill, "Duke," *The American Mercury*, August, 1929.
24. *Cocke et al. v. Duke et al.,* North Carolina Supreme Court, Spring term, 1963.
25. Duke, quoted in MacNeill, "Duke."

CHAPTER 3

1. Based upon separate studies cited in Andrews, *Philanthropic Foundations,* pp. 67–76; Eduard C. Lindeman, *Wealth and Culture,* Harcourt, Brace & World, 1936, p. 33; and upon the author's survey of trustees of the twenty-five largest foundations.
2. *New York Times* obituary, February 18, 1966.
3. Bundy, quoted in Ways and Means.
4. Philip M. Stern, "An Open Letter to the Ford Foundation," *Harper's Magazine,* January, 1966.
5. Bundy, Ways and Means, p. 414.
6. Richard H. Andres, quoted in *Foundation Relations Manual of the American College Public Relations Association,* Washington, 1962.
7. Jeanne Brewer, quoted in *Foundation Relations Manual.*
8. Charles A. Brecht, quoted in *Foundation Relations Manual.*
9. Brecht, quoted in *Foundation Relations Manual.*
10. Arnaud C. Marts, *The Generosity of Americans,* Englewood Cliffs, New Jersey, Prentice-Hall, 1966, p. 170.
11. Foundation Center, annual report for 1968.
12. The New York University Eighth Biennial Conference on Charitable Foundations; proceedings published: New York, Matthew Bender, 1967. (Eighth Biennial hereafter.)
13. Frederick de W. Bolman, quoted in *Readings in Company Contributions,* New York, National Industrial Conference Board, 1967, mimeo.
14. Warren Eisenberg, "Bungle in the Jungle," *Philadelphia Magazine,* December, 1964.
15. Ways and Means, p. 359.
16. Manning M. Pattillo, speech to the Twenty-First Annual Conference of Southwest Foundations, Galveston, Texas, May, 1969.

CHAPTER 4

1. Herbert B. West, interview with author, New York, June 18, 1969.
2. Herbert B. West, "The Art of Giving Money Away," *Foundation News,* September, 1968.
3. Fosdick, *Rockefeller Foundation,* p. 143.
4. Rockefeller Foundation, *President's Five-Year Review and Annual Report,* 1968.
5. Warren Weaver, "Thoughts on Philanthropy and Philanthropoids," *Foundation News,* May, 1962.
6. Rusk, *The Role of Foundations.*
7. Maurice Rosenberg, quoted in Walter E. Meyer Research Institute of Law, report for 1964–66.

8. Paul Ylvisaker, quoted in Proceedings of the Eleventh National Conference on Solicitations, St. Paul, Minnesota, October 19–21, 1966.
9. Fosdick, *Rockefeller Foundation,* p. 27.
10. Grant Foundation, biennial report for 1965–66.
11. Annual reports from cited foundations.
12. Bundy, quoted in Ways and Means, pp. 396–97.
13. Ibid., pp. 395–96.
14. Flexner, *Funds and Foundations,* p. 113.
15. Leonard C. Cottrell, Jr., quoted in Sixth Biennial.
16. Yorke Allen, Jr., quoted in *Proceedings,* Eighth Biennial.
17. John E. Booth, quoted in *Proceedings,* Eighth Biennial.
18. Cottrell, quoted in Sixth Biennial.
19. John Heyman, quoted in *Proceedings,* Eighth Biennial.
20. Sam C. Smith, quoted in *Proceedings,* Eighth Biennial.

CHAPTER 5

1. Matthew Josephson, *The Robber Barons,* Harcourt, Brace & Company, New York, 1934, pp. 362–63.
2. Harvey O'Connor, *Mellon's Millions,* New York, Blue Ribbon Books, 1935, p. 245.
3. Ibid., pp. 225–26.
4. *A. W. Mellon v. Commissioner of Internal Revenue,* 36 U.S. Board of Tax Appeals Reports 977.
5. Paul Mellon, quoted in Bollingen Foundation, report for 1945–65.
6. Wright Patman, quoted in Ways and Means, pp. 17–18.
7. Richard King Mellon Foundation, report for 1947–62.
8. McGeorge Bundy, quoted in Ford Foundation, annual report for 1968.
9. The Foundation Center, *Annual Report* for 1969.
10. Carnegie Foundation for the Advancement of Teaching, 1965–66 biennial report.
11. Albert Somit and Joseph Tanenhaus, *A Profile of Discipline,* New York, Atherton Press, 1964.
12. Ernest V. Hollis, *Philanthropic Foundations and Higher Education,* New York, Columbia University Press, 1938, p. 127.
13. U.S. Commission on Industrial Relations (see note 16 of Chapter Two).
14. The Foundation Center, *Annual Report* for 1969.
15. Herman B. Wells, quoted in *Foundations and the Tax Bill: Testimony on Title One of the Tax Reform Act of 1969 Submitted by Witnesses Appearing Before the U.S. Senate Finance Committee, October, 1969,* New York, Foundation Center, p. 22.
16. Wells, loc. cit.
17. Jacques Barzun, *The American University,* New York, Harper & Row, 1968; all Barzun quotes for the remainder of this chapter are from *The American University.*
18. "Foundations and Universities: A Small Symposium," *Foundation News,* May, 1963.
19. Manning M. Pattillo, "Preparing the Foundation Proposal," *Foundation News,* July, 1963.

20. Kenneth W. Mildenberger, quoted in *The Use of Social Research in Federal Domestic Programs,* a staff study for the Research and Technical Programs Subcommittee of the House Committee on Government Operations, April, 1967, Part 2, p. 136.
21. Francis Keppel, quoted in *Use of Social Research,* p. 154.
22. Maurice B. Mitchell, quoted in *Use of Social Research,* p. 219.
23. *Giving USA,* 1969 edition, New York, American Association of Fund-Raising Counsel, 1969.
24. Ronald Hilton, quoted in David Horowitz, "Sinews of Empire," *Ramparts,* October, 1969.
25. "Foundations and Universities: A Small Symposium."
26. Weaver, *U.S. Philanthropic Foundations,* p. 262.
27. Fosdick, *Rockefeller Foundation.*
28. Luther Terry, quoted in "Foundation Expenditures for Medical and Health-Related Research and Education, 1960," *Resources for Medical Research* (National Institutes of Health), November, 1962.
29. Luther Terry, quoted in House Committee on Government Operations. *Health Research and Training,* Hearings, August, 1961, p. 9.
30. *Giving USA,* 1969 edition.
31. David Hapgood, "The Health Professionals: Cure or Cause of the Health Crisis?," *Washington Monthly,* June, 1969.
32. Greer Williams, *The Plague Killers,* New York, Scribner's, 1969.
33. Henry Romney, interview with author, New York, July 8, 1969.
34. Committee on Government Operations, *The Administration of Research Grants in the Public Health Service,* Ninth Report, October 20, 1967, pp. 38–41.
35. Marshall I. Pickens, interview with author, Charlotte, North Carolina, June 11, 1969.
36. Raymond K. Wheeler, interview with author, Charlotte, North Carolina, June 12, 1969.
37. Robert J. Sailstad, interview with author, Charlotte, North Carolina, June 12, 1969.
38. Allen, quoted in *Proceedings,* Eighth Biennial.
39. Foundations' Fund for Research in Psychiatry, report for the years 1953–63.
40. Grant Foundation, report for 1967.
41. Andrew Carnegie, quoted in Carnegie Endowment for International Peace, *Basic Documents,* New York, n.d.
42. Carnegie Endowment for International Peace, *Basic Documents.*
43. John W. Byrnes, quoted in Ways and Means.

CHAPTER 6

1. Strom Thurmond, quoted in *Congressional Record,* October 20, 1969, p. S–12, 813.
2. Fred Schwartz, quoted in George Thayer, *The Farther Shores of Politics,* New York, Simon & Schuster, 1967, p. 251.
3. The quotations of Freedoms Foundation programs in this chapter are taken from more than a dozen untitled, undated pamphlets and booklets which are distributed at the Foundation's reception area.

4. Walter Cronkite, quoted in Greg Walter, "Snow Job at Valley Forge," *Philadelphia Magazine,* January, 1966, p. 117.
5. Tom P. Brady, quoted in Thayer, *The Farther Shores,* pp. 110–11.
6. W. C. Sawyer, interview with author, Valley Forge, Pennsylvania, September 2, 1969.
7. The IRS case against Rand and his foundation is contained in Tax Court dockets 4662–65 and 3034–65, filed with the court office in the IRS Building, Washington.
8. Patman, Patman IV, pp. 4–5.

CHAPTER 7

1. Learned Hand, quoted in '57 *Yale Law Journal,* p. 167.
2. *Trinidad v. Sagrada Orden de Predicadores,* 263 US 578, 582.
3. Patman, quoted in Ways and Means, p. 12.
4. Norman A. Sugarman, quoted in *Proceedings,* Eighth Biennial.
5. Harry Yolin, "The Tax Blessings of Charitable Giving," *The Practical Lawyer,* May, 1964.
6. Berrien C. Eaton, Norman A. Sugarman, Harry K. Mansfield, and Arnold R. Cutler, "How to Draft the Charter or Indenture of a Charity so as to Qualify for Federal Tax Exemption," Parts 1 and 2, *The Practical Lawyer,* October and November, 1962.
7. *Donald G. and Lillian S. Griswold v. Commissioner of Internal Revenue,* 39 TC 620.
8. Treasury Department Report on Private Foundations (published by House Ways and Means Committee), February 2, 1965, p. 58. (Treasury Report hereafter.)
9. Chauncy Belknap, letter to author, June 13, 1969.
10. "How to Use Gifts to Take Earnings Out of a Corporation Tax-Free," *Tax Planning Ideas* (New York), April 2, 1969.
11. The 1950 figure is from Treasury Report, p. 74; the 1968 figure, from the 1968 report of the Foundation Center.
12. Wright Patman, quoted in House Select Committee on Small Business, *Tax-Exempt Foundations: Their Impact on Small Business,* Hearings, October and November, 1967, pp. 2–3.
13. Treasury Report, p. 73.
14. Ibid., p. 81.
15. Wright Patman, "Subcommittee Chairman's Report to Subcommittee No. 1, /House/ Select Committee on Small Business," *Tax-Exempt Foundations and Charitable Trusts: Their Impact on Our Economy,* March 26, 1968, pp. 8–9. (Patman VI hereafter); Rose figures from *Giving USA,* 1968 edition, New York, American Association of Fund-Raising Counsel, 1968.
16. Senate Finance, p. 6148.
17. Patman, quoted in Ways and Means, p. 19.
18. Ford Foundation, *Finances 1968* and *Finances 1969* (financial supplements to annual reports for these years).
19. Ways and Means, p. 417.
20. Patman, quoted in Patman VI, pp. 12–13.

21. J. George Harrar, quoted in Ways and Means, p. 292.
22. Ibid., p. 269.
23. Senate Finance, p. 6168.
24. *Managing Endowment Funds,* New York, Ford Foundation, 1969 (A report from a special advisory committee on endowment management).
25. Senate Finance, p. 6168.
26. Byron P. Hollett, quoted in Senate Finance, p. 5680.
27. Treasury Report, p. 96.
28. Will Wilson, quoted in *Dallas Morning News,* December 15, 1962.
29. Tax returns for the Moody Foundation, the Shearn Moody Foundation, and the Robert L. Moody Foundation, 1963–67.
30. John T. Jones, Jr., quoted in Sixth Biennial.
31. Treasury Report, pp. 41–42.
32. *University Hill Foundation v. Commissioner of Internal Revenue,* 51 TC 548. Material on the operations of the University Hill Foundation is from the transcript of the trial in Tax Court—dockets 73993, 5311–65, and 1482–66—held in Los Angeles, August, 1966.
33. *Commissioner of Internal Revenue v. Brown et al.,* 380 US 568 (the "Clay Brown case").
34. *University Hill Foundation v. Commissioner of Internal Revenue.*
35. Stanley S. Surrey, quoted in House Ways and Means Committee, *Unrelated Debt-Financed Income of Tax-Exempt Organizations,* Hearings, August, 1966, p. 26.
36. *Executive Tax Report* (Prentice-Hall), June 13, 1969.
37. Robert B. Payne, letter to author, June 13, 1969.
38. Ibid.
39. For a guide to this grotesquely complex scheme, I am indebted to specialists in the Treasury Department's tax-policy division who must remain anonymous.
40. T. Whitfield Davidson, 11 Federal Tax Reports 2d, 535.
41. 218 Federal Tax Reports 2d, 567.
42. Burton Raffel, "Philanthropy and the Legal Mind," *Foundation News,* March, 1963.
43. Mortimer Caplin, "Foundations and the Government: Some Observations on the Future," *Foundation News,* May, 1963.
44. Sheldon Cohen, speech to a seminar of the Practicing Law Institute, American Bar Association, June, 1968.
45. F. Emerson Andrews, quoted in *Proceedings,* Eighth Biennial.
46. Norman A. Sugarman, quoted in *Proceedings,* Eighth Biennial.
47. Milton Young, "Tax Ethics: Some Practical Dilemmas," *The Practical Lawyer,* May, 1966.
48. Wright Patman, quoted in *Congressional Record,* August 7, 1961, p. 13755.
49. *Congressional Record,* January 22, 1962, pp. 519–20.
50. Patman, quoted in House Select Committee on Small Business, *Tax-Exempt Foundations: Their Impact on Small Business,* Hearings, July–September, 1964, p. 274.
51. F. Emerson Andrews, *Patman and Foundations: Review and Assessment,* New York, Foundation Center, 1968, p. 54.
52. Patman, quoted in Patman VI, pp. iii, iv.
53. Patman, quoted in *Congressional Record,* July 23, 1962, p. 13513.

54. Patman, quoted in Patman VI, p. 1.
55. Andrews, *Patman and Foundations,* p. 47.
56. Press release from the Fund for Public Policy Research, September 18, 1969.
57. Patman published the documents in a volume entitled "Subcommittee Chairman's Report to Subcommittee No. 1, /House/ Select Committee on Small Business," *Tax-Exempt Foundations and Charitable Trusts: Their Impact on Our Economy,* April 28, 1967. (Patman V hereafter.)

CHAPTER 8

1. Paul Hoffman, quoted in Dwight Macdonald, *The Ford Foundation: The Men and the Millions,* New York, Reynal, 1956, p. 148.
2. McGeorge Bundy, interview with author, New York, September 4, 1969.
3. Maurice R. Berude and Marilyn Gittell, eds., *Confrontation at Ocean Hill-Brownsville,* New York, Frederick A. Praeger, 1969. (*Confrontation* hereafter.)
4. Mario Fantini, "Alternatives for Urban School Reform," *Harvard Educational Review,* Winter, 1968 (reprinted by the Ford Foundation).
5. Allan C. Brownfeld, "The Financiers of Revolution," Washington, American Conservative Union, 1969.
6. David Halberstam, "The Very Expensive Education of McGeorge Bundy," *Harper's Magazine,* July, 1969.
7. Joseph Alsop, in the *Washington Post,* July 2, 1969.
8. *Foundations and the Tax Bill,* p. 4 (see note 15 of Chapter Five).
9. Michael Harrington, quoted in *Confrontation,* p. 233.
10. Ford Foundation, annual report for 1967.
11. McGeorge Bundy, speech to the annual banquet of the National Urban League, Philadelphia, August 2, 1966; reprinted as a Ford Foundation pamphlet, "Action for Equal Opportunity."
12. Fantini, "Alternatives for Urban School Reform."
13. Harrington, quoted in *Confrontation,* p. 229.
14. *Confrontation,* p. 166.
15. *Confrontation,* p. 203.
16. McGeorge Bundy, speech to the Eighteenth Annual Conference of the Council of Foundations, Boston, May 19, 1967; reprinted as a Ford Foundation pamphlet, "Government as Colleague and Petitioner."
17. *Cammarano v. US,* 358 US 498.
18. Bundy, "Action for Equal Opportunity."
19. *Cleveland Plain Dealer,* August 23, 1967.
20. Bundy, quoted in Ways and Means, p. 411.
21. Bundy, interview with author.
22. Ibid.
23. Louis Winnick, interview with author, New York, June 19, 1969 (Winnick is with the Ford Foundation's Division of National Affairs).
24. Bundy, quoted in Ways and Means, p. 411.
25. Moynihan, *Maximum Feasible Misunderstanding,* p. 190.
26. Patman, quoted in Ways and Means, p. 15.
27. Ways and Means, p. 228.

28. Frederick W. Richmond, quoted in Ways and Means, p. 1043.
29. Greg Olds, in the *Texas Observer*, April 11, 1969.
30. Gonzalez compiled into a pamphlet entitled "The New Racism" his floor speeches of April 3, 15, 16, 22, 28, 29, and May 1, 1968; these also appeared in the *Congressional Record* for these dates.
31. Mitchell Svirdoff, interview with author, New York, August 20, 1969 (Svirdoff is with the Ford Foundation's Division of National Affairs).
32. Ways and Means, pp. 375–76.
33. Rockefeller Foundation, *President's Five-Year Review and Annual Report,* 1968.
34. Foundation Center, 1968 annual report.

CHAPTER 9

1. Eric Goldman, *The Tragedy of Lyndon Johnson,* New York, Alfred A. Knopf, 1969, p. 240.
2. Edward Kennedy, quoted in the *Congressional Record,* December 12, 1969.
3. Patman IV, p. 25.
4. "Literature" quotations are from a variety of Freedoms Foundation pamphlets and handbills, all untitled and undated.
5. Tax information and charter quotations are from the J. Edgar Hoover Foundation's tax returns for 1965–68.
6. J. Edgar Hoover, quoted in House Subcommittee on Appropriations, *1970 Appropriations for the Federal Bureau of Investigation,* Hearings, April 17, 1969 (FBI reprint).
7. Fortas declined to be interviewed for this book. His statements for the remainder of this chapter are from a report he submitted to Chief Justice Earl Warren when he resigned on May 15, 1969.
8. Nicholas von Hoffman, in the *Washington Post,* May 19, 1969.
9. Byrnes, quoted in Ways and Means, pp. 1573–75.
10. "Concise Explanation of the Tax Reform Act of 1969," Oil and Gas Taxes General Bulletin Number 22 (Prentice-Hall), January 8, 1970, pp. 75–76.
11. McGeorge Bundy, quoted in Ford Foundation, annual report for 1969.
12. *Tax Reform Act of 1969,* conference committee report to accompany H.R. 13270, House Report 91-782, December 21, 1969, p. 284.
13. John J. McCloy, quoted in Senate Finance, pp. 5514–19.
14. Alan Pifer, press release from the Carnegie Corporation, June 2, 1969.
15. Andrews, *Patman and Foundations.*
16. Manning M. Pattillo, interview with author, New York, August 20, 1969.

INDEX

334

About the Author

Washington journalist Joseph C. Goulden's
previous books were *The Curtis Caper,*
written about the collapse of the *Saturday
Evening Post*; *Monopoly,* a muckraking
study of AT&T; and *Truth Is the First Casualty,*
concerning the Gulf of Tonkin incidents.
Born in 1934 in Texas, he worked for newspapers
for ten years, last as Washington correspondent
for the *Philadelphia Inquirer,* before becoming
a free-lance writer. He has written for *Harper's*
and *Ramparts* and is a frequent contributor to
The Nation. Goulden lives in Arlington, Virginia,
with his wife and two sons.